DRAGONS IN
DIAMOND VILLAGE

DRAGONS IN DIAMOND VILLAGE

TALES OF RESISTANCE FROM URBANIZING CHINA

DAVID BANDURSKI

BROOKLYN • LONDON

DRAGONS IN DIAMOND VILLAGE

Copyright © 2016 by David Bandurski

First published by Penguin Group (Australia), 2015
First Melville House Printing: October 2016

Melville House Publishing   8 Blackstock Mews
          46 John Street   and   Islington
     Brooklyn, NY 11201   London N4 2BT

mhpbooks.com   facebook.com/mhpbooks   @melvillehouse

Library of Congress Cataloging-in-Publication Data
Names: Bandurski, David, author.
Title: Dragons in diamond village : tales of resistance from
   urbanizing China / David Bandurski.
Description: 1st Edition. | Brooklyn : Melville House, 2016.
Identifiers: LCCN 2016024419 | ISBN 9781612195711
   (hardback) | ISBN 9781612195728 (ebook)
Subjects: LCSH: City planning—China. | Cities and towns—
   Growth. | China—Social policy. | BISAC: POLITICAL
   SCIENCE / Public Policy / City Planning & Urban
   Development. | SOCIAL SCIENCE / Sociology / Urban.
Classification: LCC HT169.C6 B36 2016 | DDC
   307.1/2160951—dc23
LC record available at https://lccn.loc.gov/2016024419

Printed in the United States of America
1   3   5   7   9   10   8   6   4   2

For Sara and for Tristan

In memory of
Kathryn M. Kozora and Erick Wujcik,
who had such adventures in China

CONTENTS

A NOTE ON SOURCES

All of the stories in this book, and the relationships involved, emerged naturally through the course of the reporting process, a seemingly endless series of trips between Hong Kong and Guangzhou. By 'naturally,' I mean to say that while I was interested from the beginning in urban villages, I never identified relevant stories from a distance, through news coverage or existing scholarship. My focus on the Xian Village saga was, in fact, incidental—the product of a 2012 visit to the village, long one of my favourites, along with friend and filmmaker Zhao Dayong. Our sole purpose on that visit was to photograph the village, but the more I heard villagers talk about the community's history and troubles, the more I was enchanted by what Xian seemed to represent. Once I had met Lu Qiang, other sources followed, including Lu Zhaohui and Lu Nianzu, and I circled deeper and deeper into the story. (I should also explain, perhaps, that the surname 'Lu' is an ancient one in Xian Village, along with the surname 'Xian,' which gives the village its present name. Nearly every local in Xian Village is either a 'Lu' or a 'Xian').

He Jieling, a rights defender from Guangzhou's southern Panyu District, found me first, thanks to the wonders of Chinese social media—where I remain, as much as possible, a part of China's vast conversation. Months after our first meeting in Guangzhou, she introduced me to a group of village-rights defenders, including Huang Minpeng. It was a circuitous path through the stories of He Jieling and Huang Minpeng that eventually led me to Li Qizhong, a villager holed up for months in his tenement home in the city's ancient Yangji Village. I had long assumed, having read Chinese news reports, that Yangji had been completely destroyed. What an unexpected delight it was in 2013 to find, after Huang Minpeng invited me to accompany him on a visit, that the story of Yangji Village was not finished. Inevitably, I came to know many of the sources in this book very well.

PROLOGUE

_____

In 1910, the second year of the reign of the Xuantong Emperor, fighting broke out with Shipai Village over the dragon-boat races and many people in Xian Village died. To prevent further tragedy, the elders of Xian Village decided to suspend dragon-boat racing, and two dragon boats were secretly hidden away.

—*Xian Village Chronicle*[1]

To the Chinese, the dragon is a symbol of courage, perseverance, strength and wisdom, of nation and community, of the endurance of a culture and a people. It is also a self-referential symbol: the Chinese often call themselves the 'descendants of the dragon.' For centuries, the Dragon Boat Festival—known in Chinese as *duanwu*—was the main traditional event in many Chinese villages, including Xian Village, in Guangzhou, the capital city of Guangdong Province. The festival was an exhilarating time. Each year, the Xian Villagers joined their Pearl River cousins, or *laobiao*, and celebrated with dragon-boat parades—five-day affairs that began with ritual offerings to the dragon spirits overseen by village priests in flowing golden robes. The dragon spirits, embodied in the ornately carved dragon figureheads that adorned the boats, were then marched in noisy procession through the village and out to a nearby waterway, along with shrines to Bei Di, or the 'Northern Emperor,' a god of Chinese mythology revered for his control of the elements. Everyone gathered to watch the spectacle of the boat parades. Some boats carried as many as sixty paddlers pulling in time to the thunder of cow-hide drums, accompanied by the clangour of bronze gongs and smoky salvos of firecrackers that ruptured the air.

For Lu Suigeng, who had served as Xian Village's leader since 1984, and whose immediate family members held nearly all of the other positions of power in the village, the dragon-boat parades were a more ominous gathering. They provided an opportunity for the villagers to come together and, perhaps, unite in opposition to his leadership. Already in 1999 there were rumblings over his secretive management of the village's collectively held assets and lucrative land-use rights deals. The village's farmland had been appropriated for urban development through the 1990s and auctioned off to property developers, and some villagers alleged that Lu Suigeng's family had pocketed the transfer fees, totalling the equivalent of tens of millions of dollars.

Lu Suigeng's suspicions were warranted. The most popular story of the festival's origins is rooted in resistance to corruption. According to this story, the poet and patriot Qu Yuan of China's Warring States Period (475–221 BC) drowned himself in a river to protest corruption so rife it had brought about the downfall of his beloved Chu Kingdom. The races reenact the desperate actions of the fishermen said to have paddled out in vain hopes of saving the poet. In 1999, Lu Suigeng banned the parade.

Still, a decade later, in 2009, Lu Suigeng's fears about the Dragon Boat Festival were realized. A decade after Xian Village's last dragon-boat parade, villagers organised in secret to commission three new dragon boats. When the villagers gathered in one of their ancestral halls to donate to the dragon-boat fund, they also made clear their opposition to corruption, signing a petition to be presented to the city leadership.

In 2012, I visited the boat maker's workshop, just outside Shang-jiao Village, located south of Xian Village across the main arm of the Pearl River. One of the new boats was being stored there. Lu Nianzu, a Xian Villager, described to me the mood on the day when the villagers donated to the fund and signed the petition. 'It felt like a war recruitment,' he said. 'We all lined up to sign the petition. Everyone was so happy . . . We wanted them to open up the village accounts, and for Lu Suigeng to step down. We signed it one by one, all of us. We put our fingerprints down in red ink next to our signatures. We even provided copies of our identification cards.'

On the day of my visit, the boat shone through the midday dusk of the workshop, its hull burnished to pale gold. Lu Zhaohui, another of my Xian Village contacts who, with Lu Nianzu, had accompanied me that day, stepped over to the centre of the streamlined profile, his feet scuffing through the wood shavings scattered across the earthen floor. 'The body is spruce,' he said, running his hand affectionately along the boat's polished side. I did not catch the word at first, so he traced the characters with his index finger into the yellow dust of the boat frame, leaving strokes of reddish brown behind: *shanmu*. The spruce would make the hull strong but lightweight; teak, durable and resistant to corruption, had been used for the frame. It was just the vessel to transport the hopes of the Xian Villagers on their odyssey towards justice.

The other two boats had frames and hulls crafted from tropical teak and needed to be submerged when not in use, to preserve the wood; they were stored in blankets of mud and silt on a river bottom near Xian's cousin village of Shapu. The two villages were miles apart, but the river connected them like beads on a string, and they maintained strong bonds of culture and kinship. According to local lore, Xian had mustered its men centuries before when Shapu had come under attack from marauding bandits. Now the Xian Villagers were being ransacked from within.

The warehouse opened onto a marshy backwater, where the trill of insects throbbed in the rushes on the opposite bank, and I could almost imagine that we had left the city behind. But we were in Panyu District, the southern front of Guangzhou's unrelenting urban sprawl. The city encroached from every direction, and for beleaguered rural enclaves like this, there could be only the briefest of reprieves. Lu Zhaohui motioned me over to the water's edge, where a pair of rough-hewn planks formed a makeshift slipway vanishing into the jade murk. 'This is where we launched the boats,' he said. A short way to the north, this sleepy waterway yawned out into one of the Pearl River's snaking arms.

The boats had paraded only once, three years earlier. Hundreds of villagers had gathered beside the water to witness the boats' inaugural parade. Firecrackers shattered the air like gunshots—*whack, whack, whack*—leaving a knot of curling smoke behind, just where Lu Zhaohui and I now stood. When the smoke unwound, the dragons' golden heads emerged, crowned with high crests and pairs of needle-like horns, dark eyes glaring, lips sanguine over menacing canines. The men, lining up on either side, hoisted the boats free of the trestles and marched them out on their shoulders. The crowd parted with a roar of wonder and excitement, and the dragons were lowered into the water, red flags streaming from their ornate tails. In the centre of each boat sat a large drum, a succinct message of defiance glaring from its black belly: 'Xian Village,' it said, in vivid white characters.

Lu Suigeng thwarted the new dragons with his own symbolic gesture: he ensured they never made it to the Pearl River. Once he learned of the villagers' plans, he had used his pull in Guangzhou's Maritime Affairs Office, which then refused to issue the permits necessary to take the boats into the Pearl River. They'd never made it beyond the narrow slough of water outside the boat maker's warehouse. After their stifled demonstration, the villagers vowed they would not take the boats out again until they had achieved a decisive victory in their battle against the village leadership.

A saw whined in the adjacent workshop; sawdust hung sweetly in the air. I turned back with Lu Zhaohui to the dimness of the warehouse, where the master boat maker Lu Haoying was standing on a stack of timber under the proudly curving prow of the boat. I caught snatches of his Cantonese as he explained the craft of dragon-boat making to my companions. Seventy-seven years old, Lu Haoying was a third-generation craftsman. He made his boats by hand, using traditional tools and materials, keeping the trade as it had been passed down to him from the master craftsman Huang Liao, who had made many champion boats there in the 1920s and 1930s.[2] Local dragon-boat culture dates back to the Northern Song Dynasty (960–1227), and it's rooted in a constellation of ancient rural villages that have become urban villages, slums in the city's new commercial centre—villages like Shipai, Liede, Yangji and of course Xian.

A platform with a circular well to accommodate the drum dominated the boat's centreline. Like the dragon figurehead and tail, the drum was stored in the village. But even without its ritual raiment, I could sense the dragon's power. I was struck by its size. At dragon-boat races back in Hong Kong, where I live and work, there are usually crews of twenty paddlers, ten on each side, in addition to a single drummer and a sweep, or steersman. This spruce boat, though, could accommodate a crew of around forty, as well as two drummers and at least one golden-robed priest, and it was smaller and sleeker than the boats stored in Shapu Village.

As we turned to leave the workshop, I ran my hand one last time along the boat's lustrous golden side. It felt to me like a final farewell, but I hoped I was wrong. 'I hope this dragon of yours gets a chance to parade on the river some day,' I said errantly to Lu Nianzu.

'Oh, it will!' he replied with a zeal that seemed to rebuke my doubts, his smile jagged, exposing a mouthful of crooked teeth. 'It definitely will! When Lu Suigeng falls . . . And you'll come too, as a guest of honour!'

We said goodbye to Lu Haoying, bundled into Lu Zhaohui's compact car and rumbled west along a narrow gravel road flanked by fan palms covered with ghostly dust. On our left, just past a farm shed patched with black shade cloth, stretched a rich green field of miniature orange trees in ceramic pots, which adorn the lobbies of Guangzhou's five-star hotels during the Spring Festival. Those hotels—like the opulent Grand Hyatt—stand on former village land. We passed a plot of flowering cabbage and turned left, heading for Shangjiao Village, whose tenements huddled tightly behind the fields like rusty shipping containers on a loading dock. Shangjiao is another urban village, and in all probability, it will experience the same contentious fate as Xian.

Back in city traffic a few moments later, we crossed the river and saw the towers of Tianhe District, in which Xian Village is situated, soaring on the horizon. Somewhere ahead, beneath the modern skyline, the living ruins of the village stabbed up like gravestones, encircled by a wall plastered with pro-regeneration propaganda. Behind those walls, a bitter struggle was taking place: the villagers against the village leaders and their private army of thugs—against the overwhelming power of district and city authorities, for whom the police and courts were like bludgeons wielded in either hand. Lu Nianzu's hopeful words echoed through my head, but I could not see past the fog of hardship to the victory he so clearly visualised. The villagers' battle against corruption was just beginning. The dragons, I knew, would have to wait.

The names of the following five sources in this book have been changed to protect them from possible retribution: Lu Zhaohui, Lu Qiang, Lu Huiqing, Lu Nianzu, Xian Chuntao.

DRAGONS IN
DIAMOND VILLAGE

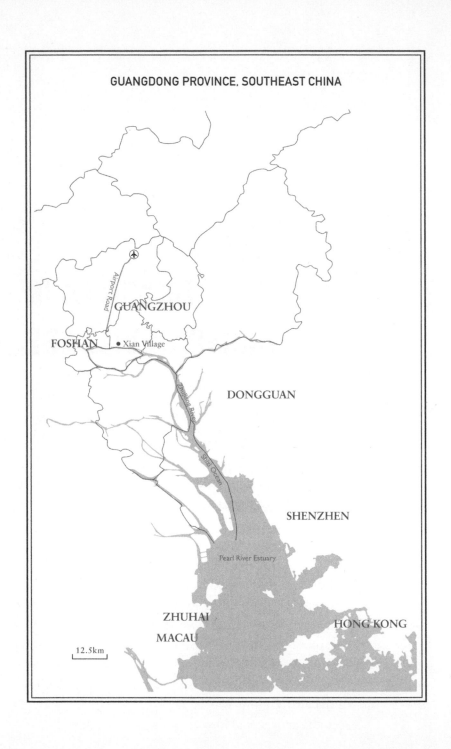

GUANGDONG PROVINCE, SOUTHEAST CHINA

Airport Road

GUANGZHOU

FOSHAN • Xian Village

Zhujiang River

DONGGUAN

Shizi Ocean

SHENZHEN

Pearl River Estuary

ZHUHAI

MACAU

HONG KONG

12.5km

INTRODUCTION

This is my Chinese dream: to have no illusions about evil, to understand that its rot will only spread; and yet, not to lose heart, not to despair—to begin from zero, from less than zero, and to build in the midst of the ruins.

—MURONG XUECUN, May 9, 2013

Glimpsed from the air, the village of Sanyuanli resembles a teardrop. At its tapering south end, it cleaves Liberation Road in two with a wedge of imposing, ugly buildings that jut out like the prow of an ocean liner. To the west, the street becomes Sanyuanli Avenue; to the east, Airport Road. City traffic bends around the oblong mass of the village, where urban tenements huddle together so closely they are called 'handshake buildings' and 'kissing towers,' the fissure-like gaps between them often so narrow even a child could not slip through. Sanyuanli stretches north for more than a mile, and as it curves around the village's northern terminus, it passes the centuries-old temple to Bei Di, restored and converted into a museum to commemorate a supposed uprising against invading British soldiers during the First Opium War in 1841.

According to the apocryphal history propagated by the Chinese

Communist Party, it was outside this temple that a vegetable hawker named Wei Shaoguang rallied the men of Sanyuanli and its environs. Displayed outside the temple, an artist's reconstruction shows Wei surrounded by a sea of peasants—muscle-bound superheroes with Manchu braids—armed with tridents and lances. The heroic rabble, it is said, marched from the temple to Niulangang, a site to the north, now most likely buried under the tarmac of Guangzhou's Baiyun International Airport. In Niulangang, far beyond the city walls of the trade port then known as Canton, Wei's peasant army surprised the British forces, killing 'a great many of the enemy' and inaugurating China's modern saga of patriotic resistance to foreign incursions.[3]

The battle at Niulangang never happened. There was no serious engagement—nothing more intense than a skirmish of some sort.[4] Nor did peasants at the time have any concept of national identity. Nevertheless, the myth of proletarian defiance perseveres, which is why the museum has been designated a 'national patriotic education site.'[5] On the day I first visited, in 2006, as I sat beside one of the old bronze cannons in the sunny courtyard, a pair of buses rolled up to the gates, disgorging waves of chattering school children.

But while the historic battle that lends Sanyuanli its modern political prestige never actually occurred, the village remains an important symbol of another ongoing struggle that will define China's future: the transformation of rural China into a modern urban polity. Sanyuanli today is an 'urban village,' or *cheng zhong cun*—literally, a 'village in the midst of the city'—a semi-urban tenement community built by rural Chinese on formerly rural land. It is a rural space caught up in a tidal wave of urban development, where the rhythms of the city merge with the cadences of the countryside. China, which had 320 cities when it began its economic reform push in 1978, had over 660 cities by 2016. Most, if not all, of these cities are hosts to urban villages. The stories in this book take place in and around the urban villages of Guangzhou, the chief city in the Pearl River Delta region, where China's modern economic development began. They explore a Gordian knot of issues facing villages and villagers in the midst of the city—land-use rights, community, identity, history, culture, corruption and justice—but they point to much deeper questions facing all of China as it makes the transition from rural giant to urban colossus. Understanding how and why urban villages came to be, and why they hold on so tenaciously, we can gain a clearer perspective of the issues shaping China's urbanisation, and by extension its modernisation.[6] The scale of urbanisation in China is so immense it beggars the imagination. As recently as 2002, just over one-third (36 per cent) of Chinese lived in cities.[7] By 2011, China's urban population had passed the 50 per cent mark, meaning that in the space of a decade roughly 160 million people—more than the entire population of Russia—had moved into cities.[8] China's rate of urbanisation is expected to surpass 70 per cent by 2050. By then, another quarter of a billion Chinese will be living in cities.[9]

Since China opened its economy to the world in 1978, the foundation of its economic growth has been industrial activity concentrated in urban manufacturing centres, and as these areas have boomed, they have become meccas for rural migrant workers, who supply the low-cost labour that sustains further industrial activity. As urban populations grow, cities must expand physically to accommodate them, and so the human migrations fuelled by industrialisation become property and infrastructure booms requiring more and more rural land.

It would seem, according to this simple logic of urban expansion, that cities are waves of unrelenting dynamism that ripple out and consume the countryside as they go. The most obvious example should be Shenzhen, the mass urban area across the border from Hong Kong where China's manufacturing revolution began. Shenzhen's urban population in 2015 was roughly 12 million, making it one of the world's biggest megacities. But of this 12 million, just 2 million people actually held urban identity cards. An estimated one-half of the remaining 10 million migrants lived in the city's urban villages. Try to picture these 5 million people, a vast sea of rural labour, living in 241 urban villages across Shenzhen, and you can understand that within the shining metropolis one might read about in business magazines, there exists a second, deeply 'rural' city.[10]

More than 40 per cent of Shenzhen's population live in urban villages—with an average of more than 20,000 migrant workers per village, though some of these (especially those closer to the centre) are far more densely populated. A typical Chinese village unit can comprise anywhere from 1,000 to 5,000 people, meaning local populations in urban villages are generally far outnumbered by migrant populations. In 2014, in Baishizhou, one of Shenzhen's largest urban villages, there were around 2,700 local villagers, but the tenements rented out by these villagers were home to close to 150,000 migrant workers, making it more populous than a sizable city like New Haven, Connecticut, in the United States.[11]

Substandard tenement apartments are the only options for migrants apart from factory dorms, where it is impossible to put down roots and raise a family.[12] Local governments have undertaken some measures to mitigate the housing crunch, but even the most ambitious efforts amount to a drop in the bucket: after all, housing Shenzhen's migrant tide alone would require a low-income housing development the size of Singapore.

Which is why urban villages number in the tens of thousands in cities across China. In 2014, for example, there were 304 urban villages inside Guangzhou alone; these villages were home to just under one million local villagers and roughly five million migrant workers,[13] accounting for almost half of the city's total population.[14] And in 2011, there were 71 villages inside the city of Nanjing, home to a local village population of roughly 240,000 people, but with migrant populations outnumbering local populations by anywhere from three to ten times, according to official statistics. And so the list goes on.

•

As low-threshold entry points to the cities that tend to attract the poorest and most vulnerable members of Chinese society, urban villages are often portrayed in China's media as 'unsanitary' and 'disorderly' founts of instability, as 'cancers,' 'black spots' or 'breeding grounds of prostitution and crime.'[15] But this dismal portrayal overlooks the villages' crucial role in the country's economic development. With their essential supply of low-cost housing, urban villages have underwritten low-cost labour in China and mitigated the associated costs of urban living.

Indeed, much of what passes for urbanisation, or *chengshihua*, in China has not been urbanisation at all—not in the sense generally understood, as an increase in the number of people *permanently concentrated* in cities.[16] Rural migrants remain 'rural' even after they begin living in the city, because that's how their status is defined under China's two-tier household registration—or *huji*—system. Dating back to the beginnings of the command economy, in 1958, but with antecedents in imperial times, this caste-like system classes an individual's residency status, or *hukou*, as either urban or rural. Before the days of economic reform, any rural labourer wishing to enter a city, even for a temporary visit, required special permission from the authorities. All of one's social benefits and prospects—education, work, medical care, food rations, even marriage—were vested in one's place of registry. The urban-rural divide was social, cultural and economic, but above all political. And that divide remains today.

The political source of this dilemma is routinely obscured by cultural melodrama emphasising emotional ties to the hometown, suggesting that rural migrants have chosen to live in a state of ambivalence between the city and the countryside. This idea culminates each year during the Spring Festival, when tens of millions of migrants return to the countryside to be with their families. One year, an apocryphal news item told the story of Li Chunfeng, a factory worker in Wenzhou, who journeyed home alone on a motorbike purchased with her meagre end-of-year wages, crossing a distance of more than 1,200 miles, to be reunited with her six-year-old son.[17] The story might have prompted deeper questions, such as: why must a young mother be permanently separated from her child and the rest of her family? Instead, it worked its magic, tugging at the heartstrings of the entire country, playing on real and enduring emotional ties to the hometown. Thus, despite the fact that the residency status system is politically manufactured, the cultural iconography of the hometown helps to rationalise the systemic discrimination that denies rural Chinese full access to urban prosperity.

Even as rural Chinese are uprooted from the land and drawn to the city as a matter of economic necessity, the countryside beckons them back as a matter of equal necessity. Rural land, even if it can promise no more than subsistence, is their hedge against the deeper uncertainty of the system itself. More than a legacy, it is a form of security, and therefore their most prized possession. Without land, they are rooted nowhere. 'The city offers nothing,' one of my urban-village contacts once told me. 'You find work if you can. You make money if you can. The land is a fallback. You can always come back and work the land.'

In 2011, while wandering along one of Sanyuanli's dim back alleys, I met a migrant labourer named Liu Jinlai. A native of Hunan Province, about 250 miles north of Guangzhou, Liu had lived in Sanyuanli for well over a decade, separated permanently from his wife and daughter. He worked as a contract labourer in the construction sector, sending money back home whenever he could. Diagnosed with cancer a few years earlier, Liu had remained with his construction crew in Guangzhou, working to finish a job on schedule and on budget. Seeking treatment locally was never an option: as a rural outsider, he was not entitled to subsidised health care, and hospital costs in the city were impossibly out of reach. He finished the job and struggled back to rural Hunan, dangerously ill, seeking treatment in a local clinic there. Men and women like Liu Jinlai—the rural workers who are building urban China and fuelling its economic growth—are what I call 'citybound.' Far from being permanent new city residents, they are permanently uprooted in the city, always bound to it (and towards it), but never quite at home. In urban villages like Sanyuanli, in cities across China, it is not uncommon these days to find two or even three generations of rural migrants still adrift in the city. Children of rural migrants are issued with rural identity cards from their parents' native village or county, regardless of where they are born.

The urban-rural divide in China's household registration system has become a form of institutionalised discrimination. It is so pervasive that few migrants even acknowledge, much less question, its absurd implications. In fact, there is a serious problem with the preferred English translation of the term *nongmingong*, 'migrant worker.' The character *nongmin* means 'farmer' or 'peasant,' while the last character, *gong*, means simply 'labourer.' As old-fashioned as the term 'peasant' might seem to the modern ear, the word captures the inferior status of China's rural people, which persists even generations after they have ceased working the land.

The 'citybound' condition is not a contingency of China's development but a crucial driver of it. Qin Hui, a prominent scholar at Beijing's Tsinghua University, has likened the household registration system to the former system of apartheid in South Africa, which also fuelled rapid but uneven growth. While there is no element of racial discrimination in China's system, in both cases, says Qin, institutionalised discrimination creates a class of permanent migrant workers, driving down the cost of labour and creating what he calls a 'low human-rights advantage.'[18] Seen in this light, as enablers of low-cost labour concentrated in urban manufacturing hubs, urban villages begin to look less like hazards and more like essential hubs of urban migration.

Over the course of nearly ten years (from 2005 to 2014), as I explored the back alleys of villages like Sanyuanli, I befriended many migrant workers. They were often, but not always, hesitant to engage with me; in these shadow communities tucked away behind the modern fabric of the city, a foreigner was still a novelty. I will never forget my first friendly encounter with village security in Sanyuanli, in a dim alley back in 2005. The pair of men, in their shabby grey uniforms, rounded a corner and stopped in their tracks as they found me photographing an old single-story shingled home wedged in among the tenements like a forgotten relic. 'Huh?' exclaimed one, his eyes bulging. 'How did *he* get in here?' But I also found migrants eager to open up about their rural hometowns and their experiences in the city. I paid back in the same coin, sharing stories of my boyhood in Oklahoma, and how I now found myself in China.

The challenge with migrant workers was not making friendships but sustaining them against the drifting backdrop of migrant life. My first friend in Sanyuanli was Lu Fayou, a migrant from faraway Jilin Province, which borders North Korea. He had lived in Guangzhou for more than a decade, finding his first foothold in Sanyuanli and settling many years later in an urban village about twenty miles to the north in Huadu District. He still regularly travelled south to the bustling area around Sanyuanli to take part in direct-sale training sessions with a local Amway chapter (his latest in a long history of ill-conceived get-rich schemes). We swapped stories over a period of months, as I made trips every few weeks from neighbouring Hong Kong. But when I called Lu Fayou in April 2007 to tell him excitedly about the birth of my son, his phone could not be reached. His daughter's phone rang, unanswered. He became a lost friend, slipping back into the migrant tide. I eventually understood this lost friendship to be part of a more significant pattern of rootlessness among rural migrants in the city. They are consistently, yet transiently, citybound. When my friends moved on, when their mobile phone numbers changed or were lost, my contact was broken—a situation only slightly improved by the dawn of social-media platforms like Sina Weibo in 2009. A migrant worker named Wang Xihuan, ultimately another lost acquaintance, introduced me to Lu Qiang, the Xian Villager and Wang's tenement landlord, who opened the door to a whole community of rights defenders in Xian Village. My eventual decision to focus this book on the stories of local villagers, as opposed to rural migrants, is owed, to a large extent, to the relative permanence of their lives in the city.

•

If migrant workers and local urban villagers are the human faces of the deep institutional divide between the urban and the nominally rural China, urban villages are the most potent visual symbol of this divide. For many rural Chinese, land has long been a delicate issue. After coming to power in 1949, the Chinese Communist Party confiscated plots from landlords dubbed 'class enemies'—poor and wealthy alike. This land was redistributed to peasants—a fulfilment, as many saw it, of the promises that had earned popular support for the Communist Party in China's civil war. But in the early 1950s, peasants were forced to relinquish their land and were reorganised into massive communes that included hundreds of households.

At present, private land ownership does not exist in China, and all land ultimately belongs to the state, but there are two kinds of classification: 'state-held,' land that can be developed for commercial and residential property as well as for public infrastructure, or 'collectively held,' rural land controlled by villages and used either for agriculture or for the collective economic activities of the village community. Rural Chinese often view the land they hold collectively as their birthright.

Even more sensitive is the status of rural people's collective-housing plots, those bits of land within the built village on which residents' homes sit. Beyond the family histories they enshrine, collective-housing plots offer rural people a lifeline to the collective community and to the benefits that it entails: their right to health care and schooling, to pensions and other benefits, to the dividends derived from the village's collective enterprises and to a share in decision making within the village community (including voting for village posts). The collective-housing plots, therefore, are not simple commodities that can easily change hands; they are at the root of rural communities and rural identities across China. In the face of rapid urban development, the plots have provided the basic foot-prints for urban villages.

In the first decades of Communist Party rule, before 'para-mount leader' Deng Xiaoping opened China's economy to the world, Sanyuanli was itself a rural village: a quiet hamlet on the northwest-ern outskirts of Guangzhou. Four main gates, one at each of the cardinal points, marked out the village's footprint. The old village grid, covering almost thirty-five acres and probably dating back to the Song Dynasty (960–1279), was a network of narrow alleys lined with squat homes, shops and ancestral temples. Beyond the village confines, in all directions, stretched the farmland that for centuries had sustained the community.

As Guangzhou expanded in the 1980s and '90s on the back of the manufacturing boom in the Pearl River Delta, Sanyuanli's col-lectively held rural land—and that of increasing numbers of other rural villages—was gradually appropriated through a series of land-use rights transfers—a process that continues to affect rural villages in the region and across the country. Under this system, parcels of collectively held land were redesignated as state-held after compen-sation was made to the village collective. Once the land-use transfer payments were delivered, the land could be used for urban develop-ment. The crux of China's landholder system, then, is not land own-ership, but land-use rights. While collectively held land is subject to many restrictions that make it impractical for the formal develop-ment of commercial and residential property, the government can grant or lease land-use rights for that kind of development.

As millions of migrant workers poured into the booming city to find jobs in the manufacturing and service sectors, the villagers of Sanyuanli (and those of Xian, Shipai, Yangji and other rural villages that had been engulfed by the city) recognised in their rural brethren a lucrative opportunity. With no rural land left to tend, they could, instead, 'farm property,'[19] building and renting out apartments to migrant workers. They began to build five-, six-, and seven-story tenements in the footprints of their collective-housing plots, knocking down the old mud-brick walls and carting away the clay roof tiles. Capitalising on space took precedence over safety and comfort: at ground level, buildings might be set ten feet apart to allow for bicycle and foot traffic, but above street level, the upper stories jutted out over the alleys, allowing for more space upstairs, which would maximise rental income. In most places, little more than a crack of sky was left visible along the rooftops—'threads of sky,' as they are called in Chinese. Electrical cables ran in tangles overhead, and the outdoor plumbing dripped into open sewers. The alleys were suffused with noxious gases and the sharp smell of urine, and garbage gathered in the gutters. In many places, refuse stacked up in the gaps between buildings as it was tossed out of windows that could open only about an inch before colliding with the walls opposite. The urban village was born.

Urban villages are black spots for the simple reason that they are policy blind spots. City governments, which generally view urban villages as problems to be contained or eliminated, have not extended services of any kind to the new populations in their midst. As a result, these collective communities have for the most part been left to their own devices, managing dense neighbourhoods with migrant populations many times their size. They handle basic sanitation and security on their own, through the village's original governing body, the village committee. Public services like education, health care and social security are offered to members of the formal village community, but the migrant workers renting tenements in the village are simply off the grid.

As urbanisation in China has become not only an inexorable trend, but also a profitable political scheme, rural land has been devoured at an astonishing rate. The official craving for speculative land deals is now routinely characterised in the press as an addiction.[20] In the

nine years from 1997 to 2006, at least 5,000 square miles of land in
China were converted into constructed urban area. This conversion
means an added urban-land area in that period was equivalent to
13 per cent of the entire landmass of South Korea, and nearly all
of this land came from rural areas in and around China's cities,
dispossessing at least three million farmers every year.[21] Since then,
urban development has not slackened. Between 2011 and 2013,
China consumed more concrete (indeed, almost 50 per cent more)
than the United States consumed in the entire twentieth century.[22]
On city margins everywhere, rural land is being paved out of
existence.

The speed and intensity of this growth often means that the
development of urban villages cheats the villagers. After all, much
of the land acquired, or requisitioned, for urban development has
been obtained for a pittance, if not taken outright. Under the current
system, rural collectives are not empowered to make private transfers of land-use rights for nonagricultural purposes. Local officials
thus have a powerful incentive to extract the maximum political
and economic capital possible from the process of public land leasing. This extraction happens in two basic ways. First, extremely low
compensation for land-use rights requisitions enables governments
to offer rock-bottom lease fees to investors in the manufacturing sector, a long-term strategy to attract economic activity. This strategy
offers scarce, if any, land-use rights revenue to local governments
in the short term, but it can bring political advancement, even if
projects turn out to be wasteful in the longer term.[23] Second, local
governments can limit the supply of land available for the real-estate
and commercial sectors through the tender and auction of land-use
rights, thereby driving up prices and reaping huge extrabudgetary
rewards, a process known as 'land financing.'

Since the turn of the century, land financing has become far
and away the top source of local government revenue in China. Pan
Shiyi, the chairperson of one of China's leading commercial real-
estate developers, once described three local governments approach-

ing him within a single month, all three wishing to find buyers for the usage rights of what Pan called 'huge amounts' of land that had been acquired from rural villages. One government official, said Pan, was trying to 'immediately' offload rights to over one square mile; another, the government of a city district, confided that it hoped to sell rights worth $24 billion within a few weeks.[24] Local governments are obsessed with urbanisation not only because it is the way of the future, but also because the construction of properties and infra-structure is hugely profitable. Naturally, they are far less concerned with the movement and naturalisation of rural populations, because these entail a knot of sensitive issues, not least reform of the house-hold registration system.

The bid to make cities cleaner, safer, more attractive and environmentally sound—to make them more civilised—is one of the core official justifications in China for carrying out 'urban-village regeneration,' which often serves as a euphemism for demolition. The current land-use rights requisition framework empowers the state to take collectively held land if its actions are in the 'interest of the public.'[25] But the exact nature of the 'interest of the public' has never been defined, allowing for widespread abuse.

In the 1990s, early in the process of reform and regeneration, restructuring was the order of the day. And, as much as state-owned enterprises were morphing into limited-liability companies, villages already in the grip of urbanisation were being nudged towards cor-poratisation, encouraged to cast off their old collective systems and embrace the stockholding enterprise as a model: according to this structure, villagers would exercise their collective rights as share-holders, and this would allow the villages to move towards greater integration with the cities. The political result of this restructuring, though, was an unprecedented consolidation of power in the hands of village overlords, officials who are generally appointed by district and city leaders from among the local village population. In one all too typical instance, a village chief had the audacity to award him-self a 20-million-yuan bonus just for inking a business proposal. By

2005, at which point the ills of the system had become painfully sa-
lient, an expert said the outcome of village shareholding reform had
been a system of 'one wagoner for three separate wagons.'[26]

To the extent that urban villages, or 'shanty towns,'[27] are squalid
and unsafe, it would seem to be in the public interest to clean them
up. In 2003, after eight migrant workers died in an apartment fire in
Xian Village, the setting of this book's central story, local newspapers
clamoured for the eradication of urban villages in favour of 'bright
and spacious modern neighbourhoods that are precisely planned.'[28]
The appeal typified the way urban development is justified in terms
of the public interest; it sounds reasonable, perhaps even humane,
until you realise that regeneration projects typically do nothing more
than enrich village officials, city and district leaders, developers, and
urban elites who make speculative investments in high-end real estate (much of which is never lived in).

Urban villages, especially those deeper inside the fabric of the
city, offer potential windfalls for local officials and property investors. They are the unpolished diamonds of land financing. In
the case of Xian Village, which lies at the heart of Guangzhou's
central business district, a small parcel of its formerly collectively
held land—less than 5 per cent the size of the tenement community slated for regeneration in 2009—was transformed in the space
of five years, between 2005 and 2010, into a commercial property
worth 1.9 billion yuan, or about $303 million. Take $303 million,
multiply it by 22, and you have a rough idea of the potential real-estate value of Xian Village. Is it any wonder that the place has been
called 'Diamond Village'?

Once local governments and property developers have dealt
with the politically sensitive collective-housing plot claims of local
villagers, urban-village redevelopment typically means that tens of
thousands of migrant workers are forced to move on—not to 'spacious modern neighbourhoods,' but to other crowded urban villages. In material terms, local villagers may fare better than their
migrant peers, whose interests are never weighed, but they are no

less deprived of their legitimate rights and interests in the regeneration process. They are in many cases pressured to accept compensation far below market value, so that purchasing property elsewhere
in the city—even on the fringes—is impossible. The loss of their
tenement properties deprives them, moreover, of what is often their
only reliable source of income. Aside from matters of restitution and
livelihood, there are complex questions of culture, community and
identity. Regeneration often spells doom for ancient village traditions, as ancestral temples yield to luxury shopping developments,
and as villagers scatter to the winds.

●

The development potential of prime sites, aided by the expedient
push for 'civilised' urban environments, has put city governments
across the country on a collision course with rural China. Nowhere
is the face-off more evident than in the conflicts over urban-village
land, which rankle at the core of all the stories in this book. But
these conflicts are ultimately about far more central issues nagging
at China's urban future: corrupt institutions and a weak civil society. These may sound like separate concerns, but the stories that
follow show how inseparable they are. In the course of researching
this book, I was astonished to discover the scale of corruption at the
village level in Guangzhou—and I have little doubt the same situation can be found just about anywhere across the country.

The 1998 Organic Law of the Villagers Committees, the purpose
of which is to 'promote the development of grassroots democracy in
the countryside and protect the legal rights and interests of villagers,'
makes it clear that a village's ruling body, the village committee,
is subject to villager supervision. Issues of core interest—including
decisions about the collective economy, the use of collective-housing
plots and the disbursement of land-use rights requisition fees—have
to be debated in the village assembly before a full gathering of legal-
age villagers. Moreover, a vote of 20 per cent in the assembly is suf-

ficient to impeach the village leadership.[29] But each time I spoke with the city's urban villagers—from Yangji, Liede, Pazhou, Maogang, Haipang, Xianchong and other villages—they told me about instances of corruption or abuses of power they'd witnessed and experienced, in many cases providing written accounts and documentation. The problems they reported became numbingly familiar. Local village chiefs monopolise village finances, sometimes paying themselves huge bonuses; land-use rights transfer fees that were paid for farmland requisitions disappear without a trace; cheap leases are negotiated with investors in exchange for off-the-books payments. To ensure they can operate with impunity, village officials cut township, district and city officials into land-use rights and regeneration deals, enjoying their protection and ushering-through of approvals and permits. Village officials circumvent checks on their power by appointing 'shareholder representatives' sure to vote their way on important village business, foregoing the need to put matters to a full village vote. They even corrupt village elections, paying off villagers with their coffers of ill-gotten wealth or with cash provided by property developers for the express purpose of vote buying. All avenues of recourse, from the courts to the petitioning system (which allows formal filing of appeals for the redress of wrongs), are slowly turning wheels of hopelessness, grinding down the resolve of villagers seeking to uphold their rights. Or, worse, complaints filed through formal channels alert the authorities to those who dare to speak up, who can then become targets for 'stability preservation,' China's umbrella term for suppression.

Fairness can be possible in the process of urban development only if those affected are able to defend their interests through open mechanisms independent of official interference. At present, however, fairness is a constant casualty of urban development in China, and the result has been a spike in social unrest.

Since 2012, China's official 'war on corruption' has been waged at the highest levels of the Communist Party, which has recognised corruption as a 'battle of life and death.'[30] The campaign is epito-

mised by high-profile cases against several 'tigers,' or senior officials, including the former security tsar Zhou Yongkang.[31] However,
while the taking-down of Party elites may bring immediate popularity gains for the central leadership, it cannot address the problem
of endemic corruption. The stories in this book suggest that corruption in the lower ranks of the Party and the government—among
the 'flies,' as they are called—has a much more direct impact on
ordinary citizens and a far more corrosive effect on Chinese society
as a whole.

Even as urbanisation is driving a fundamental transformation in
China's identity, the process of urban development in the country is
skewed in the interests of an elite few. The shift towards inclusion of
China's new urbanites will to a great extent define the kind of China
that emerges later in the twenty-first century. That shift has already
begun.

Firstly, in 2013, China's national leaders started talking about
the need for 'human urbanisation,' meaning more should be done
to ensure migrants could settle permanently in the cities with their
families.[32] The nation's premier, Li Keqiang, spoke of 'four new modernisations,' which included human urbanisation as the 'core of all
future urbanisation.'[33] He also spoke of 'new urbanisation' with a 'focus on farmers,' with the intent of broadening the provisions for public services in urban areas and eventually dismantling the household
registration system,[34] the ultimate goal being the transformation of
rural China into a modern, urban polity.

The second shift involves the more intransigent question of
power, something all of the people interviewed in this book are grappling with. Who will decide what kind of development is in the
public interest? Who will ensure private greed does not prevail to the
detriment of all? The answers to these questions are already chang-
ing thanks to one segment of urbanising China: the rural villagers
themselves—those who have been overtaken by the wave of urban
development and who form the subject of this book. In Guangzhou
alone, these villagers number around one million. Behind them

stand millions more, new urbanites whose growing sense of place and permanence will almost certainly mature into new convictions about the cities they now call home. Expected to number over one billion by 2050, these citizens will no doubt form their own sense of what it means to live in a 'civilised city.'

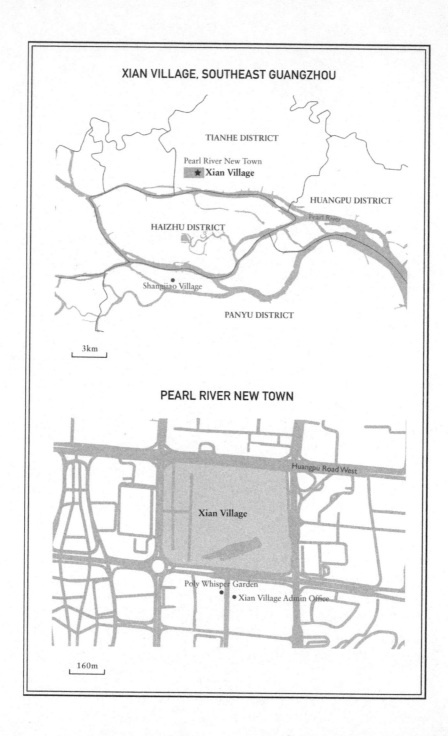

1

LU SUIGENG'S SECRET EMPIRE

Xian Village, 1999–2009

During the reign of the Hongwu Emperor (1368–98), after
the ancestors of Xian Luoshan moved into Xian Village, Lu
Yuanxun, along with his son Lu Yunan and his grandson,
Lu Dilong, left Sacred Mountain in Hua County and settled
in Xian Village. Lu Yuanxun married a daughter of the local
Liang clan and they had a son, Lu Weinan. This was the
foundation of this surname in the village.
—Xian Village Chronicle[35]

Xian Village's history can be traced back to the Song Dynasty in
the thirteenth century. As late as the 1980s, it was still a truly rural village. Fields of spring onions, celery and flowering cabbages
stretched row upon row in all directions around the village, joined
by stands of sugarcane and groves of fruit trees. But even in those
more pastoral times Xian was restless with change. Once the quiet
experiment of the 'household responsibility system' became national
policy in 1981, lowering quotas and permitting peasants to sell their
surplus goods, Xian became a model of rural dynamism. Visitors

would almost certainly have smelled the village before they spotted it, for by the middle of the 1980s Xian had achieved such unrivalled success with pig farming that it became known as 'Guangdong's richest village.'[36]

By 1995, however, the usage rights for all Xian Village's collectively held farmland, an area the size of ninety-two football pitches, had been seized by the state—for transfer fees of about 600 million yuan, about $96 million[37]—for the development of the Pearl River New Town,[38] Guangzhou's new central business district. The land could now be used legally for nonagricultural purposes such as the building of city infrastructure and commercial real estate. Some villagers alleged that the transfer fees, rather than being paid into the village accounts, had been pocketed by members of the village leadership, which was dominated by the village's Communist Party chairperson, Lu Suigeng, and members of his immediate family. Lu Suigeng, who had served in the post since 1984, had been preceded by his father-in-law, Xian Wensi. Once the farmland was gone, the village, covering the area of a city block, remained only as a tightly knit cluster of tenements built by the villagers on their collective-housing plots. Renting out cheap rooms to some of the millions of migrant workers streaming in from the countryside to seek opportunities in the city provided an essential source of income for the landless villagers and an affordable, centrally located community full of life and bustle for the migrants. Ten years later, in 2005, I made my first trip into Xian Village as an urban-village enthusiast, and I found a community still as vibrant as it must have been during the boom times in 1995. Open shopfronts glowed under the dim canopy formed by the close-set tenements—salons, restaurants, grocers, resale businesses (after all, migrants were always coming and going) and bookshops. They were arrayed along narrow alleys where electrical cables tangled overhead like fat black jungle vines, and where the pavement underfoot invariably glistened with slick, pitch-black moisture. Xian Village, home to tens of thousands of migrants, was swarming with back-alley commerce. At that time, however, I had no inkling of the troubles that were brewing in the village.

Also in 1995, as the last of the Xian farmland was seized, the village became the first in the Pearl River New Town to begin the process of reform and regeneration. Thanks to the loopholes in this process, Lu Suigeng eventually acquired the power to drive local affairs in whichever direction he chose. It took more than four years for the process of reform to run its course, but, as reported in the *Xian Village Chronicle*, an official history released in 2008 whose 'editor-in-chief' was Lu Suigeng, it was finally accomplished in 1999.[39] On August 17, the district government approved the dissolution of the village committee, Xian's rural collective political structure. From then on, the village's collective economic and political interests were, according to village and district records, bundled into a new commercial entity called the Xian Village Enterprise Group. Lu Suigeng became chairperson of the board. He now ruled over an expanding business empire built on the foundations of Xian Village's collectively held land and holdings. In theory, the assets and interests of the village—which included a rubber products factory, a sprawling furniture mall with a modern cinema, two hotels and a web of opaque land-use rights deals—were managed collectively by the villagers. In practice, Lu Suigeng's family members ran the village as a private fiefdom, monopolising its business, politics and security in league with Tianhe District officials and police, who the villagers felt certain were getting kickbacks.

As the city closed in on Xian, the villagers were locked out of their collective business dealings. But it wasn't hard to see that the numbers weren't adding up. The value of the land-use rights the government had seized in 1995 had been astronomical, and among Guangzhou locals Xian earned the nickname 'Diamond Village.' It was now positioned at the commercial nerve centre of a booming megacity, able to command enormous lease fees for collectively held properties. But the villagers' individual shares, their dividends as members of the collective, did not rise at all through the following decade of explosive growth. As late as 2012, most drew in only about 2,000 yuan a year, half the level of China's rural per capita income at the time, and roughly equal to the annual income of peasants in poorer, mountainous regions.

In 2008, Guangzhou Poly Real Estate Development Corporation, a local subsidiary of the Poly Group—a state-owned enterprise formerly under the aegis of the People's Liberation Army and controlled by the son-in-law of former 'paramount leader' Deng Xiaoping[40]—completed construction of several blocks of luxury apartment buildings on formerly collectively held farmland just south of Xian Village. With a total property area of almost 2.6 million square feet and an average sales price of more than 1,800 yuan per square foot, Poly Whisper Garden bore a price tag of 4.56 billion yuan, about $728 million. The village's parent enterprise, which according to the *Xian Village Chronicle* had been renamed as Xian Village Industry Company Limited in May 2005, was said to hold a 22 per cent stake in Poly Whisper Garden, but the details of the arrangement remained secret.[41]

In 2009, ten years after the restructuring that put Lu Suigeng at the helm of Xian's collective business empire, tensions within the village came to a head. Plans to demolish the tenements and build a new commercial and retail district—again, with the backing, it was rumoured, of Guangzhou Poly Real Estate Development—gave the villagers a greater sense of urgency. How could they allow the last remnants of their legacy and livelihood to disappear into the mist of Lu Suigeng's empire? When they demanded a full rendering of the village's business accounts, Lu Suigeng's family refused, arguing that these were 'commercial secrets.' It was at this point that the villagers secretly planned a revival of their traditional dragon-boat races. On June 19, 2009, they established a temporary registration office inside the ancestral temple of the Xian clan, on the north side of the village. Each villager entered their name on a ledger as they donated to the fund to pay for the new dragon boats. Hundreds of families contributed—even relatives in Hong Kong. (According to the *Xian Village*

Chronicle, the village leaders had gifted the village's old dragon boats to Shapu and Miaotou, villages along the river to the east, in 2003. The ostensible reason had been that Xian Village's old waterways had been filled in to make room for modern developments, and it no longer had the means to store the boats, much less to parade them.[42] And yet, neighbouring villages such as Liede and Shipai had managed against the same odds to keep their traditions alive.)

The petition that the villagers also signed that day presented four demands to city leaders, going over the head of Lu Suigeng. They wanted a clear and detailed account of the finances of the village and its associated businesses going back to 1984, along with an explanation of why the monthly dividends shared out to them were so low. They also called for the removal of the village officials and demanded elections for the formation of a new village leadership. The villagers knew by this stage that demolition, or 'regeneration,' was a certainty. What they wanted was some control over their future. On June 26, Xian Villagers journeyed to the ramshackle workshop outside Shangjiao Village where the new boats were being made, and they held a ritual to honour the commissioning of the boats. By the middle of July, more than 3,000 villagers (close to 70 per cent) had signed the petition. The commissioning of the dragon boats had inaugurated a new era of village resistance.

●

According to local media, July 10, 2009, marked the formal beginning of Xian Village's regeneration process. At the end of the month, Mayor Zhang Guangning spelled out his priorities, pledging before a gathering of city leaders that the village would be torn down before November 2010, when the city would be hosting the Asian Games, the biggest sporting event held in China since the 2008 Olympic Games in Beijing. 'Guangzhou will continue to improve its urban environment and aspect,' he said, 'striving for new results in the one-year countdown to the games.' Within five years, said Zhang,

49 urban villages would be regenerated. Within a decade, all 138 of
the city's urban villages would be cleaned up.[43]

The Asian Games were meant to showcase Guangzhou as a modern, international city on a grand scale, and, like during the 2008
Olympics, they drove a new wave of urban construction. Guangzhou spent more than $18 billion on city infrastructure ahead of the
Asian Games, excluding the costs of sports venues and running the
event itself.[44] The work included an 'urban master plan' developed
by San Francisco's Heller Manus Architects, whose philosophy em-
braced 'innovative design, grounded in a respect for continuity and
context, particularly in the urban setting.'[45] It was an exhilarating
time for Guangzhou's master planners; imaginations ran wild. As
part of their 'eco-corridor,' a strip of parkland slashing through former village fields between Zhujiang Road West and Zhujiang Road
East, Heller Manus devised open spaces with 'fountains and waterways' that would knit the master plan into an organic whole and
'reflect Guangzhou's cultural ties to the Pearl River.'[46] In 2009, as
the Xian Villagers fought to keep their culture and legacy alive—
and as the dragon boats waited for their victory parade—a sanguine
press release appeared on the other side of the world: 'With Heller
Manus Architects at the helm, the future looks bright and green for
Guangzhou.'[47]

The impact of the regeneration announcement on Xian Village
as a destination for migrant workers, and therefore on the income
of the villagers, was immediate. On August 18, 2009, a newspaper
reported that local removal companies had posted agents all over
the village, anticipating a boom in business as news of the fast-
approaching demolition drove migrants away. Most migrants, one
mover told the paper, were picking up and going to other urban villages close by, like Yuan and Shipai.[48]

The defiant petition for the removal of Lu Suigeng was the
spark that ignited a blaze of protests in Xian Village that continued through the summer of 2009. These culminated in August,
when thousands massed outside the office tower at 19 Huangpu

Avenue West that housed the village's administrative offices. White banners cascaded across the building's marble facade, visible to all who passed along the busy thoroughfare: 'Remove our incompetent village officials!' 'Return the money squeezed from our blood and sweat!' 'Expose the incomes and assets of village officials!' Flying over the whole scene was a red banner with bright yellow characters appealing for direct intervention by the city's mayor. 'We staunchly support Comrade Zhang Guangning's directives and his commitment to the interests of the villagers,' it said.[49] The sun glared over the sea of protesters as they processed along Huangpu Avenue West. They hoisted white placards with black slogans: 'Make the demolition process open!' 'Return the homesteading plots the Communist Party gave us!'

Not a whiff of the Xian Village protests ever appeared in China's mainstream media. On August 20, as protests entered a strident second day, the only article in the entire country mentioning the village was a profile of television actor Lin Yongjian, who had settled there for a time after his arrival in Guangzhou in the early 1990s. 'Coming to Guangzhou was like opening a door and seeing a whole new world,' Lin told a local newspaper. 'I settled in Xian Village to start, and at that time there was really nothing at all around it.'[50] On the internet, meanwhile, chat rooms frequented by younger villagers puffed with a sense of newfound power arising from their unified resistance. When Lu Suigeng failed to make an appearance after two weeks marked by daily sit-ins outside the office tower, one villager posted a dinner invitation full of saccharine defiance:

> Ah, Lu Suigeng! The people of Xian Village plead with you to return home for dinner! . . . Since August 19, 2009, for fifteen days already, we have surrounded your office, hoping just to see you. But still you do not show up. There are even rumours you are ill, and villagers worry it might be serious . . . If

indeed your illness has reached that critical stage, we
must begin preparations for your funeral![51]

Another villager posted a satirical poem, 'To the Cadres of Xian
Village':

Economic reforms, oh they're so handy,
Taking land is no longer a dream.
Rural acreage is passed out like candy,
So the villagers have nowhere to be.
Before, village leaders had both hands empty,
Now, they just can't take enough.
Village cadres made over as millionaires,
Put on a show and strut their stuff.[52]

Many of the posts drummed home the need for village solidarity.
'Unity is strength!' they cried, a slogan that has its origins in a fighting song that spread through communist-held territory in the 1940s,
as China fought against the invading forces of imperial Japan:

Unity is strength . . .
Stronger than steel,
Stronger than iron . . .
We fire our cannons at the fascists,
Let every undemocratic system die![53]

The oldest villagers, those who had experienced the Japanese occu-
pation of Guangzhou, remembered the song's origins. The site of a
Chinese airfield, Xian Village had been a strategic asset. After cap-
turing the airfield in 1938, the Japanese expanded it by annexing
more farmland. A few years later, as the martial notes of 'Unity is
strength' filed across the rugged hills of communist-held Shanxi,
American warplanes pounded the Japanese instalments around Xian
Village. The old fighting song now stirred villagers against corrupt

and entrenched Communist Party officials who had grown fat on the spoils of economic development. 'Problems in Xian Village have really been going on for a long time,' one local wrote on a chat forum. 'But villagers have been too soft to put up a challenge. What everyone needs right now is to stay united.'[54]

The battle cry could be heard across the city. Eight days after the August 19 protests in Xian Village, locals from Yangji Village, about four blocks west of Xian, appointed their own representatives and issued demands to their village's Party leadership that finances and collective property be declared openly.[55] A comment posted in one chat room discussing the situation was rousing: 'Villagers of Yangji! Persistence is victory, unity is strength!' Another user volleyed, 'Study from your brothers in Xian Village.'[56]

But the Xian Village protests made no impact whatsoever on the village leadership. The four demands framed in the villagers' petition were never answered. As winter approached, the villagers settled into a routine of smouldering defiance. There were daily sit-ins outside the office tower on Huangpu Avenue West. On the steps of the building, silver-haired seniors sat in quiet rows, some sporting red baseball caps with the words 'Fight corruption' glaring from the brims. Every evening, hundreds processed around the full circumference of the village, beginning at the office tower and marching counterclockwise. Their white posters became the backdrop of village life: 'Be open with us about the demolition of our personal property!' 'Be open with us about the village's property holdings!' They also took their petitions to the city government, sitting in silence outside Guangzhou's city hall, wearing their signature red baseball caps and holding up the same posters with the same demands.

It was from this time, villagers told me later, that a campaign of intimidation from the local authorities took root. Plainclothes police routinely tailed and harassed them, and some villagers claimed that they were followed any time they left the village. A few told me that district police detained them when they tried to board the city bus bound for the provincial government building, the fear being that they planned to file petitions there. The villagers described constant acts of vandalism—electrical lines cut or sewage pipes sabotaged. Some had heard that their migrant tenants' employers had urged them not to rent rooms in the village after local authorities applied pressure. I was told time and again about dead rats and mice being tossed through apartment windows or dumped in doorways.

The word 'continuity,' favoured by architects and urban planners, rolls so easily off the tongue. But away from the drafting board, it is a messy and often painful process. For the Xian Villagers, continuity was about preserving the past and making peace with the future, and that demanded fairness and openness about the change that was coming. At one point, Tianhe District leaders pledged that 'openness, fairness and justice' would govern the demolition and redevelopment of the village.[57] But the whitewash of the affair in China's mainstream media, the disregard of the protests and petition and the increasing intimidation of the locals suggested no one in the leadership—from the provincial level down to the village level—was interested in grappling openly, fairly or with justice with Xian's future, let alone with its present troubles.

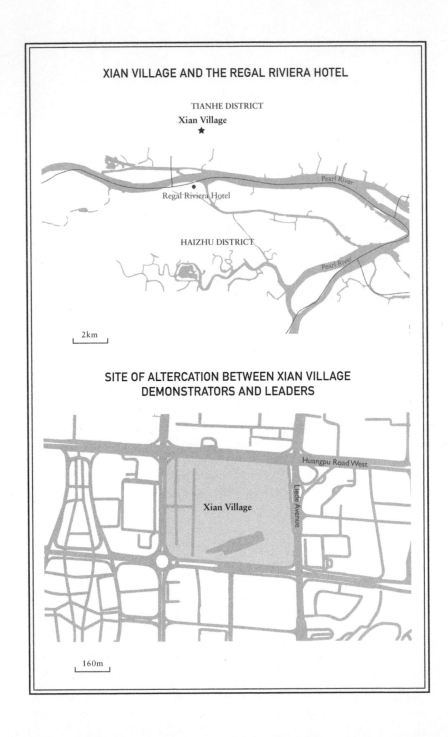

XIAN VILLAGE AND THE REGAL RIVIERA HOTEL

TIANHE DISTRICT

Xian Village
★

Pearl River

Regal Riviera Hotel

HAIZHU DISTRICT

Pearl River

2km

SITE OF ALTERCATION BETWEEN XIAN VILLAGE
DEMONSTRATORS AND LEADERS

Huangpu Road West

Xian Village

Liede Avenue

160m

2

PICKING QUARRELS AND PROVOKING TROUBLE

Xian Village, 2009–2010

On August 8, 1966, the Eighth Plenum of the Eleventh Congress of the Chinese Communist Party passed its 'Chinese
Communist Party decision concerning the great proletarian
cultural revolution' (called the 'Sixteen points memo'). After
it was publicised through newspapers and radio, Red Guard
units were organised in rapid succession on the city outskirts
to crush the 'Four Olds' . . . and there was great social chaos.
In autumn that year there was a drought.

           —*Xian Village Chronicle*[58]

On November 25, 2009, a 'concept plan' for the regeneration of
Xian Village was posted outside the office tower that housed the
village's administrative offices on Huangpu Avenue West. The plan
included three buildings for the resettlement of the original villagers, as well as designated office, hotel and retail space. Four ancestral temples in the village would be relocated and rebuilt. Lu
Suigeng, identified in newspaper reports as 'Chairman Lu,' stressed
that the plan was still only 'conceptual.'[59] In January 2010, after

months of open protests against the village leadership, district authorities formed an inspection team to explore the allegations of corruption. The team, comprising at least one hundred Communist Party cadres, descended on Xian, meeting with hundreds of villagers over a period of several days—but it failed, said district leaders, to uncover any evidence to support the allegations against the village leadership.[60] In February, the Guangzhou Urban Redevelopment Office approved the Xian Village regeneration to be completed along with eight other urban-village regenerations before the Asian Games, now just six months away.[61] Meanwhile, the stalemate in Xian Village continued. The daily protests rankled, and as before, Lu Suigeng and his clan called the shots. Tensions escalated again in April, as village leaders published the document villagers were asked to sign in order to authorise the demolition of and receive compensation for their properties.[62] The document, 'Demolition, Compensation and Resettlement Agreement for the Integral Transformation of Xian Village,' was a source of bitterness for years to come.[63] The vast majority of villagers initially refused to sign the contract. By January 2012, when I first became aware of the rights-defence movement in Xian Village, the Asian Games had come and gone, but staunch resistance from the villagers had stalled the regeneration project indefinitely.

Visiting from Hong Kong that month, I decided to photograph several urban villages with filmmaker Zhao Dayong, and Xian Village was our first stop. At that point, it had been at least two years since my last jaunt through the village. Zhao Dayong's debut fiction film, *The High Life*, which had premiered in March 2010, opened with a panning shot over the tenements of Xian Village. In that scene, the village was a living collage—gardens, trees and varicoloured laundry blooming from the cluttered rooftops. But that afternoon in January 2012, as our taxi dropped us off on Xian Village Road, we were astonished to discover a community under siege. The village was now enclosed by a high wall, and guards were posted at the entrances. They informed us that only those living in the village were allowed through the gates. Finding an undefended section of wall at the northwest corner of the village just beyond the Haitao Hotel, one of the village's collective properties, we vaulted ourselves over the top, landing in the gutted shell of what had once been a sitting room. The ground was littered with rubble, broken glass and rat droppings. From there, we made our way east along a dark and abandoned alley. Many of the tenements had already been demolished, giving the scene a ghostly quality. The ground-floor shops were shuttered, the signs faded. But further east, across from an old ancestral temple on the north side of the village—the temple, I later learned, where the 2009 petition against Lu Suigeng had been signed—we found a group of hoary villagers sitting in the maw of a gutted hair salon. Four women sat at the mah-jongg table, a crystal chandelier dipping over their heads. The plastic playing tiles went *clack-clack*. Off to one side, where a sagging sofa and several rattan chairs were crowded together, was a group of elderly men. I smiled and walked over as Zhao photographed the red banners that unfurled from the abandoned tenements—pro-regeneration propaganda urging villagers to sign their demolition agreements. My appearance brought a swift end to their chattering conversation. 'This looks like a comfortable spot,' I said.

'You speak Chinese. Where are you from?' asked a man with snowy eyebrows jagging up like dragon whiskers.

'I'm American. But I live in Hong Kong.'

'Your Mandarin isn't bad,' said another villager. A third chuckled and said with a thick Cantonese accent, 'Better than ours!'

'I'm sorry to see Xian Village in this state,' I said. 'I haven't been back in a couple of years, but this was always one of my favourite places. I suppose it will all be torn down in the next six months?'

I could see from their stiffened expressions that I had struck a nerve. 'No way!' Dragon Whiskers growled. 'They won't tear it down so quickly!'

'We're fighting them on this,' another said, leaning forwards.

After that initial visit, I returned often to Xian Village. In May

2012, sitting beside the village pond with Wang Xihuan, a migrant worker who had helped me slip into the village undetected, I met a local villager, a man in his late thirties, who was actively involved in the campaign against the village leadership. 'If you want to know about the village, here's the guy you should ask,' Wang exclaimed as the man emerged from the mouth of one of the alleys, regarding us with cautious interest.

The villager was Lu Qiang, who became one of my regular village contacts. He glanced nervously over his shoulder as he spoke about the troubles in Xian Village, about the injustice of the demolition contracts they were being asked to sign, and the veil of secrecy that shrouded the village's collective business affairs. He explained that the villagers regarded their housing plots as inviolable property, whatever the government had to say about it. 'We have ownership rights over our housing plots,' he said.

'Do you see that as the same thing as private property?' I asked.

'Yes. No one can infringe that right.' He paused. There was a fire in his eyes. 'To put it a bit less delicately, this country of ours is only sixty years old,' he said, his voice low and abrasive. 'I've been here for eight hundred years!'

Lu Qiang and I agreed to meet again the next time I came up from Hong Kong—but he insisted on meeting outside the village. When, at one of those early meetings, I saw the Xian Village demolition and resettlement contract for the first time, it was easy to understand why many were still holding out against signing. On that bright afternoon, in July 2012, I sat in the shade of a grand portico at the Regal Riviera Hotel, south of Xian Village in Haizhu District, with Lu Qiang and another of my regular Xian Village contacts, Lu Huiqing, also in his late thirties. The hotel and its adjacent residential development rose ostentatiously around us, a tacky decoupage of classical European architecture. Our quiet table looked out over the huge, circular plaza at the back of the hotel. On the other side of a stone balustrade, accented with lotus-shaped balusters, a baroque fountain displaying a bare-chested Bacchus encircled by grapevines sent water trickling down a stepped ter-race towards the plaza's central feature, a sapphire swimming pool where Romanesque cupids in blond marble blasted their silent trumpets. You could almost hear the inflated notes, a flatulent trib-ute to prosperous times.

'You know, I could agree to living in an environment like this,' Lu Qiang said finally, looking over his shoulder to the lush garden landscape of the Regal Riviera. 'That's fine. But who can say whether it's even possible? That's what I'm really afraid of.'

Lu Huiqing cut in. 'Sure, we might enjoy the new environment. But only if we could be part of the discussion and decide how to plan it and how to do the renewal. If the environment suited us, well, who wouldn't agree to that?'

'Was there any attempt at all, as far as you know, to consult the villagers on the regeneration plan?' I asked. 'The ancestral temples, for example. Do you know what they intend to do about those?'

'We were never consulted,' said Lu Qiang.

'But I seem to remember that plans on the propaganda board outside Xian Village had separate districts. One district was for the villagers, and it showed where the temples would be placed.'

'No. Here, take a look at this,' Lu Qiang said, lifting a red plas-tic bag from his lap and unwinding it on the table. He drew out a worn-looking document and smoothed it on the table before turning it towards me. It was a copy of the 'Demolition, Compensation and Resettlement Agreement.' At the top, it listed the two parties to the contract: Party A, which was Xian Village Industry Company Lim-ited, and Party B, which was left blank for each individual property holder. I quickly scanned the preamble. 'In order to effectively carry out the work of demolition of villagers' residences and resettlement for the regeneration of the old Xian Village, and in order to ensure that regeneration and construction proceed smoothly, Parties A and B have reached an agreement with the following provisions, equally, willingly and legally.' Lu Qiang turned forwards several pages in the staple-bound document and hastened a searching finger over the words. 'Right here,' he said, tapping the page for emphasis. 'It says that Party A has the right to interpret the agreement. Ultimately, they have the say. They can decide the regeneration plan "according to the specific circumstances."'

I drew the page closer and continued reading. 'Matters not explicitly stipulated in this agreement will be referred to the "Xian Village regeneration villager compensation and resettlement plan" as the standard.' This referred to a plan that had been approved by the Urban Redevelopment Office in early 2010. 'And the board of Party A will be responsible for interpretation of the content of the "Compensation and resettlement plan." If no specifics are provided by the "Compensation and resettlement plan," then arrangements will be decided by Party A according to specific circumstances.' The village leaders had dealt themselves a trump card. The agreement essentially said that in the event of any dispute over terms, the company alone had the right to decide the resolution. The board of this company, of course, was run by Lu Suigeng. Its members, villagers told me, were elected by mystery 'representatives.'

'"Specific circumstances." It's so broad!' Lu Huiqing piped up again.

I wanted to make sure I understood. 'So your reading of this is that they have the right to make the resettlement plan "specific" in whatever way they want?'

'Yes,' said Lu Qiang. 'What you saw was a concept drawing. That's all. A concept drawing. That's not necessarily how it's going to be.' He leaned forward and rested his elbows on the table, explaining how the building projects presented in the concept plan weren't possible, given the amount of available land and government restrictions on project density. 'Basically, when the plot ratio is too high, that means there's not enough space to build what you've planned. So then what do you do? You resettle the residents in another area. Resettlement in another area,' he repeated, his index finger drumming each word on the tabletop. 'What that means is that they'll find some place to put you way out on the edge of the city.'

'This is very possible,' Lu Huiqing said.

'Yes, very possible,' Lu Qiang agreed. 'Because, you know, we made our own calculations. When you look at the amount of development space, there's not enough to resettle all of us. Once, we raised the issue with an official at the Urban Redevelopment Office, and he let the cat out of the bag. We said there wasn't enough space. "Well," he said, "there won't be 100 per cent of you coming back, anyhow." He just blurted that out.'

'That was a mistake,' Lu Huiqing said. 'They promised us before that 100 per cent of the villagers could return.'

'Who made that promise?' I asked.

'Li Ming, the former district chief of Tianhe. Before, he gave us his absolute guarantee that we would all be resettled in the village. Then the official at the Urban Redevelopment Office slipped up. They want to divide us up. *You* go off to Huadu District. *You* go off somewhere else. Everyone will be separated.'

'Why won't we villagers sign this?' Lu Qiang asked. 'What are we most afraid of? It's the possibility that we won't be able to come back. In the old city centre [in Yuexiu District], they've had regeneration projects going back twenty-four years and the people still haven't been moved back as promised.'

We combed through the contract. I wanted a closer look at Article 7, which many villagers had grumbled about. It committed individual villagers to a denial of their own self-interest in the name of the nebulous notion of the 'collective interest,' which Xian Village Industry claimed to represent. It also made clear Party A's right to impose punitive measures that went beyond the scope of the agreement itself:

> In light of the complexity and difficulty of the overall regeneration task, the government at various levels has given it priority attention and support. Party A, as the representative organ of the lawful rights and interests of the whole body of villagers, and as

the actuator of specific activities, with its primary objective being the realisation of the overall interests of the village collective, has the right according to specific circumstances to make appropriate adjustments to the resettlement plan and to organise the implementation of various tasks.

Party B is bound to submit to the overall situation and actively cooperate with the work of Party A, preserving the overall interests of the village collective. If in self-interest Party B sets up obstacles, finds an excuse to cause trouble or stands in the way of Party A in the normal carrying out of its work, this will be seen as Party B's violation of this agreement. Party A has the right in such case, through the deliberation and decision of the board or the general shareholders' meeting, to determine a plan for handling Party B (including cancelling all welfare benefits enjoyed by Party B as a villager).

Imagine owning a stake in a private company that presses shareholders to sign a business contract under which they will provide property needed for an upcoming venture. The company, which is run by a self-appointed boss and his immediate family members, with no independent board, has powerful contacts in the city and district governments. The contract states that because leaders in the city have prioritised the upcoming venture, the company reserves the right to alter the contract at any time to ensure it is a success. While saying nothing about the company's obligations, the contract does state explicitly that if shareholders do not play by the company's rules—if they do not subordinate their self-interest to the greater goals of the city and district leaders—they will not only forfeit their property but will lose their stake in the company. Who would sign such a contract?

The stakes held by the villagers were political and social as well as economic. As members of the now-corporatised rural collective economic organisation, a hangover from the era of China's planned economy, they had a right to enjoy on an equal basis the benefits of membership, such as welfare benefits, in the organisation. The threat to revoke those rights amounted to direct political intimidation through a document that was ostensibly a commercial agreement under China's Contract Law—which states quite explicitly that 'parties to the contract have equal legal status, and neither party may impose its will on the other.'[64] 'They call this just and equitable,' Lu Qiang snarled.

'They tell us that any concrete plans will be determined by shareholder meetings,' Lu Huiqing said. 'But those are meetings of shareholder representatives we haven't chosen ourselves. *They* appoint them, so basically they can do whatever they want.' Lu Qiang's face reddened. 'Let me tell you,' he scoffed, stabbing at the document with his index finger. 'This is really bitter stuff, this agreement.'

'It's tyrannical,' Lu Huiqing added.

Lu Qiang stuffed the document back into the plastic bag. 'You can show that to a lawyer and see what they think,' he said, pushing it to me across the table.

A few weeks later I did exactly that. I paid a visit to Professor Fu Hualing, an expert in Chinese law at the University of Hong Kong. He turned through the pages of the agreement as he listened to my account of the village's troubles. 'Well, my immediate reaction is that this is not part of the contract,' he said. 'I mean, a contract is about an offer and acceptance of some interest. Here, we are talking about certain duties, which in a way are political. It's not . . . I would say it's not legally enforceable.'

'So if a villager was deemed troublesome in the eyes of the company, and the company used this clause to say, look, sorry, this is all null and void, I guess in that case the villager would have to bring a civil case against the company, right?'

'Yes, against the company, to say that in the first place the contract itself is not valid. That is the remedy, because there is some fault with the contract. The whole thing does not look like a contract.'

'You mean the end? Articles 7 and 8?'

'No, the whole thing, even the beginning.'

When our time was up that afternoon outside the Regal Riviera, I walked with Lu Qiang and Lu Huiqing across the gardens and out to the hotel's grand entrance, where we stood and waited for their taxi. Opposite us, just inside the marble gates of the complex, rose a grandiose bronze statue—the Angel of Peace driving a war chariot pulled by eight surging steeds. An aquamarine city taxi pulled up the drive. 'Be safe, brothers,' I said, raising my hand in farewell before turning back to the hotel and its hodgepodge of classical Western vanities.

A local journalist had told me a few months earlier how the Regal Riviera complex had been the subject of dinner-table gossip in 2011. At a meeting of Communist Party leaders discussing the issue of property prices (which had become astronomically unaffordable for most locals, to say nothing of migrant workers), the city's new mayor, Wan Qingliang, had tried to look eye to eye with the common people. He had never purchased property, he said, even though he had toiled for more than twenty years. Like so many others, he was a renter, paying 600 yuan a month for his 1,400-square-foot apartment in the luxury Regal Riviera complex.[65] On the open market, in fact, an apartment of that size in the complex rented for more than 4,500 yuan (7,000 yuan was the listed rental price in 2012). The mayor's real rent was far higher than the average gross monthly income in Guangzhou, but almost all of it was mopped up by generous subsidies only government officials enjoy. 'We need a change of mindset,' said Wan, 'from the idea of owning a place to having a place to live.' It was an insensitive moment that didn't sit well with the public. Without his subsidies, Wan's best option might have been renting a small room in the doomed tenements of Xian Village.

•

On April 28, 2010, four weeks after the contracts for property compensation and demolition were introduced in Xian Village, the official *Guangzhou Daily*, the mouthpiece of the Communist Party at the city level, reported that 70 per cent of the villagers had already signed.[66] The families, more than 900 in all, had apparently pounced on the opportunity thanks to a generous signing bonus. 'There's no need for villagers to wait until they've handed over their keys,' one unidentified village leader was quoted as saying in another newspaper. 'Right now, all they need to do is sign the agreement and they'll get a 10,000-yuan [$1,600] bonus.' Villagers who had signed, the official continued, were being notified that their money was ready to pick up.[67] Guangdong's Communist Party newspaper, *Nanfang Daily*, also citing official village sources, reported that village administrators were working late shifts to accommodate the wave of contract signers.[68] If local media reports could be believed, the Xian Village regeneration was proceeding exactly as planned. The media reports were, in fact, pure fantasy. The vast majority of villagers were reluctant to sign the contracts, bonus or no bonus. They grumbled about the fictions printed in the newspapers, which they said were spoon-fed by Lu Suigeng's nephew and second-in-command, Lu Youxing. Villagers later told me just 10 per cent had signed by the time the bonus period expired on May 5. After that, some villagers were offered 40,000 yuan to sign the agreement. Most refused to budge. The marches continued, a daily rhythm of resistance.

On May 5, the final day of the one-month signing period, the standoff between villagers and village leaders took an alarming turn. One version of the events is recorded in a verdict from the Tianhe District People's Court, which also offers documentation, rare in official records, of the villagers' struggle against the entrenched cadres of Lu Suigeng's clan. The summary argument by district prosecutors charged the five defendants—all of them villagers known to be staunch critics of the redevelopment plan—with 'picking quarrels and provoking trouble,' a serious crime often levelled against dissidents and rights defenders in China:

> At approximately 5:00 p.m. on May 5, 2010, the accused parties, Xian Zhanghai, Lu Youguang, Xian Yaoyun, Lu Zhuguang and Xian Zhangdao, came with a group of demonstrators to the road across from 101 Fanyang Avenue in Xian Village, Tianhe District, Guangzhou City. There they saw the injured party, Lu Hongzhi [a villager], who has agreed to demolition and eviction. They hurled insults at Lu Hongzhi, after which one of the accused, Xian Zhanghai, stepped forward and struck Lu Hongzhi, calling out, so that more villagers joined in the call and struck Lu Hongzhi. After Lu Hongzhi managed to extricate himself and flee, the group of demonstrators continued their march.
>
> When they reached the intersection of Liede Avenue in Tianhe District, Guangzhou, and the pedestrian walkway at the opening of Fanyang Alley Number 3, they came across Xian Village cadres Lu Bingchao and Lu Bingcan. The accused parties . . . and others then surrounded the two injured parties, refusing to let them leave. They struck and hurled insults at the injured parties. Lu Bingcan then phoned the deputy head of the public security committee, Lu Youhe, asking to be rescued. Later, when Lu Youhe arrived and prepared to escort Lu Bingchao and Lu Bingcan from the scene, the accused parties . . . and others unrestrainedly hurled insults at, chased and struck Lu Youhe, Lu Bingchao and Lu Bingcan. An official medical examination determined that the in-

jured parties, Lu Hongzhi, Lu Bingchao, Lu Bingcan and Lu Youhe, had slight bodily injuries.

It is the view of public prosecutors that the [actions of the] accused parties . . . in hurling unrestrained insults, intercepting and striking others are reprehensible in nature, and that this conduct violates Article 293 of the Criminal Law of the People's Republic of China, constituting the crime of picking quarrels and provoking trouble. [The prosecution] recommends that the accused parties be sentenced according to the facts of the crimes committed, their seriousness and the degree of contrition shown.[69]

The four accusers in this case included three nephews of Lu Suigeng: Lu Bingchao, Lu Bingcan and Lu Youhe. All three men, two of them brothers, held official village positions. Among the accused was the man I have called Lu Nianzu, whose name I have changed at his request to minimise the risk of retaliation. By the time the case went to court, on September 10, 2010, Lu Nianzu had already spent four months in prison, serving just over a third of the sentence that was eventually handed down in January 2011.

On the evening following the altercation, Lu Nianzu was at home with his family. Several villagers phoned later that evening to let him know local police were searching for him. '"They're rounding people up like crazy," that's what they told me,' he said. Lu Nianzu decided to lie low in an apartment his family kept in another urban village in Tianhe District, a place I'll call Huang Village. At around nine o'clock that night, as he hunkered down in the darkened apartment, his mobile phone flashed to life. The call was from local police in Huang Village. They told him they were checking family registration papers.

In August 2012, I sat with Lu Nianzu, Lu Zhaohui and a third, elderly villager in a roadside restaurant in Panyu District, where Lu Nianzu related his version of the events of May 2010. Lu Nianzu scoffed as he recalled the explanation the police had given him. 'Checking family registers? Hell, no one checks your residency status any more,' he said. 'When I heard that, I knew something was wrong.'

Before 2003, police frequently checked papers in major Chinese cities. That was the year that Sun Zhigang, a college graduate working in Guangzhou with registration papers from the inland province of Hubei, died in a police detention centre after being brutally beaten. When police had stopped him to check his papers, Sun had not been carrying his temporary residency permit, required of all rural residency status holders in the city. His death, exposed by the local tabloid, the *Southern Metropolis Daily*, sparked national outrage and brought the repeal of a national regulation on detention of unregistered rural migrants. These days, police almost never make sweeps to check papers.

In fact, police had been intimidating Lu Nianzu for months already. He felt sure he was being targeted, he said, because he was one of the more outspoken villagers agitating for the removal of Lu Suigeng. One month before the altercation, police in Huang Village had called him out of the blue and demanded he visit the local substation. 'They said they were making a report of some kind. They needed my statement; they wanted to talk,' he told me. 'I told them I wasn't going to go. They said, "Look, if you don't show, this will come back to you." That's how they said it. They were trying to intimidate me.'

'Did they mention any specific reason at all at the time?' I asked.
'Nothing.'
'When did they ask you to visit the station?'
'I was arrested in May. So it must have been March or April. Intimidation, that's what it was. They're still intimidating me.'
'What do you mean? How are they intimidating you?'
'Look here,' he said, sitting up and fishing a black mobile from

his pocket. He thumbed through his message inbox and leaned across the table, setting the phone down directly in front of me on the golden tablecloth. The message, sent at 1:03 p.m. a few days earlier, read, 'Hello, Lu Nianzu. Where are you at the moment? We are police from the Tianhe branch of the Public Security Bureau. We have a summons we need to deliver to you!'

Hiding in the Huang Village apartment after the 2010 altercation, Lu Nianzu had spent a wakeful night in the company of his dogs. Early the next morning, police called his mobile again. 'I didn't dare answer it. I turned off the power. After I turned it off, I looked outside and saw a whole bunch of people out there.' He repeatedly referred to them as 'their people.' Were they actually police? No one wore a police uniform, he said. But what difference did it make? He was a marked man all the same. Police, court officials, hired thugs and prosecutors—they were all 'their people,' all out to defend an urban development project he had vocally opposed. Later that morning, they barked up to his window with a megaphone, ordering him to surrender himself. He waited. And then it happened. First, silence. Then a rattling in the downstairs lock. The sound of the door being forced. 'I crawled under the chicken coop on the balcony, where I raised chickens. I covered myself up with things as best I could.' His mouth widened into a jagged grin as he told the story. 'They came up and searched around, over and over, but couldn't find me. They looked everywhere. They still couldn't find me. They were just about to leave, but they decided to have one more look around. That was when they spotted me. They spotted my feet sticking out from under the chicken coop. This guy saw my feet and started screaming, "Don't move! Don't move!"' Lu Nianzu made a pistol with his hand, levelling his index finger at me for dramatic effect.

'They pulled a gun on you?' I said, astonished.

'Guns?' he laughed, his eyes sparkling. 'They didn't *have* guns. The guy used his hand, just like this. "Freeze! Freeze!" he said. "Freeze, or I'll shoot!"' We laughed so hard the dishes on the table rattled. I glanced across to Lu Zhaohui. He was beaming. I wondered if this was the first time Lu Nianzu had ever shared the story. Basking in the success of his punch line, Lu Nianzu repeated it in Cantonese, his voice swooping up an octave. 'They couldn't see me, you know. They could only see my feet. I started to get up, but they couldn't see anything but my feet, so they shouted, "Freeze! Freeze, or we'll shoot!"' The police, Lu Nianzu said, never informed him what charges he faced. There was no sense in asking. He knew his arrest was about the village's demolition plans.

Lu Nianzu was allowed no contact with his family after the arrest. His first news of the outside world came from a lawyer's visit. 'I don't need a lawyer,' he said, mistrustfully. The lawyer explained that Lu's wife had called to engage his services after being notified of the arrest. Finally, Lu relented.

His cell was a narrow rectangle of about 485 square feet—including the open, stinking toilet at the far end. Holding thirty-two inmates in all, it allowed each prisoner an area about the size of a standard baby's crib. They slept, packed in like sardines, on mats rolled out on the floor each night. They were led out of the cell only for bathing, in five adjacent shower stalls. No exercise or other activities were permitted. Lu Nianzu's family was allowed no visits, letters or phone calls. They relayed messages through the lawyer, who visited four or five times over the course of Lu's incarceration. The date of the court date was a mystery. He didn't know until the day of the trial that three other Xian Villagers had been locked up in separate blocks of the same jail.

The first three months were the toughest, he told me. The days followed a deadening routine. Each morning, the prisoners were given a single dumpling, and each evening a bowl of rice with a small portion of vegetables and a lump of chicken the size of a toddler's thumb. In between, the time passed in a dull oblivion for which Lu Nianzu felt grateful. 'After a while, you get used to it,' he said. 'You have to. If you don't, you find it unbearable . . . You do okay if you don't think about anything. But if you start thinking, you're in trouble. You don't know what's happening on the outside. You worry about your family. You worry about what's going on in the village. My biggest worry of all was what was happening in the village. Before too long, though, I thought about nothing at all.'

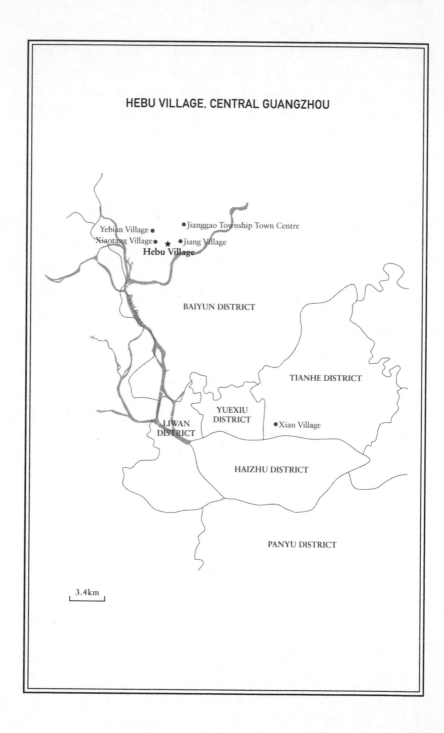

HEBU VILLAGE, CENTRAL GUANGZHOU

Yebian Village ●
● Jianggao Township Town Centre
Xiaotang Village ●
★ ● Jiang Village
Hebu Village

BAIYUN DISTRICT

Pearl River

TIANHE DISTRICT

YUEXIU
DISTRICT

LIWAN
DISTRICT

● Xian Village

HAIZHU DISTRICT

PANYU DISTRICT

3.4km

3

A SUDDEN-BREAKING INCIDENT

Huang Minpeng, Hebu Village, 1999–2010

The air-conditioned tour bus eases along Huangpu Avenue West. On the right-hand side, the tenements of Xian Village stab up like broken teeth. Many of the buildings have been gutted, the windows wrenched out, leaving shattered white tiles along the edges of gaping black cavities. The bus turns right at Liede Avenue, and when it reaches Jinsui Road, at the southeast corner of the village, it slows into a wide turn, groaning in low gear as it climbs the shallow incline and enters the village through the steel gate. A smaller bus, bearing the rest of the unofficial delegation from Sanyuanli Village, pulls in behind. More than sixty villagers have joined the tour, eager to see for themselves what city officials really mean when they talk about urban-village regeneration. The hydraulic doors hiss open. The villagers step out into the blazing afternoon sunshine and struggle up over the piles of broken concrete. Xian Village's ancient pond comes into view, a rectangle of sickly green slanting off towards the west, the glass towers of the Pearl River New Town rising in the distance. Across the pond, the tenement buildings stand shoulder to shoulder at the water's edge. Defiant red banners parodying the flag of China's ruling Communist Party hang from many of the buildings, softly but insistently contradicting the ubiquitous pro-regeneration propaganda. Whatever village leaders claim, the banners say, we have not signed the unfair 'Demolition, Compensation and Resettlement Agreement.'

As the visitors file through the alleys, they speak with local villagers, who seem nervous and desperate. They live in constant fear, they say, of thugs and secret police under the thumb of Lu Suigeng. They have tried everything. They have petitioned city, provincial and national leaders, all to no avail. 'Our situation is terrible!' they wail. For the visitors, the stories are distressing. The shadow of regeneration has loomed over Sanyuanli for many years, but now, as city leaders signal a new determination, what they hear from their brothers and sisters in Xian Village makes them warier still. 'We don't want this,' they say, again and again.

Huang Minpeng, a peasant from Hebu Village, far to the north of Sanyuanli, has joined the delegation. He understands at a personal level the brutal politics of urban development. His farmland was seized more than two years ago, in May 2010. But he is here on this blistering August afternoon to form new connections transcending any one village and any one localised grievance. An imposing, bulky man with a close-shaven head atop a sturdy neck and shoulders, he stands out in the group, looking more nightclub bouncer than rights defender. Huang Minpeng is semiliterate; he did not finish primary school. But the past three years have provided him with a rich informal education. His scattershot knowledge now covers law, land-use rights policy, community organisation. The satchel at Huang Minpeng's side, always at his side, bulges with documents telling his own story, the injustice that initiated his new sense of purpose. That original injustice is less significant now. The struggle is much bigger.

•

In 1999, the peasants in Hebu Village, located around twelve miles north of Guangzhou's central business district, drew lots to decide which men and women would serve the next term as heads of the village's collectives, and Huang Minpeng's name was drawn. Hebu was still primarily a farming village at the time, with only a few small enterprises built on land leased out by the village committee, making a modest income for the community coffers. Huang's responsibilities as head of his collective were simple. The land stretching out to the west of the huddled village until it reached the fields of neighbouring Yebian Village had to be irrigated at regular intervals. Huang scheduled the times when various members of the collective were responsible for transporting water from the irrigation ponds into the adjacent fields. For his trouble, he received an additional annual income of 200 yuan, less than $32, on top of his earnings from the fields themselves—which, at the best of times, were around 10,000 yuan a year, or just over $4 a day.

In those days, the city was far away. But urban development was already impacting rural life in Hebu. Local villagers were gradually leaving the fields, seeking more lucrative construction jobs or other work in the city. Some of the fields were now worked by migrant workers from places deeper inland, from provinces like Hunan and Jiangxi. They rented the land from Hebu locals, pitching temporary shelters in the fields. A migrant couple, husband and wife, might rent 5 *mu*, or 35,500 square feet, for between 5,000 and 10,000 yuan a year, eking out a profit of 25,000 yuan. The proximity to city markets made this backbreaking work a viable choice. Local villagers, meanwhile, could draw small but steady rental incomes to supplement their work in the city.

Not long after Huang Minpeng became head of his local collective, the frenzied logic of land development arrived, like the first hints of a coming storm. The top Communist Party leader of Jianggao Township, the higher jurisdiction immediately in charge of Hebu, assembled the grassroots leaders of many local villages at the campus of nearby Baiyun University. He spoke about the possibilities of development and the need to promote local growth. The initials 'GDP' were already on everyone's lips—like a shibboleth, or an incantation. If development was the magic potion that transformed struggling peasants into prosperous citizens, rural land was its secret ingredient. Huang Minpeng never forgot the township leader's words: 'Look, that land of yours will be of no use to you if you don't develop it. You have to develop it. There's no money in farming the land any more. You have to move on!'

I first met Huang Minpeng on a sweltering August afternoon in 2012, by which time he had become disillusioned with what he saw as the vacant promise of urban development. I had arranged that day to rendezvous with He Jieling, a rights defender from Panyu District, at a place not far from Xian Village. She asked over the phone if it would be okay to bring along 'one or two' friends. When I arrived at the designated spot, He Jieling stood, silk daisies bursting from her wide sunhat, in the midst of not 'one or two' friends but a hotchpotch company of rights defenders. Broad and thickset, with a resonant voice carrying over the others, the man they called 'Ah Peng' immediately caught my attention. As our odd flock roamed in search of a suitable meeting place—eventually settling on a nearby Starbucks—Huang Minpeng and I discussed the troubles facing Guangzhou's urban villages. I told him I had just finished meeting with two men from Xian Village, who had told me how a tour bus full of concerned and curious villagers from Sanyuanli had visited the tenements the month before. Huang Minpeng grinned. 'I was on that tour,' he said.

'Really?' I said. 'But you're not from Sanyuanli.'

'No. I'm from Hebu, up north. I went along with a friend from Sanyuanli.'

'What did the Sanyuanli villagers think?' I asked.

'They were terrified. They think they'll be the next ones to face regeneration. A lot of villagers in Guangzhou are watching Xian Village now. They're the only village that has managed to stay united.

In my village, we weren't united—and that's why we failed to hold them back.'

Ten years after the township leader's rousing speech at the campus of Baiyun University, everything had changed for Hebu Village, and for Huang Minpeng. He still lived alone in his simple stone house, just up the road from his seventy-two-year-old mother, though in another sense he had moved on. He no longer farmed the land. Like many others, he rented his fields to migrant labourers and found temporary jobs in the city to supplement his income. But in August 2009, when Huang Minpeng and the other Hebu villagers learned from local newspaper reports that an agreement had been reached for the sale of the usage rights to their farmland, it was like the earth had suddenly shifted under their feet: 'On the morning of August 23, a signing ceremony was held at the headquarters of the Jianggao Township government for an agreement on compensation for requisitioned land between the township and Guangdong Polytechnic Normal University . . . The requisition covers 1,260 *mu* of land [about 208 acres], from twenty-two economic cooperatives in the four villages of Xiaotang, Hebu, Yebian and Jiang.'[70] Top leaders from Guangzhou's Baiyun District, the administrative level above the township, had attended the signing ceremony. The township Party chairperson had also been there. While the agreement purportedly settled the issue of compensation for the rights to the village farmland, the villagers themselves had played no part in the negotiations. 'Until they made it public, none of us had any idea the land was even being sold,' Huang told me. 'That's how it started.'

In fact, the land-use rights requisition approvals had been made before, not after, the agreement was reached with the township. Land Use Permit 272 from the Guangzhou Urban Planning Bureau, dated May 13, 2008, and bearing the official chops, or seals, of both the Urban Planning Bureau and Guangdong Polytechnic Normal University, granted the university permission to use the land to build a new campus. But such permission could not have been granted legally without agreements for the transfer of the land-use rights first being reached with the four villages involved. On the website of the Land and Housing Office in Baiyun District, a notice from August 2009 about the agreement with the university said 'requisition work' had begun in 2004, but 'an agreement had never been reached due to a longstanding stalemate over the question of compensation.' The agreement of August 2009 had finally been brokered thanks to 'the tireless work of Jianggao Township, the district Land Requisition Office and other departments.'[71] But if the breakthrough had been so recent, why had the approvals been processed more than a year earlier? Also, the township government should have needed to make separate agreements with each of the four villages before it could be in a position to sign a deal with the university. Where were those agreements? When and how had they been made? What did they say? The carts, it seemed, were miles ahead of the horses.

In the weeks after the signing ceremony, *chengguan*, or 'urban management officers,' established a temporary headquarters at the entrance of the village. It was a clear signal that seizure of the land was imminent and authorities were manoeuvring to preempt local resistance. The *chengguan* are mercenary armies of quasi-police scrambled by local city governments across China to handle the dirty business of urban order and cleanliness and to tackle sensitive and, often, dangerous jobs. Unlike the police, which are part of a national bureaucracy and subject to its strictures, the *chengguan* work entirely at the bidding of city leaders. They can be counted on to do the rough, insensitive and lawless jobs that the police want to keep at arm's length. Many of those jobs deal with the rural casualties of urbanisation. *Chengguan* sweep unlicensed vendors, most of them migrants, off the streets. They execute seizures of rural land and demolitions of collectively held village structures within urban planning areas. In a very real sense, the *chengguan* are fighters on the front lines of China's urban assault on the countryside. The emergence and development of the *chengguan* paralleled the stratospheric rise of China's cities, with the first Urban Management and Law Enforcement Bureau—the city-level *chengguan* office—forming in Beijing in 1997, responding to a new law that year that empowered cities to set up their own mechanisms for enforcing noncriminal regulations.[72] In less than a decade, the *chengguan* earned a reputation for their brutal tactics and became generally despised by the public. A few months before the *chengguan* appeared in Hebu Village, one of Guangzhou's top tabloid newspapers, the *Southern Metropolis Daily*, reported the existence of a training manual for urban management forces sanctioning the use of violence. The manual stressed that the *chengguan*'s attack on victims should emerge with 'no blood on their faces and no wounds on their bodies.'[73]

As the *chengguan* appeared in Hebu, Huang Minpeng led the villagers on daily marches to confront them. They were a village rabble, with plenty of anger but little organisation. They shouted at the *chengguan*, telling them that they were doing wrong, that the approvals had not been handled properly. Huang managed at one point to make a show of force, organising around fifty protestors and running the *chengguan* out of the village for a time. 'I was the noisy one, the fearless one,' Huang told me. 'I wasn't afraid at all of making a big stink. I was so infuriated by the whole thing. But I didn't know how to speak.' For several months, the village was in a state of constant unrest. The villagers pushed as vocally as they could for township leaders to make the land-use rights requisition agreement public. The *chengguan* responded by waging a guerrilla war of intimidation. They cut electrical lines to the homes of families that spoke out. They destroyed sewage lines. They broke windows. Try as they might to organise resistance, the villagers had their hands full just repairing the damage. Township police, meanwhile, turned a deaf ear to the reports of vandalism.

Finally, in February 2010, Jianggao Township's top leader agreed to meet with a small group of villagers, including Huang Minpeng. The purpose of the meeting—ostensibly, at least—was to talk things through. The leader assured them the township had their interests at heart. There was no deception; everything would be dealt with openly. But after the meeting, matters only became worse. The intimidation continued. 'They did everything in their power to disturb the peace,' Huang said. In retrospect, he felt quite sure the leader's purpose had been to size up his most vocal opponents.

For weeks more, the stalemate in the village continued, until finally, on April 24, the authorities made a decisive play. Huang Minpeng was having breakfast that morning near a local market when five plainclothes police officers surrounded him. They told him to leave the keys to his motorbike with a friend and carted him off to the local police station. He was interrogated for hours before being charged with disrupting public order. His sentence was twenty days of administrative detention, an opaque and arbitrary process that allows police to mete out punishment without the formality of a criminal trial. It transpired that a key government meeting on the seizure of the Hebu Village land had taken place just three days before Huang's arrest. On April 21, one of Baiyun District's most senior Party officials and the district's deputy governor had met in Jianggao Township with local officials and representatives from Guangdong Polytechnic Normal University. They had been joined by officials from the Land and Housing Office, the Urban Planning Bureau, the police and the *chengguan* and had agreed on decisive action to break the stalemate in Hebu with 'a detailed plan and a fierce hand.'[74] The detention of one of the land seizure's most vociferous opponents was almost certainly part of the 'detailed plan.'

And on May 12, just two days before Huang Minpeng's release, the 'fierce hand' descended. Early that morning, hundreds of police and *chengguan* poured into Hebu Village, barricading the entrances. They ringed the perimeter of the village farmland. Inside the perimeter, *chengguan* teams levelled the fields with bulldozers, destroying the crops where they stood. In a public roster of 'sudden-breaking incidents' for the second quarter of 2010, Baiyun District eventually noted a case of unrest in Hebu Village on May 12, citing 'elements of instability' over the requisition of the rural land-use rights. The district gave the township praise for its timely handling of the incident, even using it as a case study.[75] In fact, this particular incident of unrest had been unilaterally planned by district and township officials, and executed by police and *chengguan*.

Huang Minpeng was released from jail on May 14, 2010, two days after the seizure of his land. The fields that for centuries had sustained the villagers of Hebu were now broken waves of earth, a wasteland awaiting development. It signalled a future in which Huang knew he had no part. But he would not turn his back. He would see this through, no matter the cost.

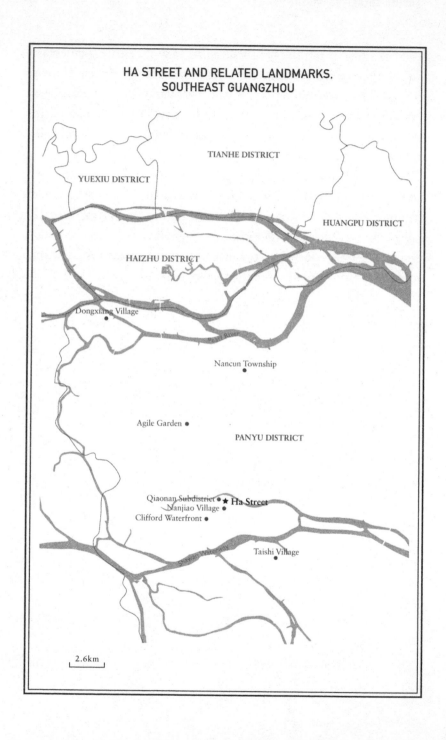

HA STREET AND RELATED LANDMARKS,
SOUTHEAST GUANGZHOU

TIANHE DISTRICT

YUEXIU DISTRICT

HUANGPU DISTRICT

HAIZHU DISTRICT

Dongxiang Village

Pearl River

Nancun Township

Agile Garden

PANYU DISTRICT

Qiaonan Subdistrict   ★ Ha Street
Nanjiao Village
Clifford Waterfront

Shiwan Waterway

Taishi Village

2.6km

4

URBAN DREAMS IN RURAL GUANGZHOU

He Jieling, Nanjiao Village, 2010–2011

The grand opening of Ha Street, a sprawling retail development in Guangzhou's Panyu District, is a turgid affair. In the plaza outside the mall's main entrance, a troupe of acrobats performs the lion dance. Four lions, red and gold, shake their shaggy heads through the din of the drums and cymbals, their bushy-browed eyes piercing the crowd. The lion dance is an old tradition, a token of good fortune. Visited by the lion, signifying power and protection, a business is promised lasting success. And if the shopkeeper's head is thrust into the creature's gaping mouth, the omen is better still. In the rosy glow beneath a red pavilion canopy, the master of ceremonies introduces the government dignitaries one by one. A drizzle of applause trails each name and title.

'Mr. Yan Zonghuo, deputy chairperson of Panyu District!'

Patter patter patter.

'Mr. Dai Yongchang, member of the Panyu District Party committee!'

Patter patter patter.

'Mr. Li Weitang, deputy governor of Panyu District!'

Patter patter patter.

A red backdrop looms behind the stage: 'Enjoyment for the entire city, a glorious getaway,' it says in bright yellow characters. Across the front of the stage, news photographers scuttle like crabs. Then a slender hostess in a traditional red gown leads an official from Qiaonan Subdistrict, for which Ha Street is a strategic development, onto the stage. He offers honeyed words of hope and felicitation. Next, the deputy governor of Panyu District takes the stage. He praises the work of Qiaonan Subdistrict. He reminds the small audience under the red pavilion that Ha Street is an exemplar of urban-village regeneration. The development will help change the perception of villages in the city; it will 'raise the overall competitiveness of the city and accelerate the development of new urban district centres.'[76] Ha Street has been billed as one of Panyu District's core 'Asian Games development projects.'[77] The theme of the sporting event, 'Thrilling Games, Harmonious Asia,' beams out from the huge television screen behind the pavilion.

Finally, during the dramatic zenith of the opening, all of the leaders present take the stage together: Peng Weimin, the Communist Party chairperson of Nanjiao Village, the village whose land has been seized for the development; Chen Hongying, the female Party chairperson of Qiaonan Subdistrict, the next level up in the government bureaucracy; Dai Yongchang, one of Panyu District's most senior officials, also making him one of Guangzhou's top bureaucrats; and, at centre stage, Cheng Liangzhou, the white-haired former deputy secretary-general of the Guangdong provincial government, the most senior official present.[78] Six months ago, he served as an honorary torchbearer during the Asian Games.[79] As they smile through a sparkling burst of rainbow confetti, every one of the dignitaries standing onstage must know the undignified truth.[80] Ha Street is a sham.

•

For a while in 2010, it seemed the advertisements for Ha Street were everywhere. In newspapers, on television. In one computer-animated commercial—accompanied by a dramatic, pounding choral soundtrack—the camera soared down from outer space towards the spinning, blue Earth; it dropped through cirrus clouds, skirted past a commercial jetliner and then, in a flash, as the Earth loomed up towards it, an expanding ring of fire consumed the misty rural landscape, revealing a lifelike rendering of Ha Street in an aerial view. The music crested. The camera panned along the length of the virtual Ha Street crowded with virtual people. Finally, the Ha Street logo came up—five handprints in the shape of a star—fireworks flowered across the screen, and viewers were given the merchant hotline that could make them part of it all. The ads for Ha Street bristled with brand names: Nike, Dolce & Gabbana, Louis Vuitton, Starbucks (none of which ever settled there, as it turned out). But the brand that really counted was the Guangzhou city government and the mall's billing as a development project for the Asian Games.[81] Ha Street was part of something bigger than itself, a history-making project that would transform the rural backwater of Nanjiao Village into a new urban commercial centre.

For He Jieling, Ha Street, about twenty miles south of central Guangzhou, seemed a golden opportunity close to home. A native of Dongxiang, an urban village halfway between Nanjiao and the city centre, she sometimes described herself as an 'N-generation peasant' from Panyu District, meaning that her family had lived in the area for countless centuries, as long as anyone could remember, as part of the peasant landlord class before the political purges of the twentieth century. She belonged to a new generation of the Panyu peasantry, born in 1981, at the outset of China's economic reform era, high-school educated with middle-class ambitions. The He family character, He Jieling once quipped when I met up with her, was of two types, stamped on the marrow of their bones. First, there were the corrupt officials; second, the unscrupulous businesspeople. Her ambition, she said, with a wisecracking glint in her eye, was to exemplify the latter. But there were plenty of officials in the extended family, too. He Tao, a distant cousin of her grandparents' generation, had been mayor of Panyu in the early 1990s (before the backwater city was formally dissolved by China's central government in May 2000, and absorbed into greater Guangzhou).

I first struck up a friendship with He Jieling in March 2012 on Sina Weibo, at the time China's most popular social-media platform. Weibo was in its heyday, and although subject to tireless censorship, it was a great watering hole where millions of people could share information and connect. At some point, probably taking note of my interest in Guangzhou villages as I posted from my account, He Jieling began tagging me in her own posts, hoping to draw my attention to issues she was engaged in, from a planned waste-incineration project on the city's south side to the demolition of village homes. I followed her account, a window onto local rights defence in Panyu District, and we started corresponding regularly. Much to the amusement of us both, He Jieling mistakenly thought I was Chinese, a misunderstanding not corrected until our first face-to-face meeting in May 2012. It was the first time I heard her songbird laugh. 'Ban Zhiyuan,' she said, using my Chinese name, her eyes twinkling under the brim of her sunhat. 'You had me convinced you were Chinese!'

Two years earlier, in April 2010, He Jieling and her husband, Tan Pei'en, also a local Panyu villager, had been considering investing in a new business venture at Ha Street. It was a time of seemingly endless possibilities—and political activism was the farthest thing from He Jieling's mind. The couple had done well over the past few years. Tai Pei'en had found a decent job in a foreign enterprise, and in the boom years since the turn of the century, they had managed to save up a good deal of money, most of which they had invested in one of the country's new favourite pastimes, real-estate speculation, known in Chinese as *chaofang*, 'stir-frying properties.' With money and connections, Chinese can pounce on mid- to high-end developments, those whose prices keep edging up, sometimes even before the apartments are formally on the market. Buyers rarely rent these properties out; in a culture that places a premium on the new and unspoiled, renting properties devalues them. So the apartments stand empty. In some cases, whole developments go dark after sundown, like vaults of invisible treasure. He Jieling and her husband had already bought two properties in Clifford Waterfront, a development in south Panyu advertising 'Venetian-style living in the city' (modern apartment blocks, in other words, dressed up with water features and kitsch Romanesque sculpture).[82] They were considering and would soon purchase two more apartments, in the fatuously named Agile Garden, a high-rise and townhouse development in Panyu billing itself as a European-style 'lakeside town.'[83] By early summer, one of their new Agile Garden apartments was home.

The time seemed right to start something new. He Jieling had little experience in running a business, but she was sensible, ambitious and eager for an opportunity. Her son, Bao Bao, born in 2007, with his mother's great big brown eyes, was now more than two years old, ready for nursery school. That would give her more time to focus on her new gamble. A project in Panyu District would be the ideal thing. He Jieling remained fiercely loyal to her local, rural roots, even as the district was being transformed by the city's relentless march to the south. She had considered investing in the Asian Games City, a cluster of residential and commercial properties next to the Asian Games sports complex, about fifteen miles southeast of the city centre. The development was out in the countryside but connected to the city with a brand-new subway line. Then Ha Street, not far from the Asian Games City, drew her attention. The surge of new construction happening around the Asian Games City would probably boost the whole area. But Ha Street had an added advantage: the state-run China Film Group, the country's biggest film enterprise and a monopoly importer of foreign films, would be opening a new multiplex there. Newspaper advertisements said the Volcano Lake Multiplex would be the second 'five-star cinema' in

Guangzhou, with eight screens and almost 1,400 seats. 'In a single stroke,' reported the *Southern Metropolis Daily*, it would give Panyu District and Guangzhou's south side their first top-grade movie theatre.[84] A steady stream of filmgoers would be a boon for merchants in the development.

He Jieling visited Ha Street a few times in April and May 2010, meeting with leasing agents at the showroom. Though nearing completion, the development was still a building site. But He could picture it all clearly in her mind. On May 29, during a special ceremony held at the showroom, she and other tenants signed their leases. He Jieling leased five shop spaces from the development's management firm, Guangzhou Jin Yue Property Management Company Limited. They were on the first floor of the west side of the development, looking out on the pedestrian street. She planned to use the space for two businesses: a high-end hairdresser, He Jieling Beauty Salon, and a ticket shop for the China Sports Lottery, a state-run network that raises funds for national sporting events. He's lease required her to pay three months' rent up front: 300,000 yuan. On top of that, she secured a deal for the exclusive sale of sports lottery tickets in the development. She had lugged the cash to the signing ceremony in her handbag, altogether more than 400,000 yuan, about $64,000.

The signing expenses were just the beginning. The grand opening date for Ha Street was initially planned for October 1, China's National Day, six weeks ahead of the opening of the Asian Games. If Ha Street had the spaces ready by August, as promised in the lease agreement, He Jieling would be able to complete renovation in time for the opening. The cost of renovation, equipment and essential inventory—hairdressing chairs, washbasins, hood dryers, salon utensils, and hair and nail products—ran to more than 500,000 yuan. She also needed to hire around thirty hairdressers and support staff, who had to be trained and ready for the October opening, which meant she would be paying their wages, room and board by August, only two months away. (It is not uncommon for some service businesses in China hiring young migrant workers to provide them with accommodation.) He Jieling estimated her employees would cost her about 100,000 yuan a month. Until she had a steady clientele bringing in a steady income, He Jieling needed a short-term loan to keep her business running. But getting credit through the traditional banking system is almost impossible in China; banks offer loans only to large, usually state-owned, companies. So, like many small-business owners, He turned to the off-the-books universe of kerbside lenders, the shadow banking industry. She took out more than 1 million yuan in loans, putting up the family's investment properties as collateral. Her creditor was a village head from Nancun Township, where the Agile Garden development is located. He had made a fortune through local land-use rights deals and had set up a loan-sharking business on the side.

By the end of August, He Jieling had hired most of her staff, migrants from provinces near and far—from Sichuan, Henan, Hunan, even a few ethnic Chinese minorities from Guizhou. She had bought equipment and supplies, worked out her services, pricing and advertising, and had even begun to sell membership cards. Ha Street, however, was suffering constant delays. Plans for the National Day grand opening were scrapped, and it was well into September, almost Mid-Autumn Festival, before tenants could get in and begin renovation work. The development's management company was technically in breach of contract for failing to deliver the spaces on time, but it insisted nonetheless on charging rent for the period of the delay. Tenants were exasperated, some furious, and several—as it emerged in the local media a year later—started legal proceedings against the development, one demanding that Ha Street return his 600,000-yuan deposit and pay a penalty for breach of contract. Considering she had put so much on the line, He Jieling was determined to stick things out. Her misgivings were softened, in any case, by the fact that this was an Asian Games project, with clear support from the government. But the Asian Games kicked off in mid-November—for Ha Street, an opportunity slipped by. He Jieling focused her energies on renovation work, determined to open her doors by December.

Soon, the warning signs were hard to ignore. The development remained in a largely unfinished state. Scaffolding covered the facade of the main wing, where the Volcano Lake Multiplex was to be located. There were constant blackouts. A fuse would pop somewhere, and the shops would sink into darkness. He Jieling began to suspect that the management company's focus was on squeezing tenants, not on making Ha Street a viable commercial development. When a pair of property managers strolled into the salon in November, prim in their dark-blue uniforms, and said He Jieling needed to pay a 20,000-yuan 'capacity fee' for an electrical upgrade, she was galled but unsure of her rights. Was her salon really a strain on Ha Street's power? Was this necessary to end her nagging electrical issues? In fact, capacity fees are generally charged, when necessary, by the public utility directly to the consumer. But He paid up, again in cash. She learned later that other tenants had been charged too, some paying two or three times as much as she had. The blackouts persisted.

It was around this time that a phone call came out of the blue from one of He Jieling's friends, one of whose contacts at the local branch of the Urban Planning Bureau had suggested Ha Street might be an illegal development. If that was true, the friend said, she needed to be really careful. He knew she and her husband were considering another major property investment. A further vexing issue was the approval of He Jieling's business licence. She had applied for it at the commercial bureau in Panyu District months earlier, but final processing of this routine matter had been constantly held up. She had no idea why.

The opening of He Jieling's salon, on December 26, 2010, a Sunday, was attended by many of her relatives and close friends. It was the culmination of months of dreaming, planning and hard work. But for He Jieling, the undercurrent of doubt was rising to the surface. She milled among her guests, eventually coming to one of her husband's former classmates, an official at a local hospital. 'So, you're in Ha Street,' he said. 'You have to be careful; the gossip in government circles is that Ha Street is working hand in hand with local criminal gangs in Panyu.' With doubts now surging, He Jieling started asking around.

Within days of her opening, He Jieling received initial confirmation of the rumours about Ha Street's legal status. One of her neighbours in the Agile Garden development was a retired military officer. He pulled some strings to get the details from the Land and Housing Office. Yes, Ha Street was a hodgepodge of violations. At least eight of the primary structures in the complex, including the unit where He's businesses were located, had no planning permits at all. Indeed, a significant amount of the land's usage rights had not even been properly transferred from Nanjiao Village. Local officials had skirted this formality—which is to say they had flagrantly broken the law—by setting up a separate company contracting with Nanjiao Village (under the villagers' noses, but without their knowledge) for the rental of the land for virtually nothing. A major commercial development on collectively held land could not possibly receive planning permission from the Land and Housing Office, and Ha Street certainly had no such permission. Every one of the tenants had been swindled, not simply over construction delays and capacity fees, but from the very start.

However, He Jieling would not bow her head and bear it; that was not in her character. And she still believed she could make this right, that the law would prevail. She tracked down the tip-off hotline for the Guangzhou mayor's office: 12345. Five digits. That was all. Five feather-light touches of her index finger to unleash the storm that engulfed her entire family, gnawed away every path she could have envisioned for herself—and gave her a new sense of purpose.

●

As Spring Festival came and went in early February 2011, He Jieling struggled to keep her businesses afloat amid a rising tide of pressure and intimidation. It was clear almost immediately after her initial complaint to the city government hotline that she had drawn attention to herself rather than to the problems at Ha Street. The first response was a call to her apartment in Agile Garden from an official from her native Dongxiang Village. While she no longer lived in the village, it was still responsible administratively for many of her affairs, because her household registration was there. Since Bao Bao's birth, family planning officials from the village had constantly badgered her about getting a tubectomy, a sterilisation surgery required under China's one-child policy. This time, though, the call was made because the official had been notified by the city petitions office of He Jieling's complaint against Ha Street. He advised her against making any further accusations. He Jieling was undeterred. She busied herself gathering documentary evidence of Ha Street's deceptions. She contacted other government agencies, including the *chengguan*, which deals with illegal city structures. The next official response was a series of visits to her home by plainclothes police, part of the local 'stability maintenance' apparatus in Nancun Township, which had jurisdiction over Agile Garden.

For its part, the Panyu District government wasn't sure how to handle the case—as He Jieling later learned from a city petitions official. Ha Street was a priority development with support at both the district and the subdistrict levels, associated publicly with the Asian Games; and yet certain departments had already broken rank and confirmed, in writing, serious violations. The Urban Management and Law Enforcement Bureau issued He Jieling with an official, chopped response in which it communicated the findings of an official investigation. 'It is the determination of the Panyu District branch of the Guangzhou Urban Planning Bureau that . . . planning and construction procedures were not followed for the abovementioned building structures,' it said, referring specifically to six major buildings in Ha Street. '[These structures] constitute illegal development . . . and do not meet the conditions for preservation under the requirements of urban planning.'[85]

He Jieling's complaints risked running foul not only of government agencies, which were wary of their possible political implications, but also of local criminal organisations. At one point, an official from the local petitions office in Nancun Township paid her a visit at Agile Garden to warn her about local gangs, saying she risked stirring up a hornet's nest if she continued to file complaints. In fact, almost immediately after her opening in December 2010, thugs visited her salon and demanded she pay for their 'protection.' They wanted regular payments and a share of her business. In January, they showed up at the salon nearly every day, 'a different face every time.' When she was away from the shop, they leaned on her employees. With her thistle-like tenacity, He Jieling was determined to clean things up. She had staked her future on the development. It had to work, and if the tenants were left in peace and Ha Street compelled to clean up its act, there was no reason it couldn't. The Volcano Lake Multiplex might still be a major draw. She filed numerous complaints about the protection racket, through phone and online petition services as well as with local police. 'I was so full of confidence,' she said, tears pooling in her eyes, when I spoke to her years later. 'I was so naïve!'

The more He Jieling pushed, the harder she was pushed back. In early February 2011, plainclothes stability maintenance officers began stalking her. They even shadowed her when she dropped her son off at his nursery. At Ha Street, meanwhile, thugs harassed her employees constantly. Calls to the local police were futile. When the thugs actually attacked one of her employees in March, He Jieling decided at last that she had no choice but to close up shop, at least temporarily, until there was some sort of resolution. She posted a notice on the doors of He Jieling Beauty Salon notifying her customers that she was suspending business. She encouraged membership holders to contact her for refunds, but she kept her employees on the payroll for the time being. She wasn't ready to retreat entirely from Ha Street, but a solution to the standoff seemed ever more elusive. He Jieling's priorities were shifting, too. She began to devote much, if not most, of her time to gathering evidence on Ha Street.

Her search plunged her into local internet forums and chat rooms, where she learned about other injustices in the district. She recognised patterns of violence and corruption similar to those in the 2005 Taishi incident, a historic dispute over illegal land seizures. In that case, peasants from Taishi Village, a community just a stone's throw from Agile Garden, gathered peacefully outside the district government offices to petition for the removal of their village chief, who had made land-use rights deals without their approval. In response, district leaders scrambled more than 1,000 riot police, who marched into the village and turned water cannons onto the protesting villagers. They arrested more than forty locals and made off with records from the village budget office. Local thugs were given a free hand in Taishi Village, just as in Ha Street. Lu Banglie, an activist from Hunan Province, was brutally beaten by men guarding the perimeter of the village, and a well-known university professor, Ai Xiaoming, was assaulted by the same rabble when she and others tried to document the struggle. In the wake of the Taishi incident—after the villagers had finally been pressured into withdrawing their demands—a law professor in Beijing, Xiao Han, expressed outrage over the government's criminality. 'For the government of Panyu to resort to violence and kidnapping . . . to beatings and the restriction of personal freedom, to looting and other tactics to respond to the reasonable demands of people in their district, this shows that it is no longer a legitimate grassroots government,' he wrote. 'In fact, it has become an out-and-out criminal gang.'[86] Dai Yongchang, the district deputy chief in charge of police and rural affairs during the Taishi incident, was well known at Ha Street. He had been the most senior district official to attend the development's groundbreaking ceremony—he had cut the ribbon—in May 2010, just before He Jieling signed her contract. The news of Dai's presence at the groundbreaking for this 'international food and entertainment street' had made the front page of the local Party newspaper, *Panyu Daily*.

In the past, He Jieling had shrugged off politics. In China, political affairs are remote. Policy decisions, made behind closed doors, are announced in mystifying slogans from the heights. But the abuses at Ha Street made politics personal. She had done nothing more than her duty as a citizen. Trusting in the government's power to do right, believing in the integrity of its laws, she had reported substantiated illegalities through the proper government channels. Her trust, the very thing the government commanded of her, had marked her as a threat. It dawned on He Jieling that trust was not enough. How could such a system command her trust? 'It was a time of awakening,' she told me. 'I saw that the situation of rule of law in China was impossible. It had to be rebuilt . . . and that meant you had to involve yourself in politics.'

A day or two after she posted the suspension notice outside her salon, He Jieling received a visit at Agile Garden from Fang Yimin, a woman who had opened an apparel shop called Autumn Waters in Ha Street with her husband, a local policeman named Chen Qingming. Fang was visibly agitated. Her concern was that He Jieling's notice risked upsetting other tenants ahead of Ha Street's grand opening, which was scheduled for April 30. Fang said her husband would pay He Jieling a visit at Agile Garden to smooth things out. Instead, Chen sought her out at Ha Street a couple of days later. He discouraged He Jieling from taking extreme measures. He could offer her protection from the thugs, he said, and he could also expedite approval of her business licence. Chen then made his personal interest clear. He Jieling first had to visit his clothing store and buy merchandise worth 10,000 yuan. After that, she could return to the Panyu District commercial bureau and ask specifically for Ms. Su, a section clerk, who would handle all the paperwork.

Though outwardly cooperative, He Jieling was incensed. For weeks, she and her employees had endured bullying by thugs while the police turned a blind eye. Now, here was a policeman offering her paid protection. But she also saw an opportunity. By playing along with Chen, she could document how the development had skirted regulations with the help of local government agencies.

He Jieling discovered that Ha Street was a mirage. It had none of the necessary planning permits and was not authorised to open for business. Nor did the development meet fire safety regulations. Even its address plate, which should have been officially issued by the Public Security Bureau, had been faked. None of the businesses in the development—not He Jieling Beauty Salon, not Autumn Waters—could obtain their business licences honestly. Turning the lie into a truth had a cost. Chen Qingming's solution offered He Jieling the real article: a fake issued by the government.

He Jieling removed the suspension notice from the door of her salon, demonstrating her goodwill to Chen Qingming and the Ha Street officials as she surreptitiously continued her crusade. 'At the time, this harebrained scheme was all I had,' she said. She made two trips to Autumn Waters, swiping her credit card each time for around 5,000 yuan. She met with Ms. Su at the commercial bureau. Her licence was expected to arrive in a few weeks' time. Meanwhile, she pushed ahead with her investigation. For the time being, though, she did not share her evidence about Ha Street's land-use rights and planning violations with other tenants. No one's interests were served by spreading panic ahead of the grand opening. But Chen Qingming and others at Ha Street must have realised before long that He Jieling had her own agenda. The thugs returned. The intimidation intensified.

The ugly culmination came on March 28, 2011. The family was home that night in their Agile Garden apartment when He Jieling received a call from an unknown man demanding she surrender her Ha Street businesses. If she refused, he said, they would exact their penalty in the morning: they would cut off her hands and feet in front of her husband and son. In the paralysed minutes that followed, He Jieling's first instinct was to sit down in front of her computer, Bao Bao sleeping soundly in the next room, and write a

jagged, disjointed online 'death note' addressed to 'the entire country.' It was an appeal for justice written through a rush of tears by
a woman convinced she was about to die, and that no one had the
power or will to prevent it.

> This whole thing goes back about half a year. I,
> He Jieling, come from a poor farming family in
> Panyu . . . Six months ago, I borrowed money to do
> business here in Ha Street. Without the aid of any
> connections, I got the rights for the sale of sports
> lottery tickets in Ha Street. After some time passed,
> these men I didn't recognise showed up and said
> they would help me look after the shop if I paid
> them a protection fee. Every employee of mine who
> was there at the time can attest to this . . .
>
> On this day, March 28, 2011, my entire family
> has been threatened. They say if I don't comply with
> their demands and relinquish without condition all
> of the lottery tickets under my name and my business
> rights to He Jieling Beauty Salon . . . then tomorrow
> morning they will have someone chop off my hands
> and feet. If I still refuse, they will kill me . . .
>
> Perhaps death is the only way I can escape from
> the clutches of these criminal gangs.
>
> I'm sorry, everyone. Please seek justice for me,
> He Jieling, after I am dead.[87]

He Jieling was spared the savage fate spelled out by the caller. She
never found out whether her public note had saved her from the
thugs, or whether she had simply called their bluff. But her stark
exposure of gang activity at Ha Street and her refusal to back out put
her under even greater pressure and scrutiny that spring. In the days
after the posting of the note, thugs from the development kept con-

stant watch outside the Agile Garden apartment. Sometimes they were replaced by a migrant from Henan whom she believed to be one of Ha Street's security guards. It was a period of chaos in which He Jieling felt she could turn nowhere and trust no one. 'I would close down the shops. I would open them again. I would file petitions online using my real identity. My employees were being pressured and paid off. My finances were crumbling. And these thugs were appearing from every direction.'

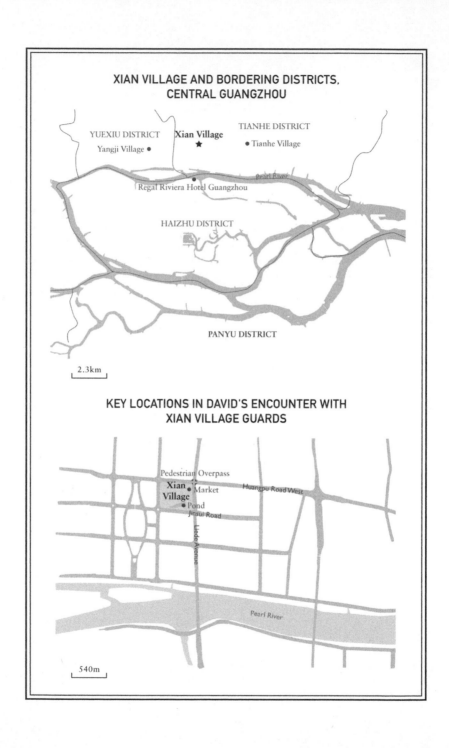

XIAN VILLAGE AND BORDERING DISTRICTS, CENTRAL GUANGZHOU

YUEXIU DISTRICT

Xian Village
★

TIANHE DISTRICT

Yangji Village ●

● Tianhe Village

Pearl River

● Regal Riviera Hotel Guangzhou

HAIZHU DISTRICT

PANYU DISTRICT

2.3km

KEY LOCATIONS IN DAVID'S ENCOUNTER WITH XIAN VILLAGE GUARDS

Pedestrian Overpass

Xian Village
● Market

Huangpu Road West

● Pond

Jinsui Road

Liede Avenue

Pearl River

540m

5

TROUBLEMAKING VILLAGERS

Xian Village, 2010–2012

In the twenty-eighth year of the Republic of China [1939], the Japanese army occupied the fields of Tianhe, Yangji, Xian Village and Shipai to expand the Tianhe Airfield.
—*Xian Village Chronicle*[88]

In Xian Village in mid-July 2010, rumours were circulating that the bustling meat and vegetable market on the northeast corner of the village was to be demolished to make way for the widening of the Xinguang Expressway, another key infrastructure project for the Asian Games. Quoted anonymously in local newspapers, village leaders said they 'could not provide a specific timetable' for the demolition.[89] But stall keepers had already received eviction notices. They were closing up shop and moving on. Uncertainty over the precise date of demolition deepened suspense and disquiet among the villagers. The market was one of a number of collectively held Xian properties. Many villagers suspected that officials had pocketed the land-use rights reclamation funds rather than paying them into the village's accounts, and they were adamantly opposed to any demolition work before the dispute over the village leadership was resolved. They continued their evening marches around the perimeter of the tenements, calling for an open reckoning of the accounts. As August came and the first anniversary of their protest movement drew near, the villagers prepared to reaffirm their demand for the removal of village leader Lu Suigeng.

The anniversary almost surely influenced the calculations of the village officials and district police. They sprang into action on August 12, exactly one week ahead of the anniversary. Riot police mobilised before sundown, around six o'clock, on the grounds of the old Xian Village Elementary School. Eyewitnesses said they sat whispering in close-set rows as the sky darkened, waiting for the command. In addition to the police, there were hundreds of *chengguan*. As word spread of the imminent demolition, villagers streamed in the hundreds over to the condemned market, massing behind the steel-framed barrier wall that surrounded the market and cordoned it off from the street. Determined to defend the only direct entrance, they armed themselves with bamboo sticks, stones and bottles of peanut oil.

The mixed police and *chengguan* force, at least several hundred strong—villagers claimed later that there were more than 2,000—mustered opposite the market on Huangpu Avenue West. After dark, men in black, domed helmets attempted to enter the market. It is unclear whether these were *chengguan* or some other temporary force; some villagers said that Lu Suigeng had hired his own force, hastily outfitted and bussed in to the city. Whatever the case, this force was unprepared for the resistance they faced from the villagers inside. They turned back quickly.

Video footage taken from a high vantage point inside the village and behind the market shows the men filing back across Huangpu Avenue West as onlookers in the street applaud and jeer.[90] The camera swings right, settling on a bristling forest of police in full riot gear about a hundred paces east of the entrance. Red and green glints shimmer from their helmets, shields and truncheons.

Here and there, under the streetlights, there are halo flashes from the rings fastened to their tall staves, instruments that can have only one purpose: to lasso human beings, making them as helpless as rag dolls, in order to drag them away from the safety of the barrier.

The air was charged with rebellion, villagers told me. Above the taunting surf of the gathering crowd in the street, gongs inside the market clanged like broken church bells, the same dissonant music that had accompanied the villagers' defiant dragon-boat launch the previous year. This was the scene before midnight, as traffic crawled along Huangpu Avenue West. But after midnight the road was closed, onlookers were urged away, and the better prepared police units advanced.

More eyewitness video, taken by a villager, clearly shows hundreds of riot police, row after row in tight formation, standing directly across the road from the market. The visors of their dark helmets are drawn down over their faces. Then, suddenly, the front of the formation peels away like a breaker as they make a running charge at the barrier, their clubs flashing in the copper lamplight. The English word 'Police' glares unmistakably from a shield. The air crackles with the sound of shattering bottles. Inside the market, voices scream, 'Save us! Save us!' The police pull back and straggle into formation, and a few officers lag behind, pitching bottles over the barrier. One stands alone, just six or seven paces from it. He draws a bottle from a white sack and launches it towards the villagers. When he realises the sack is now empty he hurls it towards the market with undisguised contempt. Finally, betraying no hint of caution, he turns his back and slouches towards the glimmering mass of his fellows. Not a single volley is returned from the barrier.

In another assault caught on video, an unarmed villager is yanked out into the middle of the street. He shields his head with his arms as the police deluge him with kicks from their boots and blows from their clubs. He is dragged further back towards the mass of police and subjected to another beating. For a moment he is left motionless, in the foetal position, in the centre of the street. Then a pair of officers step forwards and drag him off, one grabbing his languid left arm, the other his right leg. A limp fish, he vanishes into the sea of flashing helmets.

Villagers said afterwards that the police assaults on the market went on until around three o'clock in the morning. After that, the police volleyed canisters of tear gas over the barrier. They brought in bulldozers to topple it, even as villagers remained gathered inside. One villager was crushed under the structure as it fell and, according to a written account produced by the villagers, suffered multiple fractures and had one toe severed permanently from his foot.[91] Once the barrier fell, police swarmed into the market. According to eyewitnesses, they attacked anyone they encountered, young or old. Xian Chuntao, a villager in her twenties, had remained at home that night to look after the family property. Her mother and father had gone to the barrier. At around three o'clock in the morning, Xian Chuntao heard a surf-like hue and cry swell from the direction of the market. 'I knew I had to go out and search for Mum and Dad,' she said. 'As soon as I got downstairs the alley was full of those village-mafia types, the ones in uniform. They were everywhere. There was this other woman, maybe in her late forties or early fifties. She had also come out to search for her parents. The men surrounded her, ten or fifteen of them, and just kept beating her and beating her.' The lamps in the village had all been broken, said Xian Chuntao. She made her way through the gloom and managed to cross Huangpu Avenue West some distance away from the market. The road was now completely closed off. She couldn't get close enough to the market to make out anything beyond the surging tide of riot police.

By the time the sun crept into the sky on August 13, Xian Village was under police lockdown. Most of the village's men had fled, fearing arrest or attack. Lu Qiang and Lu Huiqing, the men who later showed me the village's 'Demolition, Compensation and Resettlement Agreement,' both went into hiding, not returning until the following October. 'All of the young men in the village left after the crackdown,' Lu Qiang told me. 'There was no other choice. We had to abandon our parents, our wives, our children. We never thought they would come down so hard on us,' he said, summing up the events of that night. 'But we were wrong. We underestimated their willingness to use violence. They underestimated our determination to keep fighting.'

The day after the lockdown, an account in Guangdong's Communist Party newspaper, *Nanfang Daily*, which was reprised in other local newspapers, said the Xian Village demolition had followed proper legal procedure. In May 2010, it claimed, Xian Village Industry had signed a demolition agreement with the local Bureau of Land Resources. The compensation funds had been remitted in full to the company. Nevertheless, a small number of 'troublemaking villagers' had chosen to violently obstruct the demolition. Two personnel had been injured and three excavators damaged. Fourteen villagers had been arrested for their involvement. 'During the course of the demolition, and even in the face of attempts at violent obstruction by a few people,' said district officials, 'the Bureau of Land Resources, the *chengguan*, the police and other departments maintained a high level of restraint, patience and accommodation, ultimately clearing away the property in accordance with the law.'[92] One week later, Tianhe District leaders held a press conference to address 'cyber rumours' that police had taken part in the demolition of the Xian Village market.[93]

Police involvement in forced demolitions had become a sensitive national issue, and just eight months later the Ministry of Public Security formally banned the practice.[94] At the press conference, Tianhe District's minister of propaganda urged the public to disregard the chatter on the internet. Explaining the police presence at Xian Village, he said officers had 'raced to the scene' only after they received reports of criminal acts perpetrated by a handful of 'troublemakers.'[95]

One of the troublemakers was seventy-eight-year-old Xian Zhangdao, also one of the five men arrested after the May 5 quarrel with Lu Suigeng's nephews.[96] (In consideration of his advanced age and failing health, the court had decided that spring to release Xian Zhangdao on bail.) In fact, all but one of the villagers arrested on the night of the market demolition were over the age of sixty.[97]

•

The case against Xian Zhangdao, Lu Nianzu and the three other men accused of attacking Lu Suigeng's nephews opened in the Tianhe District Court on September 10, 2010.[98] The courtroom that day was packed with villagers—mostly women and the elderly, as the younger male villagers still felt it was too dangerous to return. The men denied the charges against them, that they were party to a wilful and coordinated attack on the 'injured parties' that had impacted upon public order. Xian Yaoyun did acknowledge that he had struck one of Lu Suigeng's nephews, but he insisted he had struck no one else. The other four denied any physical involvement whatsoever, admitting only that they had surrounded the cadres and vented their frustrations. Xian Zhangdao insisted he had never hit anyone with an umbrella, as was alleged. One of the accused, Lu Zhuguang, swore he had left the scene before the alleged attack took place. He had joined the marchers initially but went home, accompanied by a friend, after his wife called to say dinner was ready. Lu Zhuguang's defence lawyer asked the court to allow his client's wife to testify. This was refused. He asked the court to allow testimony by his client's friend. Again, this was refused. Finally, the lawyer urged the court to review footage from security cameras positioned outside a local bank along his client's route home. The footage could establish beyond a doubt that Lu Zhuguang was nowhere near the scene at the time of the incident. This evidence, too, was refused.

Finding the written testimony of the prosecution's chief witness 'highly irregular,' defence lawyers had formally requested that she appear for cross-examination. But no witnesses appeared in court that day. The prosecution argued its case entirely on the basis of written testimony, including that of Lu Youzhong, a fourth nephew of Lu Suigeng, who was mentioned in the court verdict as 'an employee of Xian Village Industry Company.'[99]

Almost all the villagers in the gallery that day had taken part in the May 5 march. They had witnessed the scuffle from every conceivable angle. But no villagers were allowed to take the stand. Not a single witness stood for the defence. Eyewitnesses described to me how Lu Youhe, Lu Suigeng's nephew and the village security chief, had muscled his way through the crowd after getting the phone call from his cousins. It was only after he shoved an elderly woman to the footpath, they said, that the war of words had tipped towards physical confrontation. But it had been a run-of-the-mill scuffle, a tug-of-war, not a mob attack on the officials.

The prosecution introduced reports from the medical examiner detailing scratches and abrasions suffered by the 'injured parties.' But of course the reports couldn't possibly establish that these 'slight injuries,' as the medical examiner described them, had been inflicted by the accused. As I read the verdict two years later, I puzzled over another glaring inconsistency. If the three 'injured parties' had indeed been surrounded and menaced by a mob intent on harm, how had they managed to escape with only 'slight injuries'?

In December 2012, I arranged to speak to one of the defence lawyers involved in the case. I waited several minutes in an elegant lounge full of Chinese art and antiques, sorting out my list of questions. Finally, the lawyer arrived and greeted me with a polite handshake. He ushered me into a private meeting room and asked me to wait a moment as he stepped out. I took the opportunity to go over my dog-eared copy of the court verdict, the margins of which were crowded with inky doubts and suspicions. The lawyer returned, drawing the door shut with a click, and dropped a thick brown folder of case files on the table. 'You have the verdict?' he asked, eyeing my heavily annotated printout.

'Right here. But I don't know if this is all of it,' I said.

He glanced over the copy. 'Yes, that's the full verdict.'

'I have a lot of questions,' I said. He nodded as I dove in at the top. 'For starters, only one of the accused even admits to hitting anyone.'

'That's right,' he said. Calmly, he opened the brown folder and fanned the case files out on the table like a poker hand.

'Well, look at the case of Lu Zhuguang,' I continued. 'Lu Zhuguang, he wasn't even there. His wife called and told him to come home for dinner. First, his wife should have been called as a witness. Second, they could have submitted phone records to substantiate the call.'

'Yes, of course,' he said. His eyes fixed on me placidly over steepled fingers.

'Well, then, why was nothing submitted in support of the accused?'

'Because this whole thing . . . How can I say this? This is something that happens all the time in China.'

Though I had an inkling he was talking about political interference in the judicial system, I continued to play along. 'But a request could have been made for other witnesses.'

'Other requests *were* made,' he replied, waving his hand over the table. 'All of these are submissions made to the court.'

I studied the files. On top was an official form on which requests for the submission of evidence were listed by hand: a request that Lu Miaobing, the prosecution's chief witness, appear in court for cross-examination; requests for other witnesses; even a request, in the case of one defendant, for the admission of physical evidence that—convincingly, I thought—established his innocence. Prepared as I was with my grocery list of oddities, I was dumbfounded by the brazenness of the court's omissions.

'This was not a legal matter,' the lawyer said. 'It was a political matter.' Just as the village's 'Demolition, Compensation and Resettlement Agreement' had emphasised, the regeneration of Xian Village was a political imperative for the city. Politics trump justice. The strength of a lawyer's hand is of no consequence. The personal freedom of a villager is trivial. All five of the accused were found guilty of the crime of 'picking quarrels and provoking trouble.' With the exception of Xian Zhangdao, the old man who faced separate charges for his role in the market ruckus, and who ultimately served no prison sentence, all of the men were handed prison sentences of ten or eleven months. Feeling a rush of hopelessness for his client, the lawyer defending Lu Nianzu exclaimed in court, 'Lu Nianzu is guilty of no crime, but it is my hope, considering the current political situation in Xian Village, that you ensure his safety by keeping him in prison for another six months.'

•

By the time Lu Nianzu was released from prison, in early 2011, a wall had been erected along the perimeter of Xian Village. The construction crews, villagers said, had been hired by Guangzhou Poly Real Estate Development, the local subsidiary of China's powerful Poly Group, which built Poly Whisper Garden. Officially, no developer had yet been chosen to partner with Xian Village in its regeneration. The bidding process was still many months off. But Poly's involvement had been established hearsay, never denied, for almost two years, and in August 2009 *Southern Metropolis Daily* had reported, on the authority of 'relevant sources,' that 'Xian Village's land is already "settled" for Guangzhou Poly Real Estate.'[100] On December 1, 2011, when the public call for project bids was issued at last, the criteria ensured that Poly was the top contender: '[Bidders] must be listed domestic enterprises with registered capital of no less than 1.5 billion yuan, having assets of no less than 50 billion in 2010, and must have already successfully completed old village redevelopments nationwide totalling no less than 300,000 square metres [more than 3 million square feet].'[101] A journalist asked the village deputy chairperson, Lu Youxing, why the thresholds had been set so high.

'The position of Xian Village is very favourable, being right in the heart of the central business district,' he said. 'So naturally the villagers want to work with a capable enterprise.'[102] Xian Village Industry would decide the winning bid from among the three highest bidders. The choice, in other words, was Lu Suigeng's.

Whoever was responsible for the wall enclosing the village, there could be no doubt about its meaning. It was a hangman's knot, choking the village off from the city beyond. It announced the inescapable fact of the village's destruction—like the painted circles ringing the character for 'demolish' on the walls of condemned buildings in China. It also consigned the village to a private and savage regime of control, sanctioned by the rapacious drive to create a 'civilised city.' On the outside surface of the wall, the future was announced with larger-than-life deceits—pictures of a pair of old men playing mahjongg in a leafy courtyard, and the words 'Making real strides for the lives of the people; creating a prosperous neighbourhood'; a woman grinning through a traditional flag dance: 'I love Xian Village; I have a dream.'

In the darkened alleyways beyond the wall, fear was insistent. People spoke in timid whispers, their eyes casting left and right for any sign of Lu Suigeng's agents. Nonresidents visiting Xian Village were required to register with the private security guards at the gates, who kept detailed ledgers of all entries, noting the name, address and phone number of the person being visited. The oppressive security regime and the constant fear of forced demolition weighed heavily on Xian villagers for many months, a period Lu Qiang later referred to as 'the darkest days.' In July 2012, when I met with him and Lu Huiqing at the Regal Riviera Hotel in Haizhu District, Lu Qiang looked exhausted. His bloodshot eyes hastened left and right, lighting fearfully on anyone who happened past our spot. His shoulders hunched protectively. The villagers had petitioned that week outside the headquarters of the provincial Communist Party leadership building over plans to fill in the village pond. A key feature of traditional village design in China's south, the pond formed the heart of the village's ancient drainage system. The villagers had warned the authorities that if the pond were filled in, the consequences would be dire for the residents, who were already dealing with poor drainage and sanitation. But plainclothes police had detained and questioned Lu Huiqing's father and two other elderly villagers for several hours as they were preparing to return to the village after the petitioning visit. As they emerged from a local teashop, the three men were surrounded, handcuffed and packed into a waiting police van.

Lu Qiang threw his hands up in exasperation as he explained the pond issue. 'If they're so concerned about the problem of flooding,' he said, referring to the way city officials had in recent years listed poor flood control as another reason for pushing ahead with urban-village regeneration, 'why do they want to fill in the village pond? The whole village—80 per cent of it, at least—relies on that pond for drainage. Just imagine what would happen if they filled it in.'

'If the water didn't drain off we would have a major problem on our hands,' Lu Huiqing added. 'It would encourage a disease outbreak.'

'We've raised this issue before with leaders,' Lu Qiang continued. 'Once the pond is filled in, if there is an outbreak of some sort or another, how would they deal with that? Later, the provincial government applied some pressure. They asked local leaders not to try filling it in.'

'What's the latest word?' I asked.

Lu Qiang considered for a moment. 'Things are still really up in the air,' he said at last. 'After we petitioned, the provincial authorities gave us an emergency contact number. They said if there was any move to fill in the pond we should give them a call right away. Our village's predicament doesn't really worry the provincial government, but this danger does. They're really afraid there might be some kind of epidemic situation.'

'At present, the sanitation conditions in the village are really poor,' Lu Huiqing said. 'Basically, everything relies on our own efforts, on the villagers that are still holding out. We handle all the sewage issues ourselves.'

The village leaders had no interest in maintaining or improving conditions in Xian Village. The more desperate the situation, the easier it was to make the case for villagers signing the demolition agreements and vacating. Pro-regeneration propaganda posted around the village enunciated the promise of improved living.

A billboard on a side street showed two images of serious flooding in 2011—residents wading up to their knees in murky water. The caption beneath read 'Xian Village today.' The image next to these showed a clean architectural rendering of the conceptual Xian Village in an aerial view. The caption read 'Xian Village after regeneration.' In fact, the 2011 flooding had hit the newer areas of Tianhe District just as hard as the old ones. At nearby Jinan University, the flooding had been so serious that classes had to be cancelled.

A few days before my meeting with Lu Qiang and Lu Huiqing, I had sat with a group of elderly villagers on the shady southeast side of the village pond, where they were defending it against the demolition crews they feared would arrive at any moment to backfill it with rubble. Suddenly, a woman came hustling up the path from the tenements, wailing in Cantonese. A huddle of old women hurried over to attend her grief. 'What's the matter?' I asked the man next to me. He was stretched out on a wicker lounge chair, unfazed by the eddy of drama around us, his eyes sleepy, hands folded behind a head of tussled silver. He shifted, adjusting the toothpick clasped between his teeth. The police, he explained, had just detained the woman's husband as he stepped out of the village to pay his electricity bill.

•

On a hot evening in August 2012, one month after the petition over the village pond, I saw for myself the fear that ruled in Xian Village. Security was tight around the perimeter, guards in camouflage posted at each gap in the wall. The guards were generally unwelcoming to foreign visitors, and on the day of my photography tour with filmmaker Zhao Dayong back in January, they had said that as a matter of policy the village was off-limits to those who didn't live there, unless they could provide detailed information, including a name and phone number, about the residents they planned to visit. But on the east side of the village I finally glimpsed an opportunity to enter without registering. To the left of the gate, behind a scratched-up wooden school desk, slouched a pair of shabby-looking guards, their cap-shaded faces angled down towards their lambent mobile-phone screens. But just as I slipped past, the older of the two hopped to his feet and caught my sleeve. 'Eh, *eh, eh!*'

'Aiya, it's so hot today,' I said, gazing past him into Fanyang Main Street, a village alley crowded with market stalls. 'I'll just buy a bottle of water and come right back, okay?'

'Fine, fine,' he said, returning to his post. His eyes tracked me as I walked over to the nearest fruit stand, bought a bottle of water, then sifted with overdramatised interest through heaps of dark red lychee, newly in season. As soon as the guard's attention shifted, I darted farther up the alley, rushing past the stony face of the ancestral temple to the Lu clan and dissolving into the eddy of villagers and migrant workers. The alley gaped open a bit further on, where several properties on the north side of the village pond had been toppled into squat hills of rubble. There, small groups of migrants, many of them shirtless in the summer heat, were crouching outside a convenience stall, a hole-in-the-wall shop offering a range of basic essentials, everything from toilet paper to Chinese liquor. I bought a cold bottle of Pearl River, Guangzhou's local brew, and squatted on a red plastic stool.

'Are you American?' one migrant ventured almost immediately. (Was it really so obvious?) He dragged his stool over, close to mine, and before long a few of us were deep in conversation. The theme was China's place in the world, a subject to which Chinese often circle back apprehensively in conversation, and my native country was a looking-glass that reflected their hopes and insecurities.

Were American buildings as tall as theirs? Was it true that the American economy was still foundering while theirs was booming? How far behind was China, really? A decade maybe? Two? As the sky darkened, bats fluttered out of the shadowy ruins and wheeled in awkward circles over the pond. We talked about China's property boom, which had provided most of them with steady employment in the city. We talked about life back in their hometowns—in Hunan, Guizhou and Anhui. We even stumbled into the morass of regional security. Why had the United States supported Japan's claim to contested islands in the East China Sea? Someone asked if I wanted another beer.

And then, all of a sudden, they scattered. At my side, a migrant from Hunan Province glanced over his shoulder and broke off midsentence before scurrying across the alley and perching atop his three-wheeled pedal cart, eyes cast down.

Off to my left, in the maw of one of the smaller alleys, stood a solidly built man in a striped polo shirt, the clean white bands glowing through the dusk. He commanded a brume of fear and submission, like a wolf that had padded out of the shadows and sent the thrushes beating into the treetops. Implacably, he studied me, the only creature that hadn't properly registered terror. It was a moment before I even noticed the shorter, thickset bulldog of a man hunched obediently at his side.

Wrestling for calm against the quickening pulse of adrenaline, I passed my empty bottle to the shopkeeper, said thank you in English, and started back the way I had come. My only thought was to get out of the east gate, from where, if necessary, I could make a run for it. As I reached the edge of the alley-side market, I could feel Polo at my back. I paused at a stall selling star anise and blood-red peppers, hoping he would pass. Instead, he waited, stiff as a soldier, just inches behind my back. When I turned to move on, he brought his arm out like a level-crossing gate. 'What are you doing in here?' he asked.

I shook my head obtusely, playing the part of the innocent tourist.

'I know you speak Chinese,' he said. I shook my head again and brushed past him, not more than a hundred paces from the gate. He strode along at my side while Bulldog padded behind. 'I heard you talking with them,' he said. 'I know you speak Chinese.'

'What do you want?' I asked, giving in.

'Have you taken any pictures in here?'

'No, I was just getting a drink.'

'I need to see your phone,' he said, his tone peremptory. I quickened my steps.

'Who are you?' I asked.

'I'm a police officer.'

'Then I'd like to see your badge.'

This brought a huff of contempt from Bulldog.

'Why don't you come back with us?' Polo said, with sinister calm. 'Then I'll show you my badge.'

A bolt of fear jagged my insides. Come back with them where?

'If you're police,' I said as we neared the gate, 'then by law you have to present your badge.'

Another huff burst out of Bulldog. It was his habit, no doubt, to gnaw right through the hambone of the law.

'Come back with us, and I'll show you my badge,' Polo repeated.

I was on the footpath outside the village now, my back to the Liede Avenue. Bulldog barred the way north, towards Huangpu Avenue West. Polo stood on the other side; just beyond him was the crossing at Jinsui Road. I pictured myself darting out towards the road before spinning north for the pedestrian overpass. Could I move fast enough?

'Did you take pictures inside? I need to see your phone,' Polo said, presenting his open palm.

'This is ridiculous. What does it matter?'

'There are certain national conditions here,' he said gravely. *Guoqing*, or 'national conditions,' refers broadly to any political issue or incident regarded as sensitive by Chinese authorities—something they would rather handle quietly, away from the gaze of scrutiny.

'*Guoqing?*' I asked. 'What *guoqing?*'

'Matters of demolition and resettlement,' he said soberly. 'We need you to come back with us.'

'If you don't show me your badge, how do I know you're not con artists?' I said.

'We're police, just like them,' he said, gesturing towards the ragged pair of guards at the gate. It was a careless remark. I knew very well that the guards were private hires, migrants from the countryside with no formal police training. 'You need to come back with us,' he said again.

I felt my body tense like a torsion spring. The time had come for action, to untwist from the instant of fateful decision. *Run*, I thought. *Run*. And just then, from the edge of that moment's abyss, I saw a Westerner round the corner at Jinsui Road. 'Well, *there* you are!' I heard myself shout in English. Arms out wide, I bounded past Polo. As I reached the stranger, I gasped under my breath, 'Can you please pretend we're friends?'

'Sure,' he said, not skipping a beat.

Polo's wolfish eyes tracked us as we hurried past, but I sensed a new uncertainty in that look. Bulldog trailed us halfway up the footpath towards Huangpu Avenue West before padding back to his master. And so I was plucked from a precarious end by a Swedish furniture importer.

After that, I avoided the tenements for a while. The situation had become volatile. Those who opposed Lu Suigeng were bullied even beyond the confines of the village. On December 26, 2011, a gang of plainclothes men, presenting no identification, had broken into a villager's home in the middle of the night and cuffed both him, Xian Yaojun, and his wife, Li Meikeng, in front of their nine-year-old son. Xian had been one of the village's most outspoken champions since 2009. Li was released the next day, after hours of exhausting interrogation, but Xian was sentenced to twenty-two months of reeducation through labour—a form of administrative punishment outside the judicial system—on trumped-up charges of soliciting a prostitute, an extralegal case based on the written testimony of a single witness. Xian was kept in custody for twelve months, then released on December 24, 2012, 'for good behaviour,' but only after he agreed to drop a lawsuit against the Tianhe District police.[103]

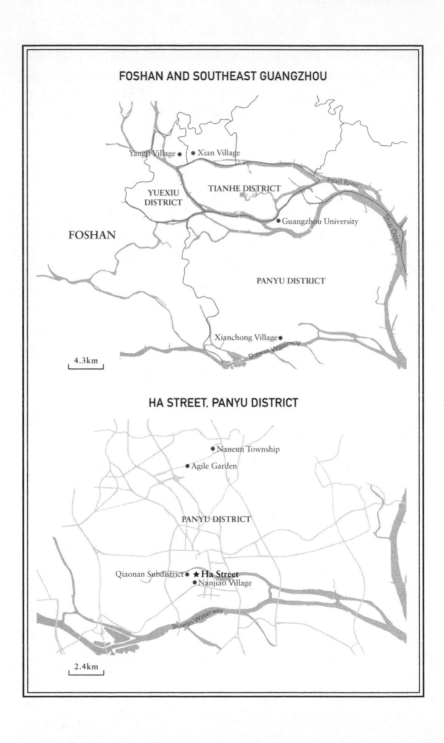

6

DANCING WITH SHACKLES ON

He Jieling, Nanjiao Village, 2011–2012

On April 30, 2011, the day of Ha Street's grand opening, the doors of He Jieling Beauty Salon were closed. He Jieling's apartment at Agile Garden was under tight surveillance by local stability preservation officers and thugs of undetermined origin. For two days she couldn't leave the apartment. Meanwhile, the grandiose ceremony went off without a hitch, and even after the drama of the past seven months, it might still have been possible to believe in the promise of Ha Street. If only the scaffolding could come down and the finishing touches be revealed. If only the thugs retreated, leaving the tenants in peace. If only new merchants came to fill the empty storefronts. If only the stores, with their illicitly obtained business licences, could fill up with customers. If only.

When I visited Ha Street with He Jieling for the first time, in December 2012, the faded characters of her name were still visible over the shuttered shopfront. Tears glistened in her eyes as she relived her wrecked dream. Despite the successful opening, Ha Street's problems, it turned out, had only just begun. In May, just a few weeks after the opening, the Volcano Lake Multiplex announced it

was closing its doors after operating for less than a month. Just as it
had seemed the development might get on its feet after all the delays
and frustrations, the news came like a crushing final judgement. The
cinema was Ha Street's backbone. It had promised to draw a steady
stream of customers to this corner of Qiaonan Subdistrict and away
from other shopping and entertainment areas in Panyu. It was the
reason many tenants had bet on the complex in the first place.

The closure of the multiplex was a shock to Ha Street tenants.
Like He Jieling, most of them had invested hundreds of thousands,
even millions, in the venture. One tenant, Ah Mei, had opened a
shop with her husband using their entire savings of about 400,000
yuan, or $64,000, scraped together over more than a decade of mi-
grant labour in the city. Many had also taken on debt to pursue their
dreams. Tenants clamoured desperately for answers. Why would a
powerful, state-owned enterprise like the China Film Group suddenly pull out of a brand-new development when its presence had
been months in the planning? He Jieling, who had the documents
confirming that Ha Street was an illegal development, knew the answer to that question. The China Film Group had abandoned Ha
Street because it could not obtain the necessary licences to operate
a cinema there. Obviously, it could grease palms like the rest of the
tenants. But the drawbacks of operating a multiplex in a development without the necessary licences—and not up to fire safety regulations—far outweighed the advantages for a powerful enterprise
that could dictate its own terms.

Most Ha Street tenants had learned the truth by the summer.
Some heard it from locals in Nanjiao Village, where there was much
internal rancour over the handling of the collectively held village
land and property, including Ha Street. Word got around. Panic per-
vaded Ha Street. Notices popped up in many of the storefronts from
desperate tenants hoping to sublet their spaces. The management
company shrugged off the incriminations, telling tenants they were
bound to their contracts unless they could find other paying tenants
to step in.

By the time I visited the complex in December, the shop spaces along the main pedestrian street were nearly all vacant. The floor-to-ceiling windows had been dressed from the inside with vinyl advertisements and generic tributes to consumerism. At ground level, several windows had been filled with banners, the colours fading, congratulating a dance studio on opening its doors in Ha Street. Directly above, a second-story window had been dressed with a banner on which dark silhouettes of female shoppers stepped to and fro in high heels. A message in perky purple characters said wishfully 'Happily buying things.'

Trailed by a distrustful security guard, He Jieling guided me on a tour of the shop spaces behind the main strip, and I saw that in fact there was nothing at all to buy at Ha Street, happily or otherwise. Through the unmasked windows of S&C, a boutique promising 'Japanese and Korean apparel,' I saw an interior stripped bare. The double doors were secured with a rusty U-lock. Next door, e-Lake, another fashion boutique, was likewise padlocked, with a discoloured sign in the window reading 'Inventory clearance: big discounts.' Next in line came Bixim, which had once been a lingerie shop—torn posters and other castaways now littering the floor. Saddest, somehow, was the gutted treat shop to its left, which some hapless entrepreneur had aptly named, in English, Taste of Love. It too was padlocked and void, dust gathering thickly on the surface of the window. Every shopfront in Ha Street, it seemed, displayed a broken dream.

In May 2011, as furious tenants went head-to-head with the management, shouting them down at an emergency meeting called after the cinema's closure, He Jieling tried to maintain a lower profile. She shared her evidence with just a few others. She hoped that by avoiding direct confrontation she might recover some level of trust with the management company and get deeper inside their operation. But despite this outward discretion, He Jieling continued her crusade against the development through government agencies— filing formal requests for information, submitting online petitions.

By July, the patience of Ha Street's management had grown thin. The doors to He Jieling Beauty Salon and the sports lottery shop were padlocked on July 22. A civil ruling notice from the Panyu District Court was posted on both storefronts saying He Jieling owed the development 270,000 yuan in rent. The shops had been shuttered and the property inside secured, the notice said, to prevent the owner from 'transferring assets.' In fact, according to her contract, He Jieling was entitled to eight months in the development rent free. She had operated for just nine or ten months, depending on how the start of her tenancy was calculated; like many tenants, she had bickered with the management company over its failure to finish the development on schedule. Under the most unfavourable scenario, the most rent He could have been responsible for was 100,000 yuan.

The real reason for the court ruling became clear almost immediately. The day the notice was posted, officials from Nanjiao Village invited He Jieling to dinner. They wanted to talk things through, they said. The dinner took place the next evening at Panlaixun Restaurant, in a village called Chentong on the southern edge of Panyu. Present were an assemblage of district officials, high and low: top leaders from Nanjiao Village; He Binghua, the chief of Xianchong Village, a little more than a mile southeast of Ha Street; a senior official from Panyu District's Environmental Protection Bureau. The men urged He to end her whistleblowing campaign. One of the local village officials offered her a stack of cash—enough money to settle her debts. If she agreed to leave Ha Street, they said, they could also offer her favourable terms on a piece of land in Nanjiao Village.

He Jieling had not come to negotiate terms; she had come for a glimpse of the men behind the development. Concealed in her purse, a digital recorder her husband had bought for her was logging the discussion. But for a moment, perhaps, He hesitated. 'I remember everything that night so clearly,' she told me later, as we sat under a concrete pavilion in a park among the tenements of Nanjiao Village, a short jaunt from Ha Street. Unlike the desolate development, the back alleys of Nanjiao were full of life. Down the street from where He Jieling and I sat, a few villagers were gathered on the stoop of a small shop overflowing with essentials, everything from mops and buckets to cigarettes. 'I had these huge debts hanging over my head,' He Jieling said, recalling her meeting at Panlaixun Restaurant, 'and I knew that if I just took the money, all of our financial troubles would disappear, and I would have powerful backers, too.' But in the end she refused. 'I chose the road to disgrace and ruin,' she said. 'All for a bit of dignity.' The dinner ended badly, a threat hovering in the sticky summer air outside the Panlaixun. 'They told me if I didn't come to terms, then I shouldn't even think about staying in Panyu,' He Jieling said. 'They thought they could buy my silence, but they underestimated my determination.'

As soon as she arrived home that night, He Jieling sat down at her computer to type out a full account of the meeting at the restaurant, including a transcript of her surreptitious recording. On Monday morning, July 25, she slipped the report into her handbag and set off for the police headquarters in Qiaonan Subdistrict, which had jurisdiction over Ha Street. She made a formal statement to the police, presenting her report on the dinner meeting. She urged them to launch an investigation and to notify the Chinese Communist Party's internal office for graft inquiries, the Central Commission for Discipline Inspection.

This time, the hammer came down hard. It is unclear who exactly struck the blow, but within days of He Jieling's report to the Qiaonan police, her loan shark—the village official from Nancun Township—ordered a surprise assault on the Agile Garden apartment. It happened at nightfall. Fortunately, three-year-old Bao Bao was out with relatives at the time. There was a flutter of voices in the corridor, a faint click as they tried the door, the rattling sound of fingers jimmying the lock. Finally, the door swung violently open, slamming against the inside wall. A group of more than ten men burst into the entryway. They were 'rough-looking migrants,' He

Jieling said, with accents from poorer inland provinces like Henan and Hebei. At first the scene was pure bedlam. Shouts and threats volleyed back and forth. But the building manager for Agile Garden arrived right on their heels, demanding to know what the fuss was about. The men said they were there to collect a debt. They weren't leaving until the business was done. Their boss demanded that He Jieling and her husband, who had put up their pair of Agile Garden apartments as collateral for their loan, transfer ownership of the properties to settle their debt. He Jieling insisted the men leave. When they refused, she called the police. A pair of officers arrived a few minutes later, but when they understood the situation they said there was nothing they could do. *Mei banfa*.

There was nothing, in fact, that anyone could do. However lawless the lender's tactics, the power of the law—in Panyu, at any rate—was on his side. The only way to end the standoff, and the only way to settle their debts, was to acquiesce to the lender's demands. In the end, the thugs forced He Jieling and her husband to sign a short-term 'rental agreement,' which allowed two of the men to remain as houseguests with them in the Agile Garden apartment until the necessary paperwork was finalised and the family's belongings removed. As a further incentive to hasten things along, He Jieling was obligated under the agreement to pay each of her lodgers 500 yuan for every day they spent under her roof. He Jieling later referred to her guests as 'the two boys.' Once things quieted down that first night, she gave each of them clean towels and toothbrushes. The next day, as she and her husband were busy packing up their belongings, 'the two boys' kept Bao Bao entertained. He Jieling said they even apologised. They didn't like imposing any more than she liked having them there. For what it was worth, they felt sorry about the whole thing. And even under the circumstances, He Jieling felt sorry for them too. In 2013, chatting on social media, He Jieling and I went back over the details of this painful episode, and still she refused to find fault with 'the two boys.' 'They were poor and afraid, that's all,' she told me. 'That's the only reason they were serving those dirty officials.' By the third day, the paperwork was finalised, their things removed. They said goodbye to Agile Garden and found temporary refuge in a cheap hotel nearby. For Bao Bao, it was all an adventure. He had no idea their world had just crumbled.

In the days that followed, as the family searched for a suitable apartment to rent, He Jieling realised—to all appearances, at least—her flippant ambition to become an 'unscrupulous businesswoman.' On August 6, the *Information Times* newspaper reported that He Jieling, the owner of a beauty salon in Panyu's Ha Street, had 'absconded' after the salon was sealed by a court order for debts owed to the development. The salon's employees were still owed a month's wages, according to an anonymous source, and membership holders had also been left in the lurch. The paper had no trouble tracking down He Jieling, who of course was no longer welcome at Ha Street. She explained to the reporter that she had never intended to leave her employees unpaid. She had started offering her members refunds months earlier, she said, and she hoped those who hadn't been refunded could be repaid once the shop's property was sold at court auction. 'Right now,' she said, 'I really have no money.'

'While speaking with our reporter,' said the paper, 'He Jieling cried uncontrollably. She told the reporter business at her salon was good at first, but things had come to this point because she had informed the relevant government authorities about illegal building in the Ha Street development, and therefore she had run foul of certain people.' This casual detail, no more than a footnote in what was otherwise a story about jilted employees—'Hair salon shut down, employees can't get wages'—was in fact the first mention anywhere in China's tightly controlled media of Ha Street's (then but alleged) misdeeds.[104]

Other coverage followed, thanks in large part to He Jieling's tireless efforts. In September, *Society Focus*, an investigative news program on the government-run Guangdong Television, ran an in-depth segment documenting Ha Street's planning and construction violations. The lead-in was a personal account from He Jieling. Her face streamed with tears. Her voice cracked under the strain. 'For more than a year, they've known everything, even where my child goes to school. Where my husband goes to work. We get phone calls in the middle of the night saying they can buy one of my husband's hands for 100,000, one of my husband's feet for 200,000. There's no-where to hide. My spirit has been strained to the breaking point over the past year. I don't want to be a victim like this any more. I would willingly sacrifice every cent my family has.'

Cut to the news anchor. The words 'Society Focus' turned slowly behind her as she introduced the segment. 'This woman's name is He Jieling. So what situation befell her? What people did she run foul of? Why would she be threatened again and again? Let us go first to a place called Ha Street. It is there, He Jieling says, that her night-mare began.' How, the program asked, had a project ruled illegal continued to stand? Why had there been no action by the *chengguan* of the Urban Management and Law Enforcement Bureau, which was responsible for dealing with illegal structures? A spokesperson for the *chengguan* in Qiaonan Subdistrict told the program they had not taken action because they had never received instructions from the district's Urban Planning Bureau. 'As soon as a report was made, we filed the case,' he said, visibly frustrated. 'We sent it to the plan-ning bureau, but as time went on there was never any decision.' The anchor ended the segment with a solemn summary. It was capped with a provocative question that shot right to the absurd heart of Ha Street: 'A commercial street doesn't go through any of the nec-essary approvals but puts out a call for tenants anyway. It is able to invite numerous leaders to lavish their praise. The government de-partments responsible for oversight see an illegal development right before their eyes, but no one does anything. No one stops it. All at once, hundreds of tenants lose out, suffering immense losses. When these tenants go through normal channels to petition, they suffer in-timidation and abuse. Exactly what sort of backing does this project have? This is a question we will continue to watch.'[105]

Two months after the television segment, the tabloid *Southern Metropolis Daily* published its own in-depth report on Ha Street, further confirming the development's planning and building violations.[106] The *Society Focus* anchor's question went unanswered, however. Before long, the question itself was forgotten. Meanwhile, Ha Street lingered, a lie whose roots stretched down to some invisible and unaccountable source of power.

•

Meanwhile, in the August 8, 2011, edition of the *Southern Metropolis Daily*, He Jieling had stumbled across an article about a dispute over land-use rights sales in the village of Xianchong.[107] Villagers there had accused the village chief, He Binghua, of skimming off at least 7 million yuan, about $1.1 million, from the land-use rights requisition funds the village had received from the state for the building of the Asian Games City. The name of the village head jumped out at He Jieling: He Binghua had been one of the local officials at her dinner meeting two weeks earlier. Scouring online forums, she tracked down a post apparently left by a representative of the petitioning villagers, named in the article as Huang Zemin. She added her own post alluding to her investigation into Ha Street. Perhaps they could join forces and share information. Were the villagers interested in meeting face to face?

'I didn't know the villagers from Xianchong at the time,' He Jieling later told me. 'But I posted my name and phone number on a chat site and said I wanted to exchange information. Thankfully, they saw it. People go online now, you know, and use new media. Even journalists go online to find information. The first time we met was at a coffee shop. We shared some information. Later, Huang Zemin and I decided to apply for a public demonstration. We thought if we stuck together that might work, right?' She shook her head and let out a carping laugh. 'We never thought we'd be targeted so fiercely for applying for a public demonstration. Once we had submitted the application, I was invited to tea several times.' In China, 'invited to tea' has become universal code for an informal interrogation and warning by security police.

He Jieling's bid to practise her constitutionally guaranteed right to public demonstration was given added support by a national law passed in 1989 in order, at least ostensibly, to ensure that citizens exercised this right 'legally' and in a way that maintained 'social stability and public order.'[108] In response to the law, Guangdong Province passed its own regulation in 1990, which reiterated these rights and specified the procedures necessary for citizens to exercise them.[109] A formal application for a demonstration had to be made at least five days before the planned date of the event. Applicants needed to specify the person in charge of the event, including a copy of valid identification. The route, number of people, starting time and ending time all had to be detailed on the application. Applicants also had to specify their methods and goals. What was the purpose of the demonstration? Would slogans be used? Placards? Posters? Floats? The regulation required local authorities to respond in writing to applications at least forty-eight hours before the start of the planned event. If the authorities failed to notify applicants of their decision, the regulation made clear that this was to be understood as tacit approval.

On January 10, 2012, He Jieling and Huang Zemin submitted three separate applications for marches to be held on January 18. They would begin at 9:00 a.m. and proceed for around four miles, with placards and loudspeakers, from the government headquarters of Nancun Township, in the north of Panyu, across an arm of the Pearl River to the campus of Guangzhou University on Xiaoguwei Island. According to the first application, 100 people would protest against the dirty land-use rights deals in Xianchong Village. A further 100 people, according to the second application, would express their disapproval of the seizure of collectively held land and property in nearby Meishan Village. The third application was for a group of fifteen people, who would demonstrate against the illegal development of Ha Street. The combined protest would mean more than 200 villagers and bilked merchants marching through the heart of Panyu District. Two days before she submitted the applications, He Jieling scribbled out a seventeen-page harangue on the rights of citizens and the vagaries of unbridled power. She even supplied her own epigraph for the document.

In China: If a Citizen Legally Applies for
a Demonstration, Will It Be Approved?

Conscience can take a person's life. But without conscience, what sense is there in being a human being?

HE JIELING, JANUARY 8, 2012

In Panyu today, only those who have fought for their rights understand that rights defence is done by those who have been brutalised into foolishness . . . In Panyu today, only those who have fought for their rights understand just how negligent the district government really is, how the petitions offices and the Discipline Inspection Office assure you things are being investigated, but it's all a deception, a process by which they exhaust you . . . In Panyu today, only those who have fought for their rights understand just how black the world will become once a complaint has been filed. In Panyu today, only those who have fought for their rights understand that behind the blackness of the 'black society' [of organised crime], there is an even greater blackness . . .

There is a district that says its people are free to hold demonstrations, but they must first apply. Now we are applying in accordance with the law,

and we hope the authorities won't find more reasons
and excuses.[110]

The applications were rejected outright. He Jieling was invited to tea.
But her failed experiment was a sort of bitter success. It was part of a
process by which she confirmed a crooked system. Her specialty was
an odd form of civil resistance—a lawful but unwelcome campaign
to press the government to live by its own laws. She was a citizen
'dancing with shackles on,' a phrase familiar to Chinese from all
walks of life who try to push the bounds. Some say it is pointless
to dance. But the music of the chains creates a meaningful form of
defiance, a bitter reminder to all that the shackles are real.

In December 2011, He Jieling had registered an account on Sina
Weibo, China's most popular microblogging platform, which is similar to Twitter, the latter having been blocked by the government in
2009. Her account name was 'He Jieling: 138 Guangzhou Villages,'
a reference to the number of villages located within the urban planning area of Guangzhou. Nearly all of these villages were suffering
in one way or another under an onslaught of urban development in
which their rights and interests were forfeit. Sharing so many problems, and sharing also a sense of local identity reaching deep into
the past, the villages could become a powerful force for change if
only they were bound by a common purpose beyond their isolated
injustices. If only they could come together. Before long, He Jieling
was involved in cases across the city, from Yangji Village (where a
handful of villagers in the middle of the city were holding out for fair
compensation) to the Guangzhou University Town (where investors
had been tricked into buying horribly substandard apartments).

In January 2013, I accompanied He Jieling to Xianchong Village,
where I met Huang Zemin and other villagers who were fighting for
answers from the government over the theft of their farmland. The
village homes gazed out over a broad stretch of unfinished road that
had been part of the Asian Games development push in 2010. The
road was empty and abandoned now, weeds rejoicing along its edges.

That evening, we had sat at a table with other Xianchong villagers—our main course a novel dish of stir-fried local field mice—as
they explained the bribery and corruption case of their former village
head He Binghua. He had been convicted five months earlier and
sentenced to twenty-one months in jail but was now apparently free
and living large. He Binghua's crime was typical: he had conspired
with an administrative superior, the deputy head of Shawan Township, to form a shell company contracting with Xianchong Village to
rent 377,000 square feet of rural land for a pittance. The plan was to
build factory and warehouse space that could be leased to other companies at enormous profit without fussing with the compulsory land-
use rights transfer to the state or applying for industrial permits.[111]

As He Jieling became more involved in rights-defence cases in
2011, she and her family were uprooted. Between 2011 and 2013
they were evicted twice from their lodgings in Panyu, as her work
ran foul of the authorities. In 2013, they were finally pushed out of
Panyu, settling to the north in Tianhe District, not far from the
beleaguered slums of Xian Village.

•

On November 29, 2012, the new general secretary of the Chinese
Communist Party, Xi Jinping, introduced a new political catchphrase, the 'Chinese dream,' during a scripted visit to the National
Museum,[112] where an exhibit called 'Road to Revival' extolled a grand
narrative of China's triumph—thanks to the glories of the Communist Party—over the vagaries of modern history and the 'century of
humiliation' that had begun with the Opium Wars in 1840.[113] In his
remarks at the museum, Xi Jinping said that, in his view, 'realising
the great rejuvenation of the Chinese people is our greatest dream
in the modern era,' and 'this dream is the common desire of generations of Chinese,'[114] The 'Chinese dream,' which rapidly took flight
in the state-run media in the days that followed, was the idea that the
Party, and the Party alone, could develop China into a prosperous

and powerful nation, strong enough that it never need fear the kind of bullying it suffered in the nineteenth and twentieth centuries at the hands of foreign aggressors.

Like those of so many other bilked investors, He Jieling's dreams had been destroyed at Ha Street. They had been hollowed out by a society in which the law was corrupted by power, and as a result her personal rights were nothing more than a fantasy. 'If an illegal building structure like Ha Street is allowed to stand,' she said in the letter supporting her application for a public protest, 'what does the law signify any more? Are we, as citizens, still expected to abide by and respect the law?'[115] But the dream gone astray set He Jieling on a dogged path of conscience—'treasured conscience,' as she called it. 'The fate of any nation is clenched in the hands of its people,' she wrote. 'If only we know in our hearts that the greatness and power of China depend on the constant striving of each and every citizen, then every act of rights defence becomes an act of hope.'[116]

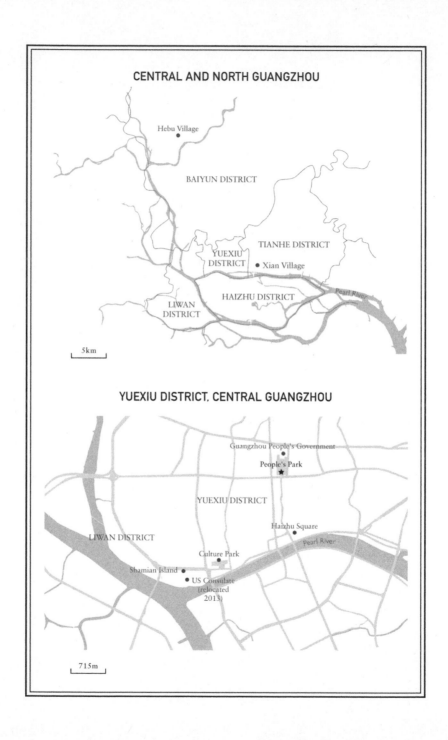

CENTRAL AND NORTH GUANGZHOU

Hebu Village

BAIYUN DISTRICT

TIANHE DISTRICT

YUEXIU
DISTRICT
Xian Village

HAIZHU DISTRICT

Pearl River

LIWAN
DISTRICT

5km

YUEXIU DISTRICT, CENTRAL GUANGZHOU

Guangzhou People's Government

People's Park

YUEXIU DISTRICT

Haizhu Square

LIWAN DISTRICT

Pearl River

Culture Park

Shamian Island

US Consulate
(relocated
2013)

715m

7

DISRUPTING PUBLIC ORDER

Huang Minpeng, 2010–2012

During the summer of 2010, as He Jieling had been busy preparing for her new Ha Street business ventures, Hebu villager Huang Minpeng was leading a double life, as a temporary labourer and part-time petitioner. He had found a job as a farmworker at an agricultural station closer to the city, not far from Sanyuanli. But his thoughts returned constantly to the events in Hebu Village three months earlier, when the village's farmland had been seized without the consent of the villagers. His mind idled over the injustice like a tongue fussing a broken tooth. He was making regular appeals to the city government. He asked repeatedly that the government intercede both in the matter of the land seizure and in what he believed had been his illegal detention, a violation of his personal liberty on the spurious charge of 'disrupting public order.' His petitions yielded nothing concrete. The responses he received were bland restatements of the government's position: that all paperwork for the Hebu Village land-use rights requisition was in order, that he had already been informed of the reasons for his detention earlier that year. But Huang Minpeng was gaining an important education in the petitioning process.

China's petitioning system, the highest agency for which is the Office of Letters and Calls in Beijing, is rooted in the country's feudal past, when those who were wronged could visit the local magistrate's office and request an audience by striking a drum. In the face of the flawed and often corrupt court system, and as the tightly controlled news media offers little relief, Chinese have turned to the petitioning system in record numbers since the 1990s, when economic development accelerated. They seek direct intervention by provincial or central authorities to deal with local grievances. But the system has been overwhelmed and is now incapable of containing the swelling tide of complaints, many dealing with land-use rights and demolition issues. The government's response has been to crack down on petitioners in a broad national campaign of 'stability preservation' designed to suppress rising social unrest, most of it stemming from basic and legitimate claims of interest.

The People's Park, a shady stretch of banyan and cypress trees directly across from central Guangzhou's golden-eaved city government building, has become an informal agora where rights defenders of all kinds gather to discuss in whispered tones the trials and tactics of social justice. Landless peasants, victims of forced demolitions or police abuse, inveterate opponents of government corruption: they sit on the park benches holding jars of home-brewed tea the colour of pond water, their tongues wagging with woes. There was once an unobstructed stone walkway between the People's Park and the steps leading up to the city government building. This proved too accommodating for petitioners, however—an open space where they could gather, unseemly, at the feet of power. The government's answer was to pack the walkway with potted shrubs and ebullient perennials, a wall of colour beaming like a false smile. So now the petitioners lurk in the cool shadows of the park. Locals call the place 'Central Park,' as it was known before 1966, the year Mao Zedong unleashed, in the name of 'the people,' the terror of China's Cultural Revolution. Even earlier, it was called simply 'First City Park.' It was the first public space in Guangzhou, created in 1918 by Sun Yat-sen, the Chinese

revolutionary revered in both China and Taiwan as a modern founding father.[117]

Sun is remembered still for his Three Principles of the People, his
vision of a free and prosperous China with a strong national identity
but also ruled by the people, under a constitutional democracy with
three independent branches of government.[118] In the leafy dusk of
the People's Park one century later, the people still huddle with their
whispered hopes of freedom, glancing over their shoulders to see if
they are being watched by plainclothes police. There is a profound
difference, in fact, between the notion of 'the people,' or *min*, in
Sun Yat-sen's philosophy and that of 'the people,' or *renmin*, in the
ethos of the Chinese Communist Party. The Party's *renmin* are its
subjects. Under the 'people's democratic dictatorship' of Mao Zedong, a dictatorship of the proletariat, the Party exercised power as a
representative of the people, who were a faceless mass. Sun Yat-sen's
min, on the other hand, are people as citizens, or *gongmin*, whose
individual rights are protected by a constitutional system in which
they are equal participants. In a sense, the People's Park is a place
where the idea of citizenship—the dream of being not a subject but
a citizen—is contested day after day.

After months of futile petitioning at the city government,
Huang Minpeng became a People's Park regular. Eventually, he fell
in with the Thursday club, a group of ten to twenty rights-defence
regulars who ate on the second floor of a restaurant just outside
the park. Over the click of bamboo chopsticks, platters of braised
fish and bowls of chicken congee, they shared news, knowledge
and strategy. Regulars included Bai Pengjiang, or Doctor Bai, a
traditional Chinese medicine practitioner and former People's Liberation Army soldier who was delving into Western systems of law
and picking up smatterings of political theory and theology along
the way. ('I'm working on two books this year,' he once told me.) It
became clear as Huang Minpeng spoke to me about his cases that
these fellow rights defenders were an important source of strength.
And Bai, in particular, was an inspiration for Huang. 'Doctor Bai

knows a lot of our cases,' he said, 'those of us who meet over at the People's Park.'

In July 2013, members of the Thursday club invited me to join them at their usual spot, the restaurant on Guangwei Road. It was a raucous rights-defence salon where the conversation rose in gales of suggestion and countersuggestion, argument and counter-argument, as spat-out chicken bones piled up on the tablecloth. How should a petition be worded? What sort of documentation would strengthen a legal appeal? The conversation, inevitably, sheered off into Cantonese, and someone, usually Bai Pengjiang, would speak up on my behalf: 'Mandarin, use Mandarin. Mr. Ban doesn't un-derstand Cantonese.' The lunch dragged on for hours as the hot, sticky air crept in through the second-floor window. At some point, one of the rights defenders, a former soldier denied his pension, re-moved his shirt and lazed back in his chair, his skin gleaming with perspiration.

Every member of the Thursday club had their own story about the injustice that had originated a life of political engagement. An-other regular was Zhou Wentian, a farmer from Maogang, a village east of the city centre on the north bank of the Pearl River. In a long list of complaints about corrupt officials and stolen land, Zhou and his fellow villagers had written, 'In a previous general meeting it was pledged that land-acquisition fees for the subway line would be dis-tributed to the villagers, but it's been years and still they avoid the issue. Where did the money go?'[119] In July 2013, less than a year after I met Zhou Wentian, Maogang's top Party leader was convicted of corruption and sentenced to twelve years in jail for colluding with a businessman to pocket close to 7 million yuan, around $1.1 million, in land requisition payments.[120]

The more time I spent with rights defenders, the clearer it be-came that pervasive corruption—to a great extent fed by the spoils of urban development—was driving not only an undercurrent of discontent but also a surge in organisation. The broken pieces were coming together. Increasingly, peasants like Huang Minpeng understood that deeper institutional change would be necessary before they could hope to resolve their individual complaints. They were part of a growing movement of rights consciousness in China. And that consciousness was networked.

•

One of the first lessons Bai Pengjiang taught Huang Minpeng was the need to document everything along the journey—what many rights defenders call 'going through the process.' The likelihood of success against the system is slight. But by travelling the maze, by documenting its twists and turns, they can map the unresponsive regime. It isn't always possible to throw light into the darkness, but they can show where that darkness is—a power of its own sort. Huang Minpeng started documenting his process more meticulously in 2011. He prepared detailed petitions laying out the facts in the Hebu Village land-use rights case and the circumstances of his detention. This was often done in consultation with Bai Pengjiang, who helped type out and finalise the documents.

Like most petitioners, Huang Minpeng's instinct was to seek out higher authorities, those who were less likely to have a vested interest in his case and had the power to pressure lower-level bureaucrats. In early November 2011, he visited the Petitions Office of the provincial leadership. The office sent him back to Baiyuan District, the jurisdiction directly overseeing his native Jianggao Township, with a letter of introduction:

GUANGDONG PETITION [2011] NO. 1286

TO THE BAIYUN DISTRICT PETITIONS OFFICE

Huang Minpeng arrived at the provincial Party committee and provincial government to express his appeal. According to the principle of 'local management and responsibility,' we request that your office accept and handle this appeal.

CHOP: GUANGDONG PROVINCIAL PARTY COMMITTEE, PEOPLE'S GOVERNMENT OF GUANGDONG PROVINCE[121]

Huang Minpeng took his letter to Baiyun District, where he received another letter of introduction, this time kicking his appeal back down to the township:

BAIYUN PETITION [2011] NO. 1666

TO THE JIANGGAO TOWNSHIP GOVERNMENT

Huang Minpeng arrived at the district Party committee and district government to express his appeal. According to the principle of 'local management and responsibility,' we request that your office accept and handle this appeal.

CHOP: GUANGZHOU CITY BAIYUN DISTRICT PETITIONS OFFICE

Huang Minpeng needed no letter of introduction in Jianggao Township. Local leaders there were the cause of his complaint. In their eyes, he was a familiar troublemaker. But he took his letter anyway. The answer arrived on February 9, 2012:

COMRADE HUANG MINPENG:

In answer to the questions you raised . . . According to our investigation, a signing ceremony was held in Jianggao Township on August 23, 2009, for an agreement on land requisition and compensation by Guangdong Polytechnic Normal University. The signing ceremony was attended by relevant leaders from the district Party committee, the district government, Guangdong Polytechnic Normal University and the township government, as well as Party branch secretaries for the four villages involved, village committee directors and the heads of various collectives, all of whom witnessed the signing of the agreement . . .

As to your request that the compensation agreement for the land requisition be made public, the township planning office has already approached Hebu Village about this, and the village committee believes that while your request is understandable, if indeed the agreement is to be made public the village collectives must make a request to the village committee.

CHOP: JIANGGAO TOWNSHIP PETITION OFFICE

To Huang Minpeng's knowledge, no one in Hebu Village had ever seen the compensation agreement. I spoke to nine other villagers who all said the same thing: the agreement was a mystery. They were embittered by the murkiness of village politics. Village elections, they said, had been rigged by township leaders, who installed their own cronies. So what hope did they have of influencing the village committee?

Events in the neighbouring village of Yebian, however, which was also affected by the contentious land-use rights transfer, offered some clues to the nature of the compensation deal. As Huang Minpeng pushed ahead with his petitions, the descendants of

Confucius in Yebian were digging in, refusing to surrender their farmland even as Guangzhou's Land and Housing Office sought a rare injunction from the Baiyun District Court to force compliance.[122] A letter from township leaders had been posted in Yebian on December 16, 2010, informing the villagers that Guangdong Polytechnic Normal University already had the legal right to develop their land and refusal to surrender that land was a crime. The letter revealed that the university had paid 190,000 yuan in compensation for each *mu* of land, which 'met national and provincial compensation standards for priority projects.' This worked out to a beggarly 284 yuan, less than $4 per square foot, but the letter insisted 'the vast majority of villagers had already agreed to the compensation.' Incensed, the locals had massed outside the village committee office four days later. They demanded to know how the land-use rights deal had been handled. Who exactly were the villagers who had agreed to these lousy terms? Show us a list, they said. We want to see a list. 'To seize land at such a price just leaves me speechless,' one Yebian villager wrote on a popular online forum. 'Can't we just buy it back for the same price?'[123] The compensation funds had been transferred directly to villagers' accounts in December 2010, finalising the deal, like it or not. In Hebu Village, too, the compensation was paid by bank transfer many months after the land was seized. 'It's like you have a house worth 300,000 yuan, and someone comes by and tosses 10,000 through your window,' Huang Minpeng told me. '"Look, we paid you for your house," they say. "It's ours now."'

At Bai Pengjiang's urging, Huang Minpeng tried to take his case off the petition hamster wheel and into the court system. He filed a lawsuit with the Baiyun District Court alleging that the township had not adequately addressed the serious questions he had raised about the land seizure. The court responded: 'This request does not, according to the law, fall within the scope of administrative actions accepted by this court.' Appeals rejected, courts closed. Where could one turn for justice? Huang Minpeng's next attempt to answer that question caused a tiny ripple in the wake of the biggest political scandal in China in a generation.

•

On February 6, 2012, Wang Lijun, a renowned crime fighter in the police force and deputy mayor of Chongqing Municipality, arrived at the American Consulate in Chengdu, a nearby provincial capital. He was disguised as a woman and was in what American diplomats later described as 'an agitated state.'[124] Wang told a disjointed story about a British businessman, Neil Heywood, being murdered by the wife of Chongqing's top leader, Bo Xilai, one of China's most powerful and charismatic political figures. The 'princeling' son of Bo Yibo, one of the Party's most senior 1980s-era leaders, Bo Xilai was a rising star, widely pegged as a candidate for China's elite politburo standing committee later that year. As Bo Xilai's chief of police, Wang Lijun had spearheaded the city's crackdown on criminal gangs, a campaign that had made both men national heroes. But Wang's visit to the American Consulate marked the dramatic collapse of their relationship. According to one version of the story, Wang had confronted Bo with news of Bo's wife murdering Heywood over a business dispute; Bo had then accused Wang of framing his wife and slapped him in the presence of other city officials. Wang feared for his life. His only route of escape was via Chengdu, where he could seek American protection until officials from Beijing arrived to escort him safely out of Bo's reach.

The Wang Lijun incident quickly became the Bo Xilai scandal, a tale of murder, corruption and unchecked power that destroyed Bo and shuddered through the Chinese Communist Party. At the same time, the incident gave rise to a popular meme on social media in China, where internet users quipped that Wang Lijun had 'petitioned' the American Consulate. Phrases like 'sneaking into the

American Consulate at night' became synonymous with the petitioning system, mocking its effectiveness and chiding China's government for failing to protect its own citizens. When push came
to shove, internet users suggested, with an unmistakable whiff of
schadenfreude, even Wang Lijun had chosen to voice his appeal to
the Americans. The online meme was everywhere, so pervasive that
even Huang Minpeng, who never used the internet or social media,
heard about it through his circle of friends.

At around eight o'clock in the morning on March 13, 2012,
Huang Minpeng left his house in Hebu Village, his satchel of documents slung over his shoulder. Among those documents was an open
letter addressed to China's premier and several government minis-
ters. Signed 'Jianggao Township peasant Huang Minpeng, March 1,
2012,' the letter included his identification and mobile-phone numbers. It began: 'The national war over land has reached Guangzhou, a
most bitter war of resistance, a war in which the smoke never settles.
Over the past eight years . . . more than 160 million peasants have
lost their land, sixty million left without homes to return to.' Huang
Minpeng rode his motorbike to the bus station in Jianggao. From
there, he took the bus south into the city, stepping off at Sanyuanli.
He took the subway to Haizhu Square, where he met up with four
fellow rights defenders. From the square, the five of them walked
west to the area around Cultural Park and sat down for an early
lunch at a street stall. With Huang were Chen Wenhua, Cui Mingyi,
Lin Jiqiang and Zhang Wenhua. All had experienced injustices of
one sort or another, and all had worn their soles ragged chasing appeals through the petitioning system. Cui was seeking justice because her husband had died shortly after his release from prison,
due, she claimed, to maltreatment while in custody. Lin Jiqiang was
demanding compensation because he had been detained without
justification for fifty days.

The petitioners talked about the scandal swirling around Bo
Xilai, who had appeared at the National People's Congress in Bei-

jing a week earlier but whose political future was now in doubt. It was then that the spark sprang casually to life. The moment is recorded in the transcript of Huang Minpeng's subsequent police interrogation: 'And then I said, "Wang Lijun, the former police chief in the city of Chongqing, went to the American Consulate, and that's how he got his demands recognised. Let's all go to the American Consulate. The consulate is right here in Shamian. Let's go and make our appeals there and see if we can fix things up." They all said okay.'

It was a short walk from the southwest corner of the park to Shamian Island. They arrived at the main gate of the American Consulate sometime before eleven o'clock. Huang Minpeng noticed a guard post to one side of the gate occupied by a single armed guard. He walked over and explained why the five of them had come. They had written appeals, he said, and they wished to hand these over to the Americans. He hoped the American ambassador to China, Gary Locke, the first Chinese-American ambassador, would turn his attention to the 'land war' and other human-rights abuses in Jianggao Township. Was it possible to go in? 'No, absolutely not,' said the guard. Huang Minpeng pulled the materials from his satchel and held them out to the guard. The guard refused to take them. 'Please, take them,' Huang Minpeng said. The guard refused again but said he would call someone to handle the situation. Within minutes, a group of around twenty men appeared outside the consulate. There were plainclothes security police, uniformed police and paramilitary police. 'A few uniformed police stepped up and asked us what appeals we had. So the five of us gave our materials to the police officers.'

Unlike Wang Lijun, these visitors were not granted an audience with American diplomats. They were taken to the local police substation in Shamian 'for investigation.' At around eleven o'clock that night, Huang Minpeng was remanded to the custody of police in Jianggao Township. After midnight the next day, March 14, he was questioned by an officer from the Baiyun District Public Security Bureau. The proceedings were taken down by an officer from Jianggao Township.

> POLICE: We are personnel from the Baiyun District Public Security Bureau and we are here to ask you relevant questions according to the law. You must answer truthfully. You have a right not to answer any questions irrelevant to your case. Is that clear?

> HUANG MINPENG: It's clear.

> POLICE: Now we are giving you a copy of the 'Notice of Rights and Obligations for Administrative Cases.' Please read it carefully so you are clear about your rights and obligations. Is it clear?

> HUANG MINPENG: Yes, it's clear. I've already read the 'Notice of Rights and Obligations for Administrative Cases,' and I am clear about its contents.

> POLICE: According to Article 82, Clause 1 of the Law of the People's Republic of China on Penalties for Administration of Public Security, you are accused of using, on numerous occasions, abnormal channels to make petitions, and you have now been remanded to the Jianggao Township Substation for questioning. Is that clear?

> HUANG MINPENG: Yes, it's clear.

It should not have been clear at all. Article 82 does deal with summonses for suspected violations of public security, but those violations naturally have to involve real charges. As the law says, police summoning a suspect orally 'shall notify the person summoned of the reasons for and the basis of the summons.'[125] Nothing in any fragment of law across the vastness of China specifies 'using abnormal channels to make petitions' as a crime. This almost certainly explains why this portion of the typewritten statement was later scratched out by hand and a correction scribbled over the top in black ink: 'disrupting public order.' 'Disrupting public order' is a real charge. But the police never made a compelling case for Huang Minpeng's guilt. In a statement to the police, the guard posted outside the consulate mentioned only that five people, four men and one woman, had arrived outside the consulate that morning; one of them, a bald man, had tried to photograph the consulate; the guard told him this was not allowed. (Huang Minpeng, who is bald but who has neither camera nor smartphone, claimed another man not known to him or his friends was there taking photographs.)

> GUARD: So then they walked up to me and handed me their materials. They wanted me to help them take the materials into the consulate. Seeing this situation, I immediately informed my superior. Not long after that, government personnel arrived and took all of them away from the scene.
>
> POLICE: Did any of these five people making appeals engage in extreme behaviour of any kind?
>
> GUARD: No, there was no extreme behaviour.

The guard's statement hardly supported the police officers' claim that the petitioners had caused a 'disturbance.' In fact, the sudden arrival of more than twenty police and government personnel outside the consulate would have been far more disruptive. Huang

Minpeng's statement also emphasised the peaceful nature of their actions: 'At the gate of the American Consulate, I complied with the instructions of the guard posted there. I didn't make any disturbance at all.'

> POLICE: In heading to the American Consulate this time, did you hand any fliers or make any appeals to the general public?
>
> HUANG MINPENG: We never handed any fliers to the general public. And when we were at the American Consulate there were no other people looking on.
>
> POLICE: Were you organised? Whose plan was it to go to the consulate to make your appeals?
>
> HUANG MINPENG: We never organised anything, and no one made a plan. It came up in conversation and we all agreed.

Huang Minpeng was detained for ten days, the maximum penalty imposed by law for 'relatively serious' cases of disrupting public order. Criminal charges were brought against Cui Mingyi, the petitioner who sought answers about the case of her husband's death; she was sentenced to three years in jail and eventually served one year. Police held Lin Jiqiang, the petitioner seeking compensation for a previous fifty-day detention, for more than six weeks before releasing him on bail and returning him forcibly to his hometown; he was warned never to return to Guangzhou.

Huang Minpeng served his time in Jianggao, in the same jail where, two years earlier, he had been detained for three weeks.

But his resolve was only hardened. On April 5, eleven days after his release, he filed an appeal with the Public Security Bureau in Baiyun District for an administrative review of his arrest outside the consulate. His application again outlined the injustices of the land seizure in Hebu, but his focus was on the charge that he had disrupted public order. Arguing that the police incorrectly applied the law in his case, he made three demands: first, that the police make available video footage taken outside the consulate, which would prove, he said, that his actions had been peaceful; second, that the original decision concerning his detention be reversed; and third, that he be awarded 25,000 yuan, about $4,000, in state compensation for the psychological damage he had endured as a result of his incarceration.

The district police denied Huang Minpeng's appeal in a decision rendered on May 14. In support, it presented a raft of incongruous evidence. There was a photograph taken outside the American Consulate showing only a car parked in front of the gates. On the night of his interrogation, Huang had scribbled a note under the picture with his signature and fingerprint: 'The place in the above photograph is the place outside the gate of the American Consulate in Shamian where I asked for an audience on March 13.' To support the charge against Huang Minpeng, police in Jianggao had presented the photograph with their own chopped and dated 'explanation': 'The photograph on the above page is the scene where order was disrupted in a public place outside the American Consulate in Shamian, Guangzhou, at around 10:30 a.m. on March 13, 2012.' In another bit of sophistry, Jianggao Township police had offered printed identity parades dated March 14 in which police from Liwan District, where the American Consulate was located, had picked out the unmistakably bald Huang Minpeng from a line-up of twelve suspects (all the others dark-haired) as 'the person who was petitioning outside the gate of the American Consulate.' The lineup violated a basic principle of fairness that fillers not all be markedly dissimilar in appearance from the suspect. But in any case the exercise was impertinent: Huang Minpeng had never denied his presence outside the consulate. What he did deny was ever having disrupted the public order. The verdict from the district police was hardly a surprise. 'It is the view of our bureau that . . . the applicant's conduct did constitute disruption of order in a public place. The facts are clear, the evidence complete and the sentence of ten days of administrative detention was a correct application of the law; the punishment was appropriate and the process legal.'

Stonewalled at the district level, Huang Minpeng tackled police authorities one level up. In a case filed two weeks after the decision by Baiyun police, he sued Guangzhou's Public Security Bureau. Among the defendants was the city's police chief, making the suit a rare case of legal action against a senior police official. More than sixty people—locals from Hebu and other villages across the city—packed into the courtroom to hear the proceedings on August 14, 2012. In recent years, the practice of sitting in on court proceedings has become a common form of collective action among rights defenders and advocates of social justice. While Article 35 of China's Constitution guarantees citizens the rights of freedom of assembly, procession and protest,[126] these rights are, in practice, virtually impossible to exercise. Sitting in on trials offers a pretext for like-minded citizens to come together around issues of common concern (such as land use, forced demolition, corruption or police violence), while skirting draconian restrictions on political activities.

Symbolic though it might have been, however, Huang Minpeng's case did not get far. He set out to argue against several factual errors in the decision document produced by the district police, the most important of which was a new assertion, found nowhere in the original police report, that Huang had 'continued to hand out materials . . . even after police arrived on the scene.' Huang Minpeng seized on this detail in his written arguments: 'This is a serious falsehood. I ask you, is it even possible that I would continue to hand out materials after the police arrive? Who exactly would I give them to?' He pointed out, quite accurately, that no language in the Law on Penalties for Administration of Public Security prevented citizens from seeking the advice of foreign missions in China.

The case fizzled on procedural issues. Once again, the core question was jurisdiction. Properly speaking, where in the rat's nest of the police-government bureaucracy should he direct his complaints? The judge believed the lawsuit should be directed against the Baiyun District Public Security Bureau, not against the city police. He called both sides into a chamber off the courtroom and advised, according to Hong Kong's *South China Morning Post*, 'Let me put it this way. If someone's son hit you, there is no point in you beating up the father. You need to figure out who you are really after in this case.'[127] The case was adjourned. The court had kicked the ball back to Baiyun District.

The path through the courts proved as circuitous as the one through the petitioning system. By late October 2012, Huang Minpeng had brought an administrative case against the Baiyun District Public Security Bureau. When the case went through the Baiyun District Court the next month, the verdict upheld the original decision by the district police: 'Our bureau has determined that Huang Minpeng's conduct did constitute disrupting order in a public place. The facts are clear, the evidence complete and the administrative punishment was a correct application of the law.'

The verdict hardly mattered any more. The only tangible hope available to Huang Minpeng was through action itself. It was the process that mattered—and the companions who were there to share and witness it. When I hear rights defenders talk about the 'process,' I am always reminded of a famous line from the twentieth-century author Lu Xun. 'It occurred to me,' he wrote in his story 'Hometown,' 'that hope wasn't something that just existed or not. It was like the paths that cross the ground. To begin with, there were no paths at all, but as more people went that way, they were made.' For a growing number of disaffected Chinese who are becoming career rights defenders, there is no path back. The struggle for personal rights is a journey that the nation has been travelling since the end of China's civil war and the founding of the People's Republic of China in 1949, a journey towards a dignity that is both personal and shared. For Huang Minpeng, it was no longer only about the land. In an open letter to the provincial and city governments ahead of his second court case, he wrote, 'In October 1949, Mao Zedong stood on Tiananmen Gate in Beijing and declared, "The people of China have stood up." Every day in Hebu Village I scream at the top of my lungs, "When will we peasants be able to stand up?"'

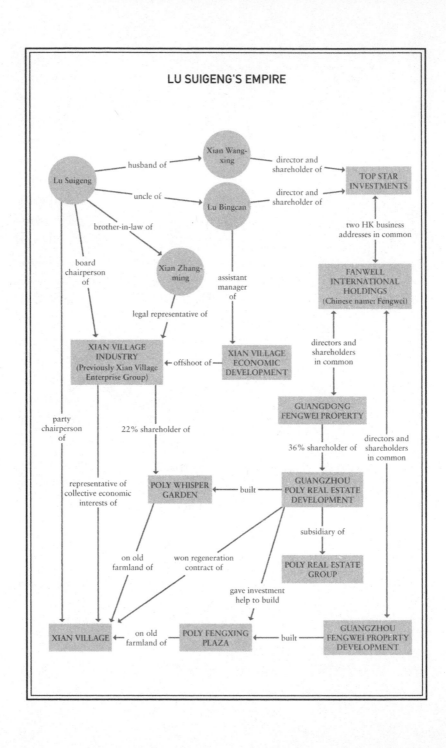

LU SUIGENG'S EMPIRE

Lu Suigeng

— husband of → Xian Wang-xing

— uncle of → Lu Bingcan

— brother-in-law of → Xian Zhang-ming

Xian Wang-xing — director and shareholder of → TOP STAR INVESTMENTS

Lu Bingcan — director and shareholder of → TOP STAR INVESTMENTS

TOP STAR INVESTMENTS ↕ two HK business addresses in common ↕ FANWELL INTERNATIONAL HOLDINGS (Chinese name: Fengwei)

Lu Suigeng — board chairperson of → XIAN VILLAGE INDUSTRY (Previously Xian Village Enterprise Group)

Xian Zhang-ming — legal representative of → XIAN VILLAGE INDUSTRY

Lu Bingcan — assistant manager of → XIAN VILLAGE ECONOMIC DEVELOPMENT

XIAN VILLAGE ECONOMIC DEVELOPMENT → offshoot of → XIAN VILLAGE INDUSTRY

FANWELL INTERNATIONAL HOLDINGS ↕ directors and shareholders in common ↕ GUANGDONG FENGWEI PROPERTY

GUANGDONG FENGWEI PROPERTY — 36% shareholder of → GUANGZHOU POLY REAL ESTATE DEVELOPMENT

Lu Suigeng — party chairperson of → (Xian Village)

Lu Suigeng — representative of collective economic interests of → (Xian Village)

XIAN VILLAGE INDUSTRY — 22% shareholder of → POLY WHISPER GARDEN

GUANGZHOU POLY REAL ESTATE DEVELOPMENT — built → POLY WHISPER GARDEN

GUANGZHOU POLY REAL ESTATE DEVELOPMENT — subsidiary of → POLY REAL ESTATE GROUP

POLY WHISPER GARDEN — on old farmland of → XIAN VILLAGE

GUANGZHOU POLY REAL ESTATE DEVELOPMENT — won regeneration contract of → XIAN VILLAGE

GUANGZHOU POLY REAL ESTATE DEVELOPMENT — gave investment help to build → POLY FENGXING PLAZA

FANWELL INTERNATIONAL HOLDINGS ↕ directors and shareholders in common ↕ GUANGZHOU FENGWEI PROPERTY DEVELOPMENT

POLY FENGXING PLAZA — on old farmland of → XIAN VILLAGE

GUANGZHOU FENGWEI PROPERTY DEVELOPMENT — built → POLY FENGXING PLAZA

8

A LIMITED-LIABILITY POLICE FORCE

Lu Suigeng

When the alleys of Xian Village became unwelcoming terrain in August 2012, I shifted my energies to the labyrinthine economic empire of Lu Suigeng, the Xian Village collective board and Communist Party chairperson. I wanted to sketch out a rough map of the various village assets and businesses that had for so many years remained hidden from the villagers. I quickly found, however, that even the simplest of questions led me down blind alleys as murky as those between the tenements themselves.

According to the 2011 *Tianhe Annual Survey*, compiled by the Tianhe District government, Xian Village Industry Company Limited—the enterprise representing the village and working with the Poly Group on its redevelopment project—was the parent company for a cluster of collective village enterprises, including Xian Village Economic Development Company Limited, Tianhe District Economic Development Company Limited, Xian Village Property Management Company Limited, Pearl River New Town Commercial Plaza Company Limited, Tianhe Rubber Products Company Limited, the Haitao Hotel and the Chundu Hotel.[128]

I had hoped my copy of the *Xian Village Chronicle*, the official
history published in 2008, would provide further details about these
businesses, but, though generous with facts about the village's rural past, the book revealed little of its dealings since the 1990s. If
your interest was the Xian Village tomato, the *Chronicle* divulged
all, tracing the plant's origins back to the enterprising work of local
agronomists in 1954. You could also read about the springtime harvesting—under a waxing moon, as the tide rose—of marine worms,
a local delicacy. The book was equally forthright about the produc-
tivity of individual peasants, like Lu Guangdi, who in 1987 farmed
4 *mu*, roughly 27,000 square feet, of land, harvesting 6,395 pounds
of green vegetables, which fetched 1,900 yuan at market. Lu also sold
five pigs that year, earning 1,100 yuan.[129] The *Chronicle*'s section on
the village holdings stated at the outset that 'after the 1990s, due to
urban construction, the village's fields were entirely requisitioned,'
and the heart of 'the collective economy shifted to property rental.'
But when I was beginning my research, the book's silence over the
exact nature of these 'collective' dealings seemed audacious. Why
had Lu Suigeng—the 'editor-in-chief' of the *Chronicle*—provided
output and profit figures for a fertiliser operation closing its doors
in 1984 and for a dairy farm shutting down in 1987 but vouchsafed
nothing about the village's lucrative properties in the commercial
heart of the megacity, where property prices were among the highest
in the country?[130]

•

The story of Lu Nianzu, who along with four other villagers had
been singled out for arrest by district police after the May 5, 2010,
protest scuffle, suggested an extremely close relationship between
Tianhe District police and the leadership in Xian Village. Also, in
their 2009 petition letter signed during the commissioning of the
three new dragon boats, the villagers had alleged that Lu Suigeng
had given a five-story tenement building on Lanqing Lane, a heavily

trafficked pedestrian street on the west side of the village, to Fan Chunming, who at the time was Tianhe's deputy chief of police, known to villagers by his nickname, 'The Handsome Prince.'[131]

One evening in August 2012, I witnessed this close relationship between Lu Suigeng and the district police during an unplanned stakeout. I had just surfaced from a pedestrian underpass onto Xian Village Road with every intention of catching a cab to my hotel, calling it quits on a day of poking around the village's edges. Suddenly, I found myself face to face with Lu Suigeng. Dressed neatly but casually in a pale-blue polo shirt and khaki trousers, he was strolling calmly and deliberately along the footpath, under a colonnade of shade trees. I knew his face from my borrowed copy of the *Xian Village Chronicle*, but his hair was now streaked and peppered with grey. Surprise must have registered on my face, but Lu was insensible to my presence. His gaze was fixed across the busy avenue, where a diesel-powered demolition excavator was rearing up its steel beak, tearing down tenements on the southwest corner of the village. The *rat-tat-tat* echoed around us. After standing for a moment to watch the demolition, Lu walked down into the pedestrian underpass. I turned to follow, at a safe distance. He resurfaced on the southeast side and walked along Jinsui Road with frequent glances across to the skeletal tenements rising above the neat hem of propaganda on the south wall of the village. He had the attitude of a commander touring the front lines. Finally, he came to Xingguo Road. He crossed the street and walked casually into a building with signs on either side of a large entryway: in black characters on the right, 'Xian Village Industry Company Limited'; in red characters on the left, 'Xian Village Industry Company Limited Party Branch Committee.' Along the curb were two police trucks, a police van and a police car.

I crossed over and photographed the vehicles from the window of a grocery store. Then I noticed Sa Mesa, an Italian restaurant with a perfect vantage point directly across the road from the Xian Village Industry offices.

I was polishing off a chicken calzone and a bottle of Corona when police streamed out of the offices. About three of them, in light-blue uniforms, jumped aboard the van, and several others got in the trucks. Behind them came nine more men, also in blue shirts and black helmets, and holding clubs and see-through anti-riot shields with 'Auxiliary Police' glaring from the fronts. They were stringy young recruits with their shirts untucked and the slouching look of yard birds engaged for the rougher work. These auxiliary officers are hired and trained by the Public Security Bureau to provide assistance, but they are not, strictly speaking, police. The striplings filed around the side of a light-gold passenger van with darkly tinted windows. They climbed in through a door directly facing the restaurant. Four men in black T-shirts were mixed in among them. One was wearing shorts and sandals. Another half-dozen or so men, in black shirts and black caps, slightly older, with a more drilled and determined look, boarded a light-blue van parked nose to nose with the gold van. These men were carrying what looked like black ballistic vests. The trucks and vans all drove off together, heading in the direction of Xian Village. Only the police car remained.

Two months later, I returned to Sa Mesa. I watched the same scene unfold once more, like clockwork—a routine deployment of district police equipped with anti-riot gear from the offices of a limited-liability company. The business of Xian Village Industry, Lu Suigeng's company, was also district police business.

•

In 2012, I asked some Xian villagers for the names of Lu Suigeng's wife and daughters, hoping the information might help me track down any business links outside China, where they were rumoured to be living. Chinese officials often use family members to keep illicit business deals at arm's length, but in the nation's sensitive political culture, even facts as elementary as names can be impossible to track down. The villagers seemed sure the wife's name was Xian Wangxing. She was the daughter of former village chief Xian Wensi, who had held a number of important Party positions from the 1950s onwards. At first, no one was certain how to write Xian Wangxing's name; eventually, however, the villagers agreed that 'Xian Wangxing' was an accurate rendering—the surname Xian, just like the village itself, followed by a pair of characters that mean 'rising prosperity.' When I filed through registered businesses in Hong Kong (the former British colony being a popular financial haven for Chinese), I located one Xian Wangxing, the director and shareholder of a company called Top Star Investments. I had already made hundreds of queries in Hong Kong for Lu Suigeng and his known associates. My costs and frustrations were mounting, and I was sure the Top Star records would bring only more disappointment. But the first document I accessed, an annual return from 1996, stopped me short. Right beside the name Xian Wangxing, scrawled in the same hurried hand, was the name of a second director and shareholder: Lu Bingcan, nephew of Lu Suigeng, assistant manager of Xian Village Economic Development (one of the offshoots of Xian Village Industry) and one of the village cadres who claimed to have been attacked by villagers in 2010.

Top Star tempted me along a winding path of searches, only to drop me right back where I had started. I could find no hint anywhere of the company's dealings, from the time of its inception in early 1995 to that of its deregistration in 1999. But those two dates did correspond with two of the most important periods in Xian Village's history. It was in 1995 that the last of Xian Village's farmland was seized and it became the first village in the Pearl River New Town to begin the process of reform and regeneration.[132] The land-use rights requisition fees for this, some villagers alleged, had not been paid into the village funds. If the money had been diverted, then Hong Kong, with its concentration of financial services, would be a logical destination. And it was in 1999 that the dissolution of the village had finally been accomplished, with the creation of the

Xian Village Enterprise Group, later renamed Xian Village Industry. On July 22, 1999, less than one month after that landmark change—which, according to the *Chronicle*, had brought 'integration with the modern society of Guangzhou'[133]—Xian Wangxing and Lu Bingcan had finalised the paperwork in Hong Kong to wind up and deregister Top Star Investments.

I ran a property search of Top Star's two registered Hong Kong business addresses. There was an outside chance that the Lu family owned one or both of the properties. The first address turned up a company called, in English, Fanwell International Holdings, which was also the owner of the second property. Had Top Star simply rented both offices from Fanwell, or was there some other connection? When I pulled out the files on Fanwell, the Chinese name for the company, which Romanises as 'Fengwei,' leaped out at me. I had already come across the Chinese name on the mainland. Poly Fengxing Plaza, a residential and commercial colossus of more than 860,000 square feet a few blocks north of the Xian Village tenements, was completed in 2007 by Guangzhou Fengwei Property Development, with investment help from the Poly Group's real-estate subsidiary, Poly Real Estate Group Company Limited. The plaza was built on what had once been Xian Village farmland. Top Star had used the same registered business addresses as the Hong Kong company Fanwell International Holdings, piggybacking the property company when it changed addresses.

In 2012, average monthly rents for office space in Tianhe District were around 9 yuan per square foot. That meant the Poly Fengxing Plaza, built on Xian Village farmland and with an unspecified connection to the village's collective business empire, was a gold mine, its annual rental income probably running into the tens of millions. But where did the plaza figure in the property rental dealings alluded to in the *Xian Village Chronicle*? What exactly was Xian Village's interest? And where did the money go? When I searched for more on Fengwei, I ran across a letter of intent from Poly Real Estate Group, sent ahead of an initial public offering on the Shanghai Stock Exchange in 2006.[134] The letter stated in its notes that a business called Guangdong Fengwei Property Company Limited held a 36 per cent stake in another business, Guangzhou Poly Real Estate Development Corporation, the local Poly Real Estate Group subsidiary that had won the bid for the village regeneration and had already completed the Poly Whisper Garden development. Guangdong Fengwei was a separate entity from Guangzhou Fengwei, the company behind Poly Fengxing Plaza, but registration records and court documents confirmed that both companies were linked to Hong Kong's Fanwell International Holdings through shared directors and shareholders. According to Poly Real Estate Group's 2012 annual report, Guangdong Fengwei was a principal shareholder, with a sizable interest, in Guangzhou Poly Real Estate Development, which meant Guangdong Fengwei had remained active in the Poly subsidiary through the period that Xian Village's regeneration was being planned and promoted.

The shared business addresses of Fanwell International Holdings and Top Star Investments in Hong Kong suggested a close relationship between Fanwell and Lu Suigeng's family, dating back to at least the beginning of 1995. In fact, the launch of Top Star had closely shadowed that of Fanwell. When Top Star was created in Hong Kong in January 1995, Guangzhou Fengwei was barely eight weeks old, and yet the fledgling company had been able to broker lucrative property deals, securing usage rights to parcels of rural land at cut-rate prices and selling them on to developers.

●

Fengwei's story, assembled from fragments of information spanning two decades, reads like a protohistory of China's property boom— and there are hints within it of that mostly invisible world in which public power swirls together with private interest, yielding an inky portrait of China under rapid economic change. In 1993, after Guangzhou's State Land Office approved the seizure of farmland in

Siyou Village, one of the city's oldest urban villages, and just west of
Xian Village, the people behind Fengwei made a play for the usage
rights of a substantial piece of land that had been rezoned for development at the discretion of the village collective, for which the villagers were entitled to compensation. In a testimony during a civil
case before Guangdong's Supreme People's Court fifteen years later,
representatives from Siyou Village's rural collective indicated that
they had first signed a contract regarding the land on December 15,
1993, with Office Five of the People's Government of Guangdong
Province.[135] Under the terms of the contract, the village was to provide 64,600 square feet of land, and Office Five was responsible for
the construction costs of a planned commercial development. Office
Five was, according to a number of sources, the intelligence division
of the Guangzhou Military Region, one of China's seven military
administrative regions (covering five southern provinces),[136] and one
of several organs of state power used by big-wheeling entrepreneurs
and the family members of Communist Party officials in south
China to advance their commercial interests. It was even alleged,
in 2011, that Office Five issued security credentials to private-sector
people willing to do business on its behalf.[137] The contract with Siyou Village was abrogated one year later at the bidding of Office
Five, which notified the village that it had set up a new company,
'subordinate to the Office,' to handle the construction project. On
December 22, 1994, Siyou's rural collective was instructed to sign
a new contract with Guangzhou Fengwei Property Development,
which thereafter would 'bear the rights and responsibilities' agreed
the year before.[138]

The Siyou Village project languished for many years—perhaps
in part because Fengwei tried, to the chagrin of its village partners,
to transfer its rights and responsibilities in the deal to a third development company just six months into the contract. In fact, mis-
fortune seemed to shadow Fengwei. Xian Village's Fengxing Plaza,
for which Fengwei started preselling properties in 1999—meaning
the land-use rights transfer from the village occurred during the pe-

riod Top Star shared its Hong Kong address—was in dire straits by 2002. The residential blocks had been completed and sold, but work had ground to a standstill at the construction site of the offices in the complex.[139] In March 2002, Fengxing property buyers picketed outside Guangdong's Department of Construction, demanding reparation. They wanted to know why the project was unfinished more than two years after its promised date of completion. Fengwei threw up its hands. It no longer had the funds, it said, to finish the project.[140] It was three more years before the deep-pocketed Poly Real Estate Group stepped in, and two more after that before Poly Fengxing Plaza was completed at last.[141] In May 2006, Fengwei was blacklisted, along with eighteen other property development companies that had defaulted on major construction projects.[142]

•

It is impossible to grasp the full saga of Fengwei and the cause of its financial woes without knowing the story of its founder, Chen Buzhong, who for the company's first year was its majority shareholder and legal representative. In 1987, when Guangdong was at the vanguard of reforms in China, 'former soldier' Chen Buzhong was among the province's leading business barons.[143] He began his climb as head of the real-estate division of the Guangdong International Trust and Investment Corporation, or GITIC, the investment arm of Guangdong's provincial government, and by the second half of the 1980s he was the general manager of GITIC's real-estate subsidiary, Guangdong International Leasing Corporation. In those heady early days, GITIC was one of just a few 'windows' through which foreigners could invest in China, and property was one of GITIC's biggest businesses.

The Guangzhou city government decided in 1987 to explore the sale of requisitioned usage rights for rural land as a source of revenue. For this purpose, the government seized 247 acres of land in Fang Village, on the western fringes of the city—an area that since the

Han Dynasty (206 BC–AD 220) had been known for its fragrant jasmine flowers—and set the minimum bid at 60 million yuan, about $1 per square foot. In a public bidding war described colourfully as 'dragons and tigers vying in the land of flowers,' the land went to Chen Buzhong's Guangdong International Leasing for the staggering sum of 280 million yuan. The sale, dubbed 'China's biggest property miracle of the 1980s,' was the most dramatic in a series of pioneering land sales in Guangzhou and Shenzhen that drove a wave of reform through China's land-use rights system, clearing the way for the property boom of the 1990s and the rapacious land-financing system on which China's cities became largely dependent by the turn of the century.[144]

GITIC reached the height of its corporate stature in May 1994, and its collapse, at the end of 1998, was the biggest corporate failure of China's reform era. It sent ripples through the region and across the world. Of GITIC's estimated $4.4 billion of debt, more than $1 billion was owed to Western lenders.[145] An official investigation into GITIC's dealings reported that without proper authorisation from the central government, the company had borrowed substantial sums of money at high rates and, as its debts loomed, had tried to make up ground with real-estate gambles and other risky investments.[146] In the end, no one knew how vast GITIC's empire had been. Liquidators uncovered 240 subsidiaries, almost twice what GITIC had publicly claimed. But certainly there had to be others. In December 1997, one year before the bankruptcy was announced, top Party officials in Guangdong launched an investigation into senior executives at GITIC.[147] Included was Fengwei founder Chen Buzhong, the former GITIC vice-president who had died, untouched by scandal, in 1995. Fanwell's Chen Buzhong connection would not necessarily have identified the company as one of GITIC's prodigal orphans. But during the Siyou Village case heard before the Guangdong Supreme People's Court in 2008, Fengwei, which alleged that the village had never actually delivered the land into its hands, demanded compensation for related economic losses.

It presented a raft of its own internal documents to substantiate the claim, none of which the court regarded as credible. Then, in a gambit equally rejected, Fengwei presented the court with expense receipts from Guangdong GITIC Property Management Company, suggesting Fengwei might be a GITIC subsidiary equally under Chen Buzhong's thumb.

I was dealing with a bewildering knot of connections. The wife and nephew of Xian Village chairman Lu Suigeng had operated a company in Hong Kong sharing several offices with a company whose mainland counterpart, Fengwei, had been founded by GITIC property magnate Chen Buzhong. Fengwei had been founded, moreover, under the auspices of Guangdong's Office Five, establishing the company's early link to China's sprawling military-industrial complex. Up close, the details were mystifying. And although there was no direct evidence in this tangle to prove that any of the people involved had violated the law, from a distance it resolved into a portrait of the privileged access to power and opportunity enjoyed by those who, like Lu Suigeng, could monopolise local politics, and therefore local assets and resources, without any expectation of oversight. The exact nature of any possible meeting between Chen Buzhong and Lu Suigeng was probably lost in the mists of time. But as I read about Chen's early days, in the 1980s, as a property boss in Guangzhou, when the 'square-faced' and 'tawny-skinned' veteran soldier of the Communist revolution would ride his bicycle through the alleys of old Dongshan District, just west of Yangji, I couldn't help but imagine him wheeling up to the still very rural Xian Village and considering the possibilities. As Chen once said while weaving the yarn of his success story to a rapt audience, 'For me, Chen Buzhong, the sale of land-use rights brought liberation.'[148]

•

In September 2012, I stood on the western edge of the Pearl River New Town, waiting to meet with my Xian Village sources. All around me, clean, modern landmarks jutted into the sky, including the crystalline tower of the International Financial Center, designed by the London firm Wilkinson Eyre Architects, and the sleek, reflective Pearl River Tower, by the American company Skidmore, Owings & Merrill. The structures epitomise what former Tianhe District government leader Cao Jianliao called 'civilised construction' during a planning meeting in December 2000. Cao warned that urban villages in his district were breeding grounds for 'problems and maladies' that 'seriously impacted civilised construction and coordinated development.'[149] Many saw him as a champion of 'sustainable development.' As Communist Party chairperson of Tianhe's Shahe Township from 1987 to 1995, Cao was Lu Suigeng's immediate superior. The men were pictured side by side in the *Xian Village Chronicle* in a photograph taken in 2007, during Cao's tour of the village as part of a propaganda campaign to designate Guangzhou as a National Hygienic City.[150] By 2012, Cao was Guangzhou's deputy mayor and had recently been appointed to a concurrent post as Party chairperson of Zengcheng, a satellite city to the south of Guangzhou. He was a rising star in the regional leadership—confident and charismatic.[151]

Cao Jianliao also emerged as a person of interest in my Xian Village investigation. In a detailed petition addressed in 2009 to the Central Commission for Discipline Inspection, the Beijing office charged with fighting official corruption, the Xian villagers alleged that Lu Suigeng had given Cao Jianliao a seven-story tenement building on Lanqing Lane, a pedestrian street on the village's west side. This property was handled, the petition said, by a trusted go-between who collected rent for Cao and made deposits into a designated bank account. The alleged exchange of a lucrative rental property secured for the village's 'ruling family' political backing that insulated them from charges of corruption and abuse of power.[152] 'Let me tell you, Cao Jianliao and Lu Suigeng are part of the same chain of interests,' an elderly Xian villager once told me with vehemence, wagging a bony index finger. 'Cao can protect Lu Suigeng, but he also knows that Lu can pull him down with what he knows.'

The villagers pointed me also to an enigmatic property company with shares in village developments all over Tianhe District, Cao Jianliao's old stomping grounds. According to a press release announcing a recent joint venture, the firm, Nanya Property Development Company Limited, had 'a wealth of experience in the regeneration and development of urban villages.'[153] But I could find nothing to link the company to Cao Jianliao or other district or city officials, and a brief about Nanya Property Development on a major Chinese property website said only that the developer 'holds many plots of land in the Pearl River New Town, but maintains a low profile.'[154] When I polled Guangzhou journalists for a list of Cao Jianliao's family members to match them against associates of the mystery company, everyone drew blanks. In China's cult of official secrecy, nothing is guarded so religiously as the particulars of the powerful.

Whatever the gossip in the back valleys of Xian Village, Cao Jianliao was, by all public accounts, a capable and creditable leader. He was a local Party veteran who 'dared to speak and dared to act.'[155] He was an ardent bibliophile, which might explain how he managed to earn a doctorate in international relations from Jinan University, not far from Xian Village, while serving as Party chairperson of Tianhe District. On one occasion, Cao urged his Party colleagues to aspire to what he called the 'three cores': love of the Party, solicitude for the people, and personal integrity. And in February 2012, during a leadership conference on 'clean government,' he sounded a stern warning against corruption, saying 'those who are corrupt must be decisively removed from the Party's ranks.'[156]

The rights defenders of Xian Village had fought for more than a decade to decisively remove Lu Suigeng and supplant what they referred to bitterly as the village's 'dynastic clan.' In their 2009 petition, the villagers had written: 'For more than ten years, we villagers have petitioned and made written appeals, but as Lu Suigeng has strong, entrenched backstage supporters offering him protection, we are constantly persecuted in response to our appeals, and we continue to suffer profound indignities.'[157] For the villagers, the barrier that stood between them and the end of Lu Suigeng's reign of tyranny had a name: Cao Jianliao.

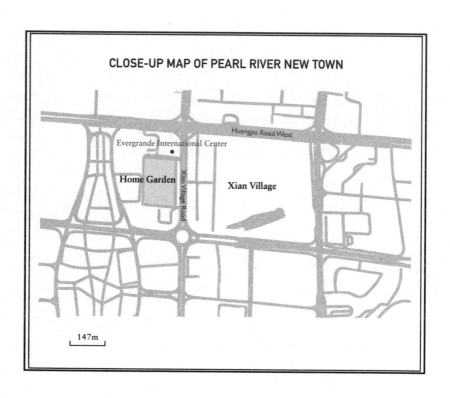

CLOSE-UP MAP OF PEARL RIVER NEW TOWN

9

DUBIOUS RICHES

Home Garden

The baffling matter of the sprawling Home Garden complex, a furniture mall situated on a tract of old farmland on the west side of the village across Xian Village Road, came next in my research into Xian Village's business dealings. The complex was mentioned in the *Xian Village Chronicle* under a section on 'collective holdings,' but the book provided only a paltry handful of facts accompanied by a few photographs of the space and its glossy marble interior. It was built in 2003, and with a total area of almost 323,000 square feet it was one of the largest malls of its kind in Guangzhou. It was home to a cinema megaplex with seven screens and close to 1,000 seats.[158] Though I could locate no public record of a land-use permit for the property, I came across some prospectuses of the Guangzhou Jinyi Film & Television Group (ahead of its listing on the Shenzhen Stock Exchange), which said the property was built 'by Xian Village Economic Development Company Limited [one of the offshoots of the village's industry group] . . . on collectively held land in its possession, zoned for commercial office, business and financial services use.' The village enterprise had obtained the necessary building permits and had 'leased the property to Pearl River New Town Commercial Plaza Company Limited, permitting the subletting of the property.' The latter had turned right around and leased the complex's 'luxury' cinema to Guangzhou Jinyi Film & Television Group, which was operating cinemas in first- and second-tier cities across China, for a minimum annual rent of 1.1 million yuan, about $175,000, or 10 per cent of cinema ticket sales. The rest of the mall's cavernous space was leased to high-end furniture retailers.[159] Home Garden's operator, Pearl River New Town Commercial Plaza, was identified in village and district sources as a 'collective village enterprise.' But the company, established in September 2001, two years before construction of the complex was completed, had never in fact been 'collective.' Registration files showed it was held by two private shareholders, Xu Shouwei and Li Xiaojian, who controlled 68 and 32 per cent respectively.

Casting about for connections between these shareholders and village interests, I discovered that the June 2012 Guangzhou Jinyi prospectus disclosed the relationships of its core owners and executives and made clear that Li Xiaojian was the son of sixty-year-old Li Genchang, who, along with his sister Li Yuzhen, controlled not just Guangzhou Jinyi but also the sprawling Jiayu Group,[160] the parent company of a corporate empire spanning property, hotel management, tourism and entertainment.[161] Its subsidiaries included Jiayu Real Estate Development, founded in April 1995, which by 2012 had become the Pearl River New Town's largest landholder.[162] Xu Shouwei, the principal shareholder of the ostensibly 'collective' company operating Home Garden, had married into the Jiayu business empire, becoming the husband of Li Yuzhen's daughter. Guangzhou's *Time Weekly* newspaper had recently reached out to Xu for background information on Li Genchang and Li Yuzhen, but he had refused to breathe a word; he was bound, he said, by a nondisclosure agreement.[163]

The *Time Weekly* story poked in a desultory fashion around the edges of Jiayu Real Estate Development, marvelling that a company

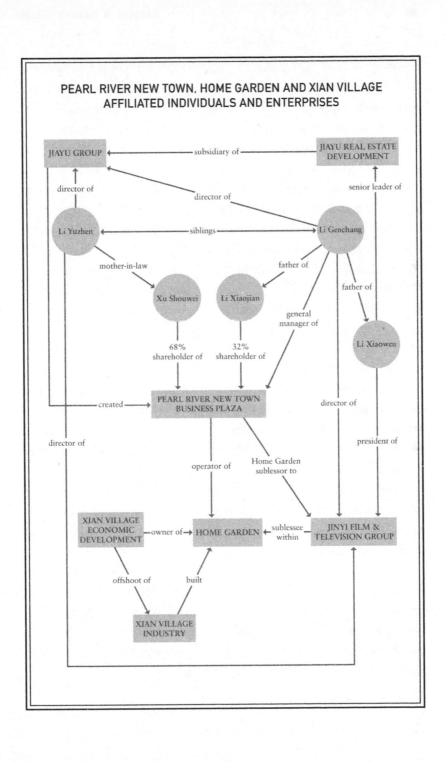

PEARL RIVER NEW TOWN, HOME GARDEN AND XIAN VILLAGE
AFFILIATED INDIVIDUALS AND ENTERPRISES

founded in 2008 with capital of just 10 million yuan had invested 10 *billion* yuan in second- and third-tier cities across China in the space of four years. 'How is it conceivable,' the paper asked, 'that a totally unknown property company could become the dominant landholder in Guangzhou's central business district, where land is as valuable as gold, and then march right into second- and third-tier cities with its dubious riches? . . . When we look into the face of the Jiayu property empire, what are we looking at exactly?'[164]

The Jiayu Group was essentially a family business. Li Xiaowen—the brother of Home Garden shareholder Li Xiaojian—had held a senior leadership position at Jiayu Real Estate Development at the boyish age of seventeen and was now president of the Guangzhou Jinyi Film & Television Group.[165] And it was apparent from newspaper coverage going back through the years that the Jiayu Group's most senior executives were involved directly in the Home Garden venture. Li Genchang was identified in a 2007 article in the local *Yangcheng Evening News* as the 'general manager of Pearl River New Town Commercial Plaza Company Limited.'[166] The grocery list of land parcels the Jiayu Group cited among its Pearl River New Town holdings did not, however, include the Xian Village land occupied by the Home Garden complex. So what were the arrangements?

According to China's Land Administration Law, state-held land (as opposed to collectively held rural land) can be used when necessary for 'construction purposes.' The only exceptions allowing for such use of rural land, or 'land owned by peasant collectives,' are cases in which 'collective economic organisations' have 'lawfully obtained approval' to use the land in question for 'township or town enterprises or to build houses for villagers.' Rural land held collectively can also be used for the construction of 'public utilities or public welfare undertakings' at the village or township level. If usage rights for rural land are appropriated for construction projects of a commercial nature, the law requires approval from 'people's governments of provinces, autonomous regions and municipalities directly under the Central Government.'[167] The rural land enveloped by China's expanding cities is a scarce and valuable resource—especially in first-tier cities like Guangzhou. When the usage rights for such land are 'expropriated by the state' and the land is made available for development, the rights are generally auctioned off to established developers like the Poly Group or R&F Properties (though not always competitively, as there are always back doors). *Time Weekly*'s wonder and suspicion over the Jiayu Group's rapid advances in the Pearl River New Town were rooted in this commonsense understanding of how the contest over land development unfolds. How could such an upstart out-manoeuvre established property giants on a primary battlefield?

The immense value of the usage rights for the land parcel on which Home Garden sat could be understood by looking at the decade-long saga of a significantly smaller site on its north side, a shred of state-held land on the corner of Huangpu Avenue West and Xian Village Road. I discovered records from Guangzhou's Land and Housing Office showing that this small portion of land, its footprint amounting to 75,000 square feet, was rezoned as state-held land and assigned in 2005 to Guangzhou Jiaxing Industry Company Limited, identified in business listings as a 'manufacturer and seller of LCD timers and other LCD electronic products.'[168] Here again I had found a virtually unknown company with no ascertainable experience in property development snatching up the usage rights for a valuable land site in the centre of a first-tier city. Curiously, the company's only public trace outside business listings was an entry in the 2012 interim financial report for Shanghai-listed Qinghai Xiancheng Mining Company Limited, controlled by a recently disgraced mining magnate. According to that report, Guangzhou Jiaxing Industry was a joint-liability guarantor for a sizable bank loan in Guangzhou.[169] The magnate, meanwhile, faced investigation for providing illegal loan guarantees and hastening his listed company 'towards the abyss.'[170] He had disappeared just months before my search, and in late 2013 his name appeared alongside Guangzhou Jiaxing Industry in a no-

tice published in the official *People's Daily*. Both were sought for
indictments in a civil case in Guangzhou's Yuexiu District Court
concerning the aforementioned bank loan. The trial, said the notice, would be held in their absence in a few months' time, as their
'current whereabouts were unknown.'[171]

In July 2006, the land-use permit for the small sliver of land was
transferred to Jiasui Housing Company Limited, a firm held through
a series of subsidiaries by Kaisa Group Holdings, a mainland property
developer listed in Hong Kong.[172] Kaisa Group Holdings developed
a soaring forty-seven-story commercial property called Guangzhou
Kaisa Plaza on the site. Before the finishing touches were made to the
building, however, it was sold for 1.9 billion yuan to a second major
property developer, Evergrande Real Estate, the owner of Guangzhou's
local football team.[173] The building was renamed the Evergrande International Center. In the space of five years, this modest plot of state-
held land had been transformed into a property interest worth $300
million. By comparison, the Home Garden complex, with its far more
substantial footprint, occupying the remainder of the same plot and
most, if not all, of the next one, had to be a treasure trove.

The partnership between the Jiayu Group and Xian Village
seemed to date back to the construction of the Home Garden complex itself. A listing on the Jiayu Group's website said the group had
created Pearl River New Town Commercial Plaza in September 2001
as 'an important first step in [the group's] advancement into the commercial sector.'[174] The arrangement for the Home Garden complex
had clearly been a seminal one for the group, establishing its commercial profile at just the moment the creation of the city's new central
business district was underway. An entry on the group's website said
it had put 'massive investment' into the Home Garden complex,[175]
suggesting the Jiayu Group was not just a tenant but the property's
developer, having found a way to work directly with village leaders to
build a large-scale commercial project from the ground up, without
fussing with the transfer of land-use rights through the competitive
auction generally required.

The villagers knew nothing about the arrangements for the ostensibly collective Home Garden. It was whispered, however, that the village leadership had struck up numerous partnerships in which companies were awarded protracted leases at favourable terms in exchange for under-the-table payments and personal gifts. So what terms had the executives at the Jiayu Group negotiated with Lu Suigeng for the use of Xian Village's collectively held land? This question brought me once again to the blind end of an investigation alley. I could be sure only that Jiayu Group executives viewed the arrangement as 'favourable.' In the prospectus ahead of its 2012 share offering, the Guangzhou Jinyi Film & Television Group had reassured investors that arrangements for its primary 'place of operation' in Guangzhou—the Home Garden location—were secure. The agreement with Xian Village would not expire until 2019, and 'stipulations in the lease contract concerning contract renewal are such that once the lease period for the theatre [property] terminates, [we] have the right to extend the lease at the same favourable terms.'[176] Given the enormous value of property in the central business district, it was difficult to imagine that such terms, forged and fixed more than a decade earlier, could possibly be favourable to the interests of the villagers so far into the unforeseeable future.

The interests of the villagers, in fact, did not figure at all in the calculations of Lu Suigeng's business empire, headquartered in the collective Xian Village Industry, the umbrella enterprise outside whose offices I had watched the mustering of Lu's proxy police force. Poly Fengxing Plaza and Home Garden were separate tiles in a sprawling mosaic of business deals brokered by Lu Suigeng and his brother-in-law Xian Zhangming. In the 2009 petition to the Central Commission for Discipline Inspection, villagers had alleged misconduct by Lu Suigeng and other members of the village's (family-based) leadership team across an array of business relationships,[177] but tracking down even the most rudimentary information about these deals was a laborious process. In separate email exchanges with me, the Hong Kong–listed Miramar Hotel and Investment Company Limited twice denied ever having had any involvement in the Haitao Hotel, a collectively held Xian Village property. For Lu Zhaohui and other villagers, for whom Miramar's past management of the property was unassailable fact, that assertion was absurd—and several detailed allegations concerning Miramar were laid out in the 2009 petition.[178] It was only after weeks of digging that I was able, thanks to a Hong Kong booking number on one of the Haitao's brochures, to track down the village's Hong Kong joint-venture partner,[179] Grand Fortune Food & Beverage Company Limited, in which Albert Young, the scion of Miramar founder CW Young, had purchased a 70 per cent stake through an offshore company in 1994,[180] the year the joint-venture deal over the Haitao was settled.[181] Albert Young was serving as both executive director and general manager of Miramar at the time.[182]

Lu Suigeng's business dealings were an endless terrain of secrets and guileful half-truths, and when I finally pulled the business registration records for Xian Village Industry, I was hardly surprised to find another deception. According to the *Xian Village Chronicle*, the village's parent company had been created in May 2005.[183] In fact, the company had not been registered until March 11, 2010, just two weeks before it was listed as Party A on the villagers' demolition agreements. For almost five years, Xian Village's parent company had been a ghost.

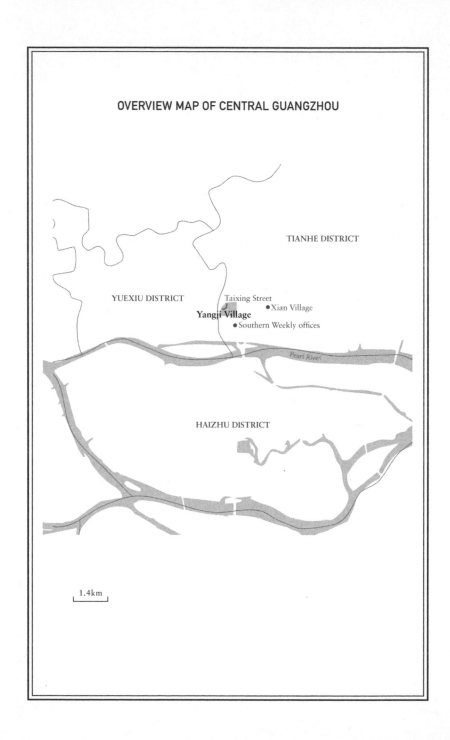

OVERVIEW MAP OF CENTRAL GUANGZHOU

TIANHE DISTRICT

YUEXIU DISTRICT

Taixing Street

●Xian Village

Yangji Village

●Southern Weekly offices

Pearl River

HAIZHU DISTRICT

1.4km

10

KICKING THE PIG

Li Qizhong, Yangji Village, 2012–2013

In her bright fuchsia blouse, Li Jie'e is a bolt of colour against the blue-grey sky. She stands five stories up, on the rooftop of one of the last remaining tenement buildings in Yangji Village, which is about four blocks west of Xian Village. Her soft shout carries down: 'How can they just lock you up and take your home? Just lock you up and take your home?' Weeks of fruitless petitioning have only deepened her despair—Li Jie'e, who once adored pretty things, who idled away her afternoons at the mah-jongg table, who joined the dancing club in the evenings.[184] She clasps some sheets of white paper in her fists and holds them high over her head before tossing them free, her arms thrown out in the arc of an embrace as the papers flutter down.[185]

A handful of villagers have converged at the foot of the building, but, fearing to further agitate Li's frayed nerves, no one dares climb up. Liang Yongquan knows already what those papers say.[186] He rushed out to search for Li Jie'e almost an hour ago, after he discovered a copy in his sitting room. Li Jie'e has been staying at his house ever since her release from the Paramilitary Police Hospital seven weeks ago. Her own house, a small walk-up three stories high, was demolished a few days before her release. It was everything she had. In Yangji's heyday, by renting out her rooms, Li Jie'e had made a modest income, enough to support her son and two daughters.

From the distance, sirens approach. Li Jie'e raises her arms over her head in a gentle oval shape, like a ballerina in fifth position. She steps to the edge of the roof, planting her black slippers on the ridge of dingy white tiles, then bends her knees into a slight crouch, her legs held neatly together. As a fire engine comes to a stop nearby, she drops her arms and suddenly thrusts them forwards, launching her body out into the open air. For a moment, she makes an arc. Her hands stretch out, fingers splayed open in a gesture almost serene, as though she is reaching for and expecting something. Her frizzy black hair flows behind. And then.

Minutes later, as doctors and nurses in their white coats work helplessly on Li Jie'e's body, a few hundred feet away Yangji villager Li Qizhong climbs onto the rooftop of his own five-story 'nail house,' the term given to a home whose owner has rejected property developers' compensation offers and refuses to allow their property to be demolished. Out of 1,400 village families who used to have tenement buildings atop their old village parcels, there are just a handful left. Yangji was once one of the city's most densely populated urban villages. Even on the brink of demolition work in 2010, it was home to some 40,000 migrant workers living in an area of about 1.27 million square feet.[187]

Li Qizhong has not left his tenement for months, fearing that if he steps out, even for a moment, the local authorities might compel him to accept their unfair terms so they can demolish his property. Like the other remaining villagers, who are living in no more than ten properties in all, he contests the legality of the planned 'urban-village regeneration' project undertaken by the local government and the Hong Kong–based commercial real-estate developer R&F Properties. He views his home, built in the 1980s on a village plot that has been in his family for generations, as his private property. But the once-bustling village of Yangji, just eight years shy of its one thousandth year, is now, in May 2012, a bleak expanse of rubble and red earth bound on all sides by high-rise office buildings, hotels and residential blocks. Police and reporters are milling about below. Just off to one side lurks the hulk of a yellow wrecking machine. Li Qizhong screams at the blue-clad figures, 'Do you even know what humanity is? Are you human beings? You drove her to her death! You fools!' Faces swivel up, looking towards him. Li Qizhong's anger rises. His voice twists into a scream. 'The people's police should serve the people. But instead you take the lead in breaking the law!'

As the police clear the scene, Li Qizhong ducks into the top floor of his property. What was once his sitting room has become his central command. A small room at the top of the stairs houses the monitors connected to his surveillance system, his eyes and ears against encroaching police, demolition crews, court officials and R&F personnel. To one side of the bathroom, what used to be a small bedroom bristles with his cache of explosives, fashioned roughly from fireworks, tanks of petrol and gas canisters. The smell of black powder permeates the upstairs rooms. Carefully opening a window covered with browning newspapers, Li Qizhong lights the fuse of one of his smaller petrol bombs, a glass jar filled with honey-coloured fuel and fitted with a cotton fuse. He steps back, and seconds later, *boom*, a tongue of flame licks across the outside wall. His fiery display carries a message he hopes the officials outside will take to heart. They are prepared to use violence to steal what is rightfully his. But if those are their rules, he is ready, too.

Outside the police cordon, a young officer walks over to a group of journalists and bystanders who have gathered to read the crumpled sheets of paper that Li Jie'e threw down just before she jumped. Stony-faced, without a word, he confiscates the papers, straightening the edges as he shuffles back across the police line and stands with his back to the crowd. The letter reads:

My home was forcibly demolished by [village lead-
ers] Zhang Jianhao, Liang Qixiong and Yao Baoyu,
and by the court. My son now has no home to return to and no income. I have no health insurance
and no pension. To live on, I had only the income
from renting my house out. My appeals case over
the house was being considered, and I meant only to
wait for a result. But at 5:00 p.m. on March 20 . . .
six men without police uniforms, presenting no
identification and no warrant, detained me along
with villager Yao Muchang as we were leaving the
Tianhe Mall. They took me to the Yuexiu District
Court and then to the Yuexiu Detention Centre.
Eventually, they took me to the Paramilitary Police
Hospital.

   During my time in the detention centre, I was
forced to wear handcuffs and shackles day in and
day out, even when sleeping and washing. The paramilitary police had these electric prods. It was terri-
fying. I was really afraid. And then one day, a man
from the court came and said if I signed a letter
of contrition they would let me go. My body was
so weak I couldn't write, so one of my cellmates
helped me copy it out. I was so scared. Someone
called Judge Lin asked me to sign a bunch of things
and then they just dropped me at the gate of the
hospital.

   When I finally made my way back to Yangji
Village I realised my home had already been demolished. They demolished it while I was locked
up . . . That home was everything I had . . . My
son, my daughters: Mummy owes you so much.
The matter of the house is something you will need
to pursue on your own now. I'm truly sorry . . .

I have to go. And once I go, there will be no more pain.

Li Jie'e, May 9, 2012

•

'What are you doing tomorrow?' Huang Minpeng asked me on one of my visits to Hebu Village in January 2013. 'I'm visiting a friend over there at Yangji Village in the morning,' he continued. 'We could meet there if you want to go. Li Qizhong is one of the last villagers holding out. He hasn't left his house in more than a year.'

The signs of a stalemated conflict at Yangji Village were evident even before we reached the north gate on Taixing Street. A red banner, faded to pink, sagged on the empty shell of a walk-up that had once housed a travel agency and a driving school: 'Heaven will not tolerate those who hold ransom the legal interests of their village kin!' More slogans had been spray-painted on the wall beneath. When I paused to take a photograph, Huang Minpeng turned and grumbled. 'Don't pay any attention to that,' he said. 'The corrupt village leaders put those there because Ah Zhong and the others have refused to sign.' Ah Zhong was the name by which Li Qizhong's friends called him.

I knew already that Yangji Village had been desolated. In fact, I had been surprised to learn from Huang Minpeng that villagers were still holding out there. Who could forget the agonising images from the previous year? The suicide of Li Jie'e had become one of the most iconic tragedies of China's urbanisation drive. But as we walked through the unguarded steel gate, it was a shock nonetheless to see the crater of Yangji Village open up before us. The ancient village had been gouged right out of Guangzhou's heart.

There were just a few ragged buildings left. Huang Minpeng led the way, guiding me through heaps of rubble and red earth. The nail-house villagers had constructed a footpath through the mud using castoff bricks, seven across. It wound, crossing a trench filled with muddy brown water, towards a pair of tenements. The first had a shop space underneath, now a sitting area for villagers Liang Jinheng and Kuang Chunlian. They had paved the whole area in front of the building with bricks and had even set out a lacquered redwood sofa, an oddly civilised touch in the midst of the devastation. Ahead of me, Huang Minpeng's diesel voice boomed a greeting in Cantonese to the couple, who were sitting just inside on a pair of lounge chairs. I said hello in Mandarin. 'How long do you expect to be staying?' I asked.

Liang grinned, but there was a hint of truculence in his voice. 'We don't expect to be leaving any time soon,' he said.

We walked on, past a few piles of concrete rubble. Weeds and wildflowers had sprung up among them. Just ahead was a narrow nail house surrounded by ridges of russet earth. To the southwest, a mountain of soil rose up maybe five stories, a sheer cliff of clay scooped out at its base. A tower crane nodded in the distance be-hind. The windows of Li Qizhong's tenement were masked from the inside with rags and old newspapers. Outside the fourth-floor win-dows, dark plastic bottles dangled next to brown rags that sagged like tongues from the window ledges. The rags, I supposed, were meant to catch fire once the fuel inside the bottles was ignited. Our approach brought out a tawny dog with a wolfish face, the tip of his tail as black as a Chinese calligraphy brush. He stood on a mound of overgrown rubble, raised his head and barked as we made our way along the path.

We reached the front of the nail house. The rubble had been cleared away, making a rough embankment around the entryway. The dog stood guard before the tarnished aluminium double doors, baring his teeth. Several newspaper pages, now sun-bleached and peeling away, had been pasted onto the brick wall to the left of the door. They included an old front page from Guangdong's official Communist Party newspaper, *Nanfang Daily*. 'No one has the right to infringe on the legal property rights of the peasants,' said the bold headline. There was a hollow rasping sound as the deadbolts slid free and the door groaned open. Li Qizhong's wife, Yu Lirong, edged her head cautiously around the door, her face framed by a bob of jet-black hair, then ventured out from the dimness of the stairwell. Her eyes made a precautionary survey of the landscape. 'Good morning,' she said finally, motioning us inside. I followed Huang Minpeng up the stairs while Yu Lirong secured the door. The dog padded ahead of us. Against the walls of the stairwell were piled jumbles of broken furniture and other junk. These, I guessed, could be thrown down at short notice to form barricades against intruders. The dog was ken-nelled on the second floor: another line of defence. Otherwise, the bottom floors were empty, the rooms covered thickly with dust. The masked stairwell windows allowed light to suffuse the space with a filmy amber glow. The sulphurous tang of black powder became more pungent as we climbed.

Li Qizhong was waiting for us on the third floor. His eyes, nar-rowing under a bony brow etched with a fine scar, were as dark as Buddhist prayer beads. The edges of his full-lipped mouth turned down into a slight scowl, accentuated by his threadbare moustache. He reminded me of the dark warrior Xuan Wu, the sword-wielding Taoist deity who mastered the elements. But this balding Xuan Wu wore cotton pyjamas and grubby plastic slippers. 'Mr. Ban. Thanks for coming,' he said.

'I'm surprised you're still here. I thought Yangji Village was de-molished long ago,' I replied.

'There are only eight properties left now. You passed Liang Jin-heng's place on the way in. Li Jianming's house is out that way.' He gestured past the small sitting room and a south-facing balcony in the next room. 'Li Jianming should be coming over in a bit. Have a seat.' Li Jianming had spearheaded opposition to the eviction and demolition terms dictated by the Yangji Village Economic Union, a company claiming to represent the collective economic interests of all villagers in Yangji. In March 2011, the Economic Union had sued Li Jianming and fifteen other Yangji Village homeowners, including Li Qizhong, in the Yuexiu District People's Court. Their homes, the company had argued, sat on collective village property required for an urban-village regeneration plan agreed in 2010 with R&F Properties, which had the blessing of the city government.

More than 90 per cent of the villagers had signed the agreement within the first few months, many with a sense of desperation—they had been told that those who signed first would be given priority in choosing apartments in the resettlement block planned alongside R&F's commercial development. In a district where property prices per square foot had already soared to almost 2,800 yuan, villagers were offered rock-bottom compensation of 93 yuan, and only for the ground level of their property. The area on the upper floors was not factored in, because the government deemed it 'illegal construction.' But if this was true, if these properties were violations, why had they stood for more than twenty years? And why had the villagers been obliged to pay taxes on them over all that time?

Li Jianming had fought the lawsuit by devouring every law book he could find. He had pored over China's Constitution, its Civil Procedure Law, its Land Administration Law, its Property Law. He had prepared an eleven-page brief and presented it to the court, serving as his own legal counsel. He had lost the case, but he gained substantial expertise—and earned the support and admiration of other rights defenders and beleaguered villagers in the city. The Economic Union had claimed that by refusing to sign the agreement, the nail-house villagers were impinging on the rights of those who had signed and who were waiting anxiously for the completion of the resettlement blocks, which had been indefinitely postponed. Some of those villagers were staying in apartments on the remote outskirts of the city, because their meagre resettlement allowances were far below rent levels in the city centre.

Li Qizhong and Li Jianming had insisted still that their homes were private property. They had refused to sacrifice their rights under the tyranny of a village majority that had rushed blindly and fearfully into a project agreed to behind their backs. Announced to the villagers for the first time in March 2010, the project had been approved behind closed doors by sixty-nine 'stockholder representatives' of the Economic Union. But a Guangzhou regulation on village redevelopment passed in June 2012 required approval by at least 90 per cent of the village collective in a general vote before redevelopment could go ahead. That vote, by the admission of the village leaders, had never taken place.

Li Qizhong poured cups of tea and pulled a stool up directly across from the drab sofa where I had sat down. His daughter and son, ten and eight years old, flitted around us, shy but curious. 'Do you study English in school?' I asked the girl.

She rocked on her heels. She was skinny, almost as tall as her father. 'Yes,' she said in English, smiling.

'What's your name?'

'Fan Fan. And he's Lang Lang.'

'Do you have an English name?' I asked. It is common for schoolchildren in China to be given Western names in English class, which is a compulsory part of the curriculum.

'No,' she said, in English again. She pointed to her brother. 'His . . . name . . . is . . . John. He is small.'

'Very good,' I said.

She translated for everyone. 'He says, "Very good."'

Li Qizhong's face flushed with pride. Fan Fan enjoyed school, he said. She was a member of the drum corps, which was preparing for the school's Spring Festival celebration. But earlier that week she had been called to the principal's office and told she could not perform with the group, because her parents had refused to sign the demolition agreement. She had come home in tears. 'Can you believe that?' Li Qizhong shook his head. 'If they want to take things out on me, I can understand that. But they're just children.' Things were tough enough already on the children. The family was often without water or electricity for days on end. A few weeks before, a group of signed-up villagers with excavators had destroyed the main waterline and had dug moat-like trenches around each of the remaining properties. For a time, going to and from school had meant the children scrambling up and down a muddy embankment, sometimes in the dark.

Li Qizhong hadn't set foot off his property since early December 2011, when the district court had ruled against the owners of the sixteen remaining village properties and said the Economic Union of Yangji Village had the right to seize the properties for the general collective interest of the village. Li Qizhong, Li Jianming and the others were ordered to surrender their homes within three days of the court's decision.[188] Li Qizhong had used the time to dig in, fortifying his property against the police, developers and village leaders, who had their own contingent of thugs. He installed a security system. He stored up water and food. He manufactured an arsenal of deterrent force. That explosive stockpile was now directly over our heads. 'I don't advocate violence, Mr. Ban,' Li Qizhong explained. 'But if you want to get a pig to walk straight, violence is sometimes necessary. We are all from the countryside, you know. When I was a boy, that's how things were. To move a pig along you had to give him a little kick. If you want the pig to walk straight, violence is unavoidable.' The 'pig,' in this case, was the Chinese Communist Party and the entire corrupt political system over which it ruled. Li Qizhong's idea was that the system had to be nudged in the right direction.

Huang Minpeng groaned with cynicism. The Party was beyond redemption, too fat on the spoils of growth to be goaded in any direction, he said.

'Look,' said Li Qizhong. 'You can say that the Chinese Communist Party is bad. But it's not all bad. When the Party took power, it was the vanguard. It won the hearts of the people.'

'No,' Huang Minpeng protested in his deep, guttural Cantonese. '*Moh-ah!*'

'Just listen to me. This is not about opposing the Communist Party. It's about opposing corruption.'

'Don't defend them, Ah Zhong. Don't defend them.' Huang Minpeng had unzipped his jacket. I noticed he was wearing a white 'Freedom, democracy and constitutionalism' T-shirt, a steel-blue image of the Statue of Liberty in the centre.

'I'm not defending them,' said Li Qizhong. 'But they were able

to rally the people. They were able to lead the people to revolution.'
He forged ahead with his line of argument. The question of regime
was not important. The Chinese had to unite against corruption and
demand greater autonomy. This was the only way everyone's rights,
including his own, could be adequately protected. Society had to be
remade. In an oddly subversive way, the popular support amassed
by the Chinese Communist Party in Li's grandparents' generation
had inspired a new movement for change—an organised citizenry
nudging the Party in the direction of the future.

'We should all hope that Chairman Xi [Jinping, soon to become the nation's president] moves towards constitutionalism,' said
Li Qizhong. 'The way I see it, if my resistance succeeds, this is a tiny
step on the way to democracy. You just don't see this level of corruption in a democratic system. Everyone lives together more harmoni-
ously. For us right now, this kind of democracy is really important.'

We were interrupted by a shout volleyed up from outside. 'Ah
Zhong! Ah Zhong!' Soon after, Li Jianming appeared at the top of
the stairs with a stack of papers under his arm. He pushed in next to
me on the sofa, sorting through the documents on his lap. On my
left, at his father's elbow under the hooded window, Lang Lang was
playing with a set of coloured blocks, carefully arranging the rectan-
gles and triangles into a cityscape. 'Okay, so this is the latest thing,'
said Li Jianming. He passed me the printed image of a large poster
I had seen on the way in, pasted on the wall just outside the village
gate—a call for vigilante action written in black calligraphy against
a deep red background:

NOTICE

Fellow villagers, uncles and brothers:

So that we can resettle as quickly as possible, we call
on everyone to unite together to clear out and demolish the remaining eight nail houses beginning

on December 16 at the site of the old village. Please
pass this message along once you have seen it.

Signed,

THE RIGHTS DEFENDERS OF YANGJI VILLAGE

'This is the village committee's development company calling on all
of the villagers to oppose us,' Li Jianming explained. He turned to
a typewritten letter dated November 15, 2012. The letter's tone was
menacing: 'We villagers sternly call on you to vacate the old village
within a month's time,' it said. 'Otherwise, we will strike a firm blow
against this repugnant conduct of yours!' The letter was signed 'All the
villagers,' below which were hundreds of individual signatures. Li Jianming waited, watching my eyes as I scanned the page. 'Can you see
it?' And suddenly, it was obvious what he meant. The signatures had
clearly been scribbled by only a handful of people; they were a shallow
farce. But there was something ruthlessly clever about how the local
authorities—working hand-in-hand with a property developer whose
chairperson was on the *Forbes* list of global billionaires—sought to
swindle away the moral high ground. They stood for the 'true rights
defenders,' while villagers like Li Qizhong and Li Jianming, they
claimed, had ransomed the collective interest out of 'selfish desire.'

  'This is the same argument you find in Xian Village,' I said. 'The
idea that the collective interest overrules all private rights.'

  'That's right; but you can't use a majority to trample the rights of
a minority,' said Li Jianming. 'I guarantee you, the contract we have
in Yangji Village is even worse.' He winnowed through his pile of papers until he came to a document called 'Demolition, Compensation
and Resettlement Agreement for the Urban-Village Regeneration of
Yangji.' 'Look here,' he said, running his finger over a portion of the
agreement he had underlined. 'Party A [Yangji Village Economic
Union] has a right to make appropriate adjustments to the resettlement plan "according to specific circumstances."'

'Just that little bit of language, and none of the rest of it matters,' Li Qizhong growled.

'Yes. Here, it says they can do so for the "overall collective interest,"' I said, reading the beginning of the clause. 'According to the contract, they get to decide what that interest is.'

'And look here,' Li Qizhong continued. 'Party B has a "duty to submit themselves to the overall situation." So *they* have the *right* to interpret it how they want, and it's our *duty* to follow along.'[189]

Another of the documents in Li Jianming's stack was a defence argument presented to the Guangzhou Intermediate People's Court by Wang Cailiang, a prominent Beijing lawyer who had agreed to help the nail-house villagers fight their case on appeal. The six-page document, 'Urban-village regeneration cannot proceed illegally,' laid out a series of legal points so fundamental that it seemed a naked mockery the court had upheld the verdict against the villagers. The original plaintiff, the Economic Union, was an economic body without proper administrative authority over village affairs—and which, moreover, was registered in the neighbouring Tianhe District. Legally speaking, said Wang, the appropriate plaintiff was the Yangji Village committee, an administrative body under the proper jurisdiction of Yuexiu District, in which Yangji is located.[190] Also, China's 1998 Organic Law of the Villagers Committees stipulates that proposals for the use of collective-housing plots has to be debated and decided in a general meeting of villagers aged eighteen or over.[191] But during the proceedings, the Economic Union had supported its claim to the land-use rights for Yangji Village's collective-housing plots by presenting the minutes of a meeting of 'stockholder representatives.' Wrong plaintiff, wrong procedure.

The most egregious problem was the fact that neither the village committee nor the Economic Union actually owned the usage rights to the land in question any more. In June 2010, three months after the redevelopment proposal was announced, Guangzhou's Land and Housing Office had approved the transfer of Yangji's collective-housing plots to state-held status, which was legally necessary for development to proceed. In December 2010, the same office had listed the land-use rights for auction. Finally, in January 2011, in a competitive sale in which R&F Properties had been the only bidder, the land-use rights had been sold. By the time the Economic Union filed its initial lawsuit in March 2011, the collective-housing plots had been no longer collective. And yet somehow, in the midst of the appeals process, the Economic Union had managed to present another document from the Land and Housing Office, dated July 24, 2012, that purported to show that the contested land was still collectively held. 'Surely, the regeneration land cited in this document must be state land, because only state land can be allotted for use,' Wang Cailiang wrote. 'But for this document to say that the ownership rights for this land are still collective points to clear illegalities. There is no law in our country that empowers Guangzhou's Land and Housing Office to transfer state land back to collective land.' If the land had indeed been redesignated by the city as collectively held, said Wang, this would amount to a serious criminal act resulting in the loss of state-held assets. In his closing remarks, Wang made clear that his clients were not opposed to urban-village regeneration; however, they believed that regeneration had to proceed legally, with respect for the legal rights and interests of those concerned.[192]

In fact, the Guangzhou Intermediate People's Court never really heard the case on appeal, entrusting it instead to the Yuexiu District Court, the same court that had already ruled against Li Jianming and the other property holders. The court upheld its own verdict on January 16, 2013. As with the first verdict,[193] the villagers were ordered to vacate their homes and hand them over to the Economic Union within three days.[194]

'For the sake of peace in society, the government should pursue justice in our cases,' Li Qizhong said after lunch that afternoon. 'Actually, the course we're taking isn't real violence. True violence is what happened in Libya, right?' The others nodded. He continued. 'If the system can change itself, if we no longer have this problem of corrupt officials, and if we can all do our part and have our little piece of happiness, then no one needs to fight.

'So, about this *Southern Weekly* incident.' In the first week of January, staff at Guangzhou's *Southern Weekly* offices, located in the southeast corner of Yangji Village, had begun a strike action to protest draconian controls that threatened their legacy as one of China's most progressive newspapers. Li Qizhong went on, 'Actually, Mr. Ban, if I could have set foot outside, I might not have had the courage to join the protest. But I would have looked on. Looking on is its own form of power.' He was referring to what Chinese call the 'surrounding gaze,' the idea that if the public masses attention around an event or issue, either online or in the real world, this can exert pressure on the government or others to change their conduct, even without more direct activism. 'So, online there's this woman named He Jieling. You probably know about her, right?'

'Yes, yes,' I said, taken by surprise. Just two days earlier I had spent the entire day with He Jieling in Panyu District.

'He Jieling,' Li Qizhong repeated, nodding. 'I often have contact with her. Her way of thinking is like mine. She changed the name of her Sina Weibo account to "He Jieling, 138 Guangzhou Villages." And I told her, you mustn't change it. Because we have 138 villages in Guangzhou, and we are a powerful force. We are a source of local strength, born here and raised here. So we need to use this strength to push the government towards democracy. This is why I've proposed online that villagers using social media all put Guangzhou and the name of their villages in front, and after that their names. That way, we all have a common *logo*.' He used the English word. 'And that gives us a sense of identity. We are all locals. We represent local strength. First, we need to get everyone around us to band together, like a massive dragon. That will make us strong. It's not that we want to overthrow the government; it's just that we want to protect our interests. We can only protect our legitimate rights and interests if we are all bound together. My idea, like He Jieling's, is that we do what we can to connect all of these people. Maybe we can't be a real organisation. But we can still have our own identity. We are all Guangzhou villagers. We are attached to this land. When there are thirty thousand of us, we won't need to petition the government. We'll just mass outside the offices of *Southern Weekly* and shout, "Down with corrupt officials! Stop the insolent demolition of our homes!" They'll feel the ground tremble. Once they see our strength, what can they do? Unite, gather your strength, and then make your voice heard. Actually, this is the way it was in the early days of the Chinese Communist Party.' As far as Li Qizhong was concerned, a corrupt system had shoved villager Li Jie'e off the roof of that abandoned tenement eight months earlier, the day he had ignited one of his firebombs in protest. The system had isolated and crushed her, leaving her no options. 'Apartments are selling over 10,000 yuan per square foot here in the Pearl River New Town. She was fifty-four years old, with no education. Without her home, she had no way of fending for herself. What choice did she have?'

After Li Jie'e's death, He Jieling had told me, many Guangzhou villagers dealing with land seizures or forced property demolitions had gathered together. Reaching out on Sina Weibo that very day, He Jieling had met Pazhou villager Xu Zhihao, who had fought an unsuccessful court battle to save his home the year before, and Chen Qingqiu, a university instructor who was embroiled in a dispute over a property investment in Guangzhou University Town. 'The only way to keep tragedies like that from happening again is to join up all of these local village forces,' said Li Qizhong. 'Guangzhou first, then the Pearl River Delta, then all of Guangdong, then the entire country. With that kind of strength, corrupt officials won't dare run roughshod over us.'

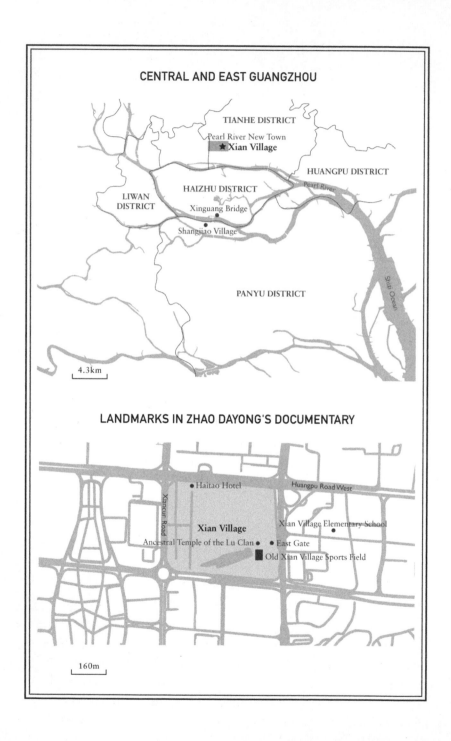

11

TEAR DOWN THIS WALL

Xian Village, 2012–2013

On the eve of liberation [in 1949], Xian Village organised a 'May 1 Music Society' and taught the villagers the revolutionary song 'The march of the volunteers.' Xian Village created a Forward Committee, made initial arrangements and prepared to welcome the People's Liberation Army.

—*Xian Village Chronicle*[195]

I caught up with Lu Zhaohui and Lu Qiang, my Xian Village contacts, in a restaurant on the western edge of the Pearl River New Town in September 2012. I had booked a private room upstairs and was waiting for the men outside the main entrance. Modern towers soared up all around me where once there had been farmland: the Leeden Hotel, one of several properties in the area built by the Jiayu Group,[196] and the luxury King Thai Centre Apartments. When Lu Qiang and Lu Zhaohui strode up to the door a few minutes later, I could sense that the fortunes of Xian Village had in some way shifted. Lu Qiang was no longer careworn; the bloodshot eyes I had looked into at the Regal Riviera Hotel a month earlier were gone. Lu Zhaohui wore an insouciant smile. 'Have you seen the flags in the village?' He asked, as we settled into our seats at an enormous round dining table.

I had indeed seen some simple red flags sagging over the tops of the tenements the evening before. 'What do they mean?' I asked.

'The village officials claim almost all of us have signed the [regeneration] agreement,' he said. 'This is our way of showing how many are still holding out.'

The goal posts had moved in the game of numbers that summer. The new city-planning policy stipulating that demolitions for urban-village regenerations required the consent of at least 90 per cent of villagers had been announced in June.[197] A few weeks later, the *Guangzhou Daily*, the city's official Communist Party newspaper, had reported that Xian Village had already reached the 90 per cent threshold. Villagers I spoke to had insisted this was a lie cooked up by Lu Suigeng's nephew Lu Youxing, the village's Party deputy chairperson, and that close to a quarter of them were still refusing to sign their 'Demolition, Compensation and Resettlement Agreement.' The *Guangzhou Daily* story also reported that the Poly Group had paid out an additional compensation fund of 150 million yuan, about $24 million, to 'shore up the trust of the villagers.'[198] If the project was progressing so well, what could explain this unasked-for act of largesse from a publicly listed enterprise? And where had the money gone?

'How many of you are still holding out?' I asked.

'About 20 per cent,' said Lu Qiang. 'Eighty per cent at the most have signed, but a lot of them regret it now. They only signed in the first place because they were frightened.'

'So the flags are to show leaders higher up that you are still holding out?'

'We want them to know that what the village leaders are claiming is wrong,' said Lu Zhaohui.

'And we want to show our solidarity,' Lu Qiang added.

The opposition movement in Xian Village had never been about compensation. The core issues remained, as ever, corruption and accountability. The villagers continued to insist on the ousting of Lu Suigeng and his cronies, as well as a full and open accounting of the village's assets. The law, in theory, empowered them to accomplish both; off paper, the law meant nothing. Insulated by his powerful friends, Lu Suigeng had ruled in his own interest for decades, through 'shareholder representatives' he had appointed himself.

The red flags could equally be understood as signal fires to the leadership. Red is the hue of revolution, the Communist Party's chosen colour. But the flags flying over the village were devoid of sickles and hammers, the symbols crossed on the Party flag to illustrate the sacred compact between rural peasants and urban workers. The time had come, the villagers believed, for the Party to decide where it stood. If it stood only for itself, the compact was broken. Red is also, of course, the colour of blood, the colour of ancestry. In Xian Village, ancestral lines ran deep into the past, into the red earth that had sustained them for so many centuries. Those ties bound the villagers more decisively than political pledges or the promise of financial reward.

Our conversation lulled as a hostess in a bright silk cheongsam wafted into the room, proffering an enormous menu book. Assiduously, I studied the tome of Cantonese delicacies, most of them alien, before ordering a soup, a steamed fish and a few other recommended dishes. As soon as the hostess left the room, Lu Zhaohui said, 'We're hearing now that there might be an investigation under way into corruption inside the city government.'

'Are they investigating the Xian Village leadership?'

'We don't know exactly. But it appears something is going on.'

'How do you know?'

'A friend from another village has good contacts in the city government,' he said. 'Something is happening, but they can't tell us any more than that.'

A text buzzed in from Xian Chuntao, the young villager who

had given me her account of the market demolition that night in 2010, when she had hurried through the pitch-dark alleyways of Xian Village in search of her parents. She was waiting downstairs in the foyer. I hadn't seen her for months. The last time we had met, in June 2012, she had been apprehensive about being seen walking with me on the village side of Huangpu Avenue West; there was a risk plainclothes police might see us talking and summon her for questioning, assuming she had been speaking about matters in Xian Village. As I escorted her up to the dining room, she seemed more at ease as well. 'Is your family flying a red flag too?' I asked.

She laughed. 'We actually put two of them up on our roof.'

It was clear from our conversation that afternoon that tensions remained high in the village. There were occasional clashes between villagers and demolition personnel. Lu Qiang showed me a video he had taken secretly that morning: a line of men in camouflage jackets and domed white helmets slouching past a blue barricade surrounding a demolition site, as several villagers shouted at them, calling them traitors. Like the guards at the village gates, the demolition men were migrants from the countryside, villagers from far-flung outposts pitted for a meagre wage against villagers on the urban front lines. I thought of a political cartoon I had seen making the rounds on Sina Weibo. In the first frame, an elderly peasant clutched his mobile, cowering under the baton blows of a land-seizure team as he made an emergency call to his son. The next frame pictured the son answering the call in some distant city, clad in full riot gear, truncheon in hand, with some poor peasant or rights defender stretched out at his feet, motionless. 'I'm out on a job right now, Dad,' the son said. 'Is something wrong?'[199] But even as tensions lingered, the tide seemed to be turning in the villagers' favour. Less than two weeks earlier, they had even received the busload of villagers from Sanyuanli Village, plus Huang Minpeng from Hebu Village, to whom they had given firsthand accounts of the horrors of 'regeneration.' Three months earlier, during what Lu Qiang had called 'the darkest days,' the visit from the Sanyuanli delegation would have been unthinkable.

Why had the darkness retreated? It was possible that Lu Suigeng had indeed suffered a dramatic reversal of fortune. It was also possible—and more probable, I thought—that the vagaries of national politics had made local leaders more cautious. These were jittery times, notwithstanding a curious absence and reemergence of Xi Jinping, soon to become the Party's general secretary and then the nation's president. In March, the dramatic Bo Xilai scandal had exposed deep factional divisions within the Party leadership and had left officials everywhere with a harrowing sense of insecurity. Until the waters calmed, officials in Guangzhou could be expected to navigate with utmost caution. The smallest eddy of turmoil in a place like Xian Village could have ruinous consequences, drawing national attention at a time when factional rivals sought any opportunity to pull an opponent down.

•

One afternoon in January 2013, Lu Zhaohui met up with me and Huang Minpeng at Li Qizhong's Yangji Village nail house and afterwards drove us through the glimmering towers of the central business district until we reached the northwest corner of Xian Village. 'Waaah!' Huang Minpeng exclaimed as we rounded the corner. The scene that greeted us looked like an open-air carnival. More than a hundred villagers were huddled near the busy intersection just beyond the village gate. The footpath on the other side was lined with makeshift billboards pasted with photographs, documents and declarations, and it was teeming with onlookers. They paused before the displays, reading documents and news articles, lingering over images.

Lu Zhaohui stopped the car, and we got out. On one of the display boards I spotted a familiar photograph taken during the violent police crackdown of August 2010—an old villager with blood streaming down his face. There were eyewitness accounts of police violence, open letters to corruption investigators and in-depth reports from forbidden Hong Kong newspapers. Photograph collages bore testament to alleged beatings and intimidation. It was a museum to the Xian Village resistance, a history spanning almost four years. In a country where dissidents are detained at a pin drop for 'disturbing the public order,' the spectacle outside Xian Village was audacious, to say the least. And yet the police were nowhere to be seen. Private security guards in military fatigues were slouched on either side of the village gate. They watched me as I photographed the displays. But the cocksure alertness was gone; there was a languid impotence in their eyes. They no longer bothered to register those going in and out of the village. 'Should we go in?' said Lu Zhaohui, at my side. For the past six months, he and I had taken great care to meet only outside the village, usually in neighbouring Yuexiu District, across the Pearl River. And even given these precautions, we had still been wary, glancing over our shoulders to see whether we had been tailed by police. Lu's suggestion now that we enter the tenements together seemed the clearest sign that things had changed.

But my insides still tugged with the anxiety of my last trip into the village that July past, when I had narrowly escaped the clutches of Polo and Bulldog, the pair of plainclothes village security who had insisted on taking me to an unspecified location for questioning. 'Is it safe to go in?' I asked.

'Of course,' he said.

For the first time in nearly six months, I strolled through the dim alleys of Xian Village. And for the first time, Lu Zhaohui was my guide. The tenements remained in a half-abandoned state. Doors and windows were torn jaggedly from the walls, surrendering the interiors to an almost feral darkness. Villagers had cleared the rubble away from the footpaths, which were now fastidiously lined with walls of salvaged brick. In the gaps where tenements had been demolished, January sunlight cascaded into the ruins. Fear, it seemed that afternoon, had retreated. I had no idea how to interpret the astonishing change. The sense of oppression had lifted, and there were unmistakable signs of life: a young migrant in a pressed white shirt locking the steel door of his apartment with a hollow clang before heading off to work; a woman hunched under the sickly light of a tobacco stand, knitting a pair of baby slippers. As we walked along the cleared paths, Lu Zhaohui even hoped out loud that the dragon-boat parades might be possible by the summer. 'We'll just have to see,' he said. Perhaps, I thought, hope could also be salvaged for these villagers bound by the city.

On our way back around to the villagers' exhibition, we crossed paths with a pair of grim-looking security men, red bands slashing across their shoulders. My thoughts flew instantly to my encounter with Polo and Bulldog. 'Those guys don't worry you?' I asked Lu Zhaohui as they approached.

He dismissed the idea with a brusque sweep of his hand. 'There's absolutely nothing they can do,' he said.

•

As the Year of the Dragon drew to its festive close in mid-February 2013, there was still no definite news of the rumoured investigation into the Xian Village leadership, and there was no hint of the circumstances or whereabouts of Lu Suigeng. But the weather in Guangzhou was unseasonably mild, as though the gods had blessed Xian's next mass rally, an outdoor New Year's banquet to be held at the old sports field beside the ruins of Xian Village Primary School. More than sixty round tables were set out for the banquet on February 19,[200] draped with festal red cloths and ringed with red plastic stools. A few tables were set aside for visitors from other Guangzhou villages facing their own land-use rights and corruption struggles. 'Cousins,' said the brush-written characters on squares of red paper. Close to 1,000 people, most of them local villagers, attended the celebration. It culminated in a gutsy revival of a practice not seen for sixty-one years, since the early days of Communist Party rule in China: the names of male children born over the past year were formally entered into the ancient clan records of the village's ancestry.[201] As a cannonade of firecrackers was set off from a rooftop across from the sports field, a sense of gathering momentum filled the air.

It was from a Xian Village cousin that I received the quietly 'confirmed' news several weeks later of Lu Suigeng's suspension as de facto village chief and head of Xian Village Industry. My source was Li Qizhong, the nail-house inhabitant from Yangji Village. Between my visits to Guangzhou we had kept up correspondence on Sina Weibo. In mid-March, Li wrote to me, 'According to an authoritative government source, all official responsibilities of the Xian Village official Lu Suigeng have been suspended and he is now under investigation.' Li's source was another Yangji villager, with contacts inside the city government. When I called Xian villagers Lu Zhaohui and Lu Qiang, they had already heard the news and said the villagers regarded it as credible. Lu Zhaohui spoke of an 'official notice,' although no one could claim to have seen it firsthand, and so far nothing had been made public.

Once again, weeks passed without definite news. Meanwhile, the village was suspended in an uneasy truce under which each side quietly sought advantage. Guards still loitered in pairs at the entrances to the village, but their logbooks were closed; visitors seemed to wander in and out now without so much as a glance. Here and there, ragtag demolition crews still made incursions on the village, dismantling vacant tenements whose owners—so the crews claimed—had given consent. But the villagers were confident that the momentum in their resistance movement was building. With impish grins, some told me they had prevented demolition crews from withdrawing their heavy machinery. Atop one hillock of rubble, a yellow digger hunched like a sheepish prisoner of war.

The next mass rally on the old sports field was planned for April 20. Five days before the event, a message pinged into my phone from Li Qizhong, sequestered in his Yangji nail house. The message, which Li was passing on from another Guangzhou cousin, was a general invitation to join the rally:

We encourage all nail housers, victims of demolition and eviction, and rights defenders from villages
throughout the city to take part in the banquet . . .

We must believe that victory can be ours. Only
if all villagers join together can corrupt officials be
effectively opposed. We hope someone from your
village can attend the banquet. This is an opportunity for exchange over how to oppose corrupt officials. The more people the better.

The response to the general invitation proved so enthusiastic, however, that the Xian Village organisers finally decided to postpone it,
fearing a strong backlash from authorities already on edge. Conflicts
over land-use rights were growing violent throughout the region. In
January, riot police armed with clubs and electric prods had been
scrambled in Jiangmen City, just south of Guangzhou, to scatter
hundreds of peasants in Nan'an Village who had barricaded a road
to protest against local corruption, including the apparent theft of
70 million yuan, about $11 million, of compensation for farmland
seized to build a factory.[202] Brutally attacked by police, the villagers had fought back with bricks and stones.[203] And just three days
before the planned Xian Village banquet, riot police in the city of
Zhanjiang, about three hours west of Guangzhou, had joined in the
forced demolition of village homes and fields for a tourism project.
Peasants from Xiaozhi Village, violently beaten back with clubs and
other instruments, could only look on as the machines levelled their
homes and fruit trees.[204]

The next occasion for a Xian Village banquet was the Dragon
Boat Festival, in early June. On April 16, a preview of the festivities in the tabloid *Southern Metropolis Daily* offered a glimpse of the
tensions still present in the village. 'The subdistrict would like us
to organise dragon-boat parades,' an unnamed village official told
the newspaper, 'but we haven't yet determined a time.' The official
said they had 'done some mobilising' and acknowledged 'it had been

tough to muster enthusiasm among villagers refusing to sign the demolition agreement.'[205] If the news of Lu Suigeng's ousting were true, who was this unnamed official?

Three days after the *Southern Metropolis Daily* article, the strained relations to which it alluded finally culminated. The uneasy truce in Xian Village collapsed. I heard it first from He Jieling, who called me just before sundown on May 23, gasping the news before I could get a word out. 'They've murdered a villager, Mr. Ban! They've murdered a villager!'

'Where?'

'In Xian Village!'

'Are you sure? Where did you hear it?'

'It's all over Weibo,' she said.

'Okay. I'll call the villagers straightaway,' I said.

Lu Zhaohui answered immediately. His voice strained above a surf of confusion in the background. 'Mr. Ban, you've heard?'

'I heard a villager was killed,' I said. 'What's going on?'

'Those demolition thugs beat an old villager unconscious. He's in the intensive care unit.'

'Will he be okay?'

'We don't know yet.'

It had started, he said, with an ill-tempered exchange between the villager and members of a demolition crew. In their carelessness, the crew had damaged buildings and blocked the way to the villager's home. The men had suddenly turned on the old man, beating him and knocking him to the ground. 'We called the police, but they didn't come,' said Lu Zhaohui. 'Now we're gathering on Huangpu Avenue West to demand the government do something. The villagers are sitting in the middle of the road. Things can't go on like this.'

Social media buzzed with news of the incident. As images and eyewitness accounts scudded across Sina Weibo, hovered briefly, then disappeared, I scurried to capture them like a child chasing opalescent bubbles through the air. An image of the white-haired victim stretched out on a gurney, a mass of villagers crowding around as the ambulance crew worked, villagers marching along Huangpu Avenue West by the hundreds, villagers squatting on the pedestrian crossings at the intersection of Huangpu Avenue West and Xian Village Road, blocking rush hour traffic in all directions. Finally, the images recorded the summary end of two and a half years of forced isolation. Villagers under the dusky titian bloom of the sodium lamps pressed forwards against section after section of the village wall, their palms and fingers flattened against the hated surface. Piece by piece, the wall fell and shattered as onlookers cheered.[206] By the time riot police arrived to calm the situation, much of the enclosing wall that had symbolised Xian Village's isolation and oppression lay in ruins. The sheets of propaganda that had promised a dazzling future were buried facedown under heaps of brick and mortar.

Rousing cries of support appeared on the internet, though no news whatsoever of the incident was reported inside China. 'The wall around Xian Village could not imprison the hearts of the villagers; nor could it stop the spread of justice,' one Sina Weibo user wrote. 'Everyone has to pass this along,' another urged. 'We need to tell the provincial and central governments, and the entire country, what's actually happening in Xian Village.' Most provocative, perhaps, were echoes of a challenge spoken almost exactly twenty-six years earlier to crowds in Berlin, against a hated symbol of communist oppression: 'Tear down this wall!'[207]

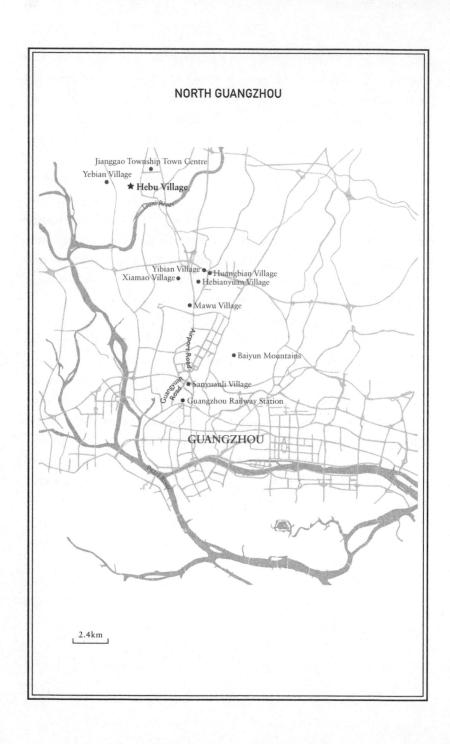

NORTH GUANGZHOU

Jianggao Township Town Centre
Yebian Village
★ **Hebu Village**

Gaxi River

Yibian Village ● Huangbian Village
Xiamao Village ● Hebianyuan Village

● Mawu Village

Airport Road

● Baiyun Mountains

Guangyuan Road

● Sanyuanli Village
● Guangzhou Railway Station

GUANGZHOU

Pearl River

2.4km

12

THE CHINESE DREAM

_____

Huang Minpeng, 2012–2013

As I made my way across the sprawling plaza in front of the Guangzhou Railway Station in December 2012, brisk rays of sunlight
topped the entrance hall. Completed in the final years of the Cultural Revolution and too plain to even be demonstrably ugly, the
building is a faultless example of Maoist architecture. The slogan
on the top of the station once read 'Long live the all-conquering
thought of Mao Zedong, long live the glorious Chinese Communist
Party.' In 1986, as reforms seized the country, city leaders deemed
the slogan unsuited to a railway hub now at the heart of a different
revolution, of industry and commerce. They hoisted a fresh rallying
cry, to the hope of national recovery in the wake of three decades
of upheaval: 'Unifying the motherland, revitalising the Chinese
nation.'

For three decades, the Guangzhou Railway Station has been a
window of possibility for tens of millions of migrants from across
China. The station offers a fresh start at the end of the line. From
here, millions of migrant workers disperse to fill the factories of
the Pearl River Delta, to staff its restaurants and to build its high-

rises and commercial plazas, its roads and subways. They crowd into its urban villages, forming new communities on the margins of an imagined future they are building brick by brick. There are other railway stations, in the east and south of the city—bolder modernist statements gleaming with confidence—but the Guangzhou Railway Station is where the rougher dreams begin, and this gives the place an unwashed beauty. The austere station tower, with its clock face blankly telling the time, is no nonsense. It does not sell a polished dream of personal fulfilment; it opens the back door to the city and lets you through with the rest of the crushing masses.

Already, at 7:30 a.m., the station plaza was buzzing with travellers—migrants from inland provinces mixed in with traders from Africa. Many of them lugged massive bags of consumer goods purchased at local wholesale markets. From here, cheap clothing, homewares and electronics make their way to distant markets in Nigeria, Ghana and the Ivory Coast. The goods are often manufactured in sweatshops close by, in urban villages like Mawu, where I once saw hundreds of rural girls (most looking to be in their teens) bent over sewing machines, under sallow fluorescent lamps, in scores of workrooms arrayed along the village alleys.

I was making my first visit to Hebu Village, on the northern edge of Guangzhou, a bus journey of about an hour from the City Bus Station. We set off, rumbling up Guangyuan Road until we passed the northern tip of Sanyuanli Village. On Airport Road we turned north. The Baiyun Mountains rose in smoggy blue swells on the horizon. In the 1990s, before China's urban boom began in earnest, Sanyuanli was a busy rural enclave on Guangzhou's northwestern fringe. I had no idea where the edge of the city was now, but as we rattled north, the bus feeling at times like it would jostle itself apart, the developments went on seemingly endlessly. We passed Baiyun New City, then Cloud Mountain Metropolis. Even way out there, at least six miles north of the city centre, a modest two-bedroom apartment of 915 square feet bore a price tag of over

2 million yuan, nearly $350,000. But the urban villages seemed to be everywhere too, hemmed in by the newer developments and of-fering affordable alternatives to the migrants that gave this outlying section of the city its character. There was Wanggang Village, or Prospect Mound, which by now, I supposed, had lost its prospect in the crush of high-rises. There was Yibian Village, Huangbian Village, Hebianyuan Village. Before long, the bus, which had left the station empty, was crammed full of migrants. Many lugged the red, white and blue plastic bags that are iconic symbols of Chinese migrant life. One boy I guessed to be thirteen or fourteen, his bangs sagging over his sun-swept face, carried a bulging bag of clothing at least twice his size.

We passed the gate of Mawu Village, which had been chosen as the site of the recently completed Museum to the Migrant Worker, a government project to encourage urban-village regeneration. Built at a cost of 230 million yuan, or $36 million, the museum was meant as a testament to the immense contributions made to the nation by migrant workers. In preparation for the museum's opening, a local university professor, Xu Hui, had produced a short film in which construction workers talked about their gruelling lives. The film had been dropped in favour of a video, more palatable to propaganda apparatchiks, in which a young worker lamented his meagre pay and was berated by an older worker, who told him, 'Young people must learn to face hardship. When I was your age, I worked twelve hours a day, and never once did I complain. If it's money you're after, just work overtime.'

The youth's face brightened. 'Yes, if I work overtime I'll be richer!'

A Hong Kong magazine had been aghast at the museum's tone: 'After thirty years of relentlessly exploiting peasant labourers,' it said, 'the glorious city has finally remembered its humble workers, and it has decided to reward them by building a crystal coffin.'[208]

On the road to Hebu, the idea of urbanisation was inescapable. Displayed on the rear window of every public bus we passed were depictions of modernist cityscapes overset with the slogan 'Building a national civilised city.' Where, I wondered, would the city ease away and the countryside begin? Hebu Village was over twelve miles to the north of the central business district, far from the restless industry of places like Mawu and Sanyuanli, and yet, even there, the pull of urbanisation had been inexorable. Like Huang Minpeng, many villagers in Jianggao Township had lost their land-use rights. Rural life had become impossible long before urban life was anything more than an idea.

After we passed Xiamao Village, about halfway to Jianggao Township, our surroundings became semi-rural. Standing off to the west, Xiamao was a bundle of close-set tenements with vegetable fields at their feet. In five more years, I thought to myself, it would be a fully fledged urban village, enclosed by the expanding city. We rumbled past more fields interspersed with housing plots. Newer developments were appearing less frequently. But further north, just as the city seemed to let go, we reached the narrow band of the Liuxi River, and a sign at the foot of the bridge welcomed us with another urban promise: 'Jianggao, working hard to be a civilised satellite city.'

When the bus finally pulled into the Jianggao Bus Station, Huang Minpeng was waiting nearby on his red motorbike. He kicked the motor to life, and we sped off through the dusty rural landscape. Away on our right, a group of farmers in sloping sun hats bent over a dark-green plot of strawberry plants, the elevated high-speed railway line towering above their heads. A few minutes later, we skirted the edge of Yebian Village before darting over a crossing under a highway. Huang Minpeng brought the motorbike to a stop. 'This is it,' he said. Rolling out before us was a massive wasteland, an expanse of broken earth stretching away to the horizon. The soil had been heaped up into piles, gouged out to create waterlogged trenches, polluted with garbage and fragments of brick and concrete. A few solitary figures wandered among the mounds of barren soil, probably scrounging for scrap. A yellow bulldozer sat indolently off to our right. 'In the distance there, that's Hebu Village,' said Huang. He pointed straight ahead to the horizon, where a line of squat homes rose behind a group of buildings that I assumed formed the new campus of the Guangdong Polytechnic Normal University.

'And that's the university?' I asked.

'That's right,' he said. 'Those buildings are on Hebu Village land. The land we're standing on here is Yebian Village land.'

The university campus was dwarfed by the colossal expanse of idle land. Why, I wondered, had they taken the usage rights to so much land all at once? 'How much did they pay for this land?' I asked.

'The villagers got anywhere from 10,000 to 20,000 yuan each. But what good is that anyway? Once the money is gone, you have nothing.'

'So they paid 60 yuan or so per square foot,' I said. 'That's incredibly cheap.'

'It's not about cheap or not cheap,' he grumbled, gesturing over the wasteland. 'Look at this. All of it is sitting idle, waiting for real-estate development. But people have to eat. How are we supposed to be productive now? This land will no longer yield anything for us. It's not about the price; it's about our livelihoods.'

I wondered if the university would create other sources of income for the villagers. Hebu Village was too far from central Guangzhou to attract migrant renters, but perhaps students from the university would eat in village restaurants or buy essentials in village shops.

'No, look. They've already built halls of residence,' Huang Minpeng said. He pointed out a pair of six-story buildings to the side of the main complex. 'The few students they have get board and lodging. They have nothing to spend. There's nothing out this way. Did you notice all those motorcycle taxis at the bus station? I was waiting there for half an hour, and in all that time maybe one or two had customers.' Huang voiced his suspicion that the university had used its new campus as a pretext to seize usage rights to more land than necessary, knowing the rights could be resold sometime down the track at an immense profit. 'First, they use the name of this university to get the land. As for how they use the land later, they might have other things in mind. It won't necessarily be for the university. It might be a commercial project.'

'So you think they'll sell off the rights to bits of the land to developers?'

'If they came right out and said it was for a commercial development, more people would be up in arms,' he said. 'So they say it's for the university.'

We stood silently for a while. Behind us, the traffic whooshed past on the highway. The location of the land certainly seemed ideal for development. It was less than a mile northwest of the township centre, close to the high-speed railway line and sandwiched between two arterial highways. If Jianggao's ambition was to become an important 'satellite city,' then this was prime real estate. 'Development has to conserve resources,' Huang Minpeng said finally. 'If you push development, it has to be workable development. You can't do so much all at once. If you move too fast, people can't catch up with you.' The remark reminded me of the January 2012 cover story of Guangzhou's *Vision Weekly*, a magazine published by the *Southern Metropolis Daily*. The story, 'Slow down, China,' had included a series of photographs of the last remaining residents of Yangji, the urban-village home to Li Qizhong that was being demolished to make room for a commercial development. In the photographs, the villagers posed in the rubble outside their homes. Behind each villager, the photographer had placed a studio backdrop of glimmering modern high-rises. The accompanying article read, 'Slowing down is so we can see clearly the road ahead, and make sure we don't lose sight of our original intentions . . . Slowing down is about making sure every life has freedom and dignity, and that no person is abandoned by the times. In 2012, slow down, China!' The image chosen for the cover was that of villager Li Jie'e, wearing a bright red blouse and grinning under a yellow umbrella.[209] Li had killed herself four months after the piece was published. As we gazed across the wrecked fields of Hebu, Huang Minpeng talked about how the dream of development could lead to destruction if it was not balanced against the rights and interests of individual citizens. 'If this is how things are done,' he said, 'if people lose their land at one blow . . . How are they to survive? People can't adjust like that. They have no way of making the transition.'

Huang took me on a motorbike tour through Hebu Village. We whirred through the alleys, where the newer village houses reached across at second-floor level, forming tunnels reminiscent of those in classic Guangzhou urban villages such as Shipai and Xian. We passed the offices of the village committee, where Huang and other villagers had gathered in April 2011 to protest the reelection of the village secretary. They alleged that he had rigged the vote with the help of township officials and local thugs. Beneath the building's garish pink portico, the protesters had unfurled a red banner that read: 'They've sold and devoured our fields. No land means no yield!'[210] A small plaza opened up a bit further on. Construction workers were outfitting a six-story palace faced with light-brown tiles, a more sumptuous interpretation of the village walk-up. The building had balconies jutting out on every level, accented with columns. 'Whose place is that?' I shouted over Huang Minpeng's shoulder.

'It belongs to a village cadre,' he said above the whirr of the engine.

'It's so massive. It looks like a hotel.'

'Yeah.'

'Is it the village leader's?'

'No,' he said. 'It's the village accountant's.'

Turning left, we passed an ancestral temple that had fallen into hopeless disrepair. Only its ancient facade and entryway remained, the shingled roof sloping artfully under the newer houses towering behind. The temple's stone post-and-lintel entryway, set neatly in its ash-coloured brick face, was disfigured with Cultural Revolution slogans, fading away, almost ghost-like. Only the characters across the lintel were legible: 'Serve the people.'

Huang Minpeng's house was a rustic stone structure overlooking a fishpond so strangled with withered and flowerless hyacinth that scarcely a drop of water was visible. A redbrick outhouse perched on the pond's edge, just to one side of Huang's front door. Inside the house, the main room had high walls of flat-stacked stone, whitewashed many years earlier. A pair of windows on the pond-side wall drew in the crisp winter sunlight. The wall was lined with shelves supporting stacks of newspapers and petitioning documents, some snapped into plastic boxes to shut out the humidity. The sitting area—a slumping wicker sofa and a coffee table cluttered with essential odds and ends—was partitioned from the sleeping area at the room's far end by a wooden bunk bed draped with a grey cotton quilt. Huang's only luxuries, it seemed, were his old cathode-ray-tube television and DVD player.

We sat for a while and sifted through the piles of letters and documents from Huang Minpeng's recent case against the police. 'How do you write all of these letters and petitions?' I asked.

'I don't,' he said, grinning. 'I don't even know how to write. I didn't finish primary school.'

'Really?' I thought suddenly of how I had sent him a text message before arriving at the Jianggao Bus Station, and how he had called me back instead of texting.

'Other people type them out for me.'

'You dictate them?'

'Not quite. I lay out the situation and the facts, and they help me work out the wording. They think it's so strange, that someone of my educational level can write stuff like this.' His chest rumbled with a laugh. His eyes sparkled. 'Not in their wildest dreams did they ever imagine that a country bumpkin like me would file a lawsuit against them. Never.'

'But you can read a newspaper? And write a bit?'

'Yes.' He chortled. My surprise clearly gratified him. 'I know most of the basic characters I see in the newspaper. Not all of them, though. These documents may look simple to a lot of people, but they took a lot of effort for me.'

I asked Huang how he managed to press ahead with his rights-defence work in the face of constant setbacks and defeats, and he talked about his personal character and circumstances. He had never married or had children, so he was unburdened, he said, by the demands of family life. He had no mouths to feed but his own. He had always had an independent streak. He recalled being put off by his primary-school textbooks, which stressed his obligations to the Chinese Communist Party and to the nation but never acknowledged his rights and freedoms.

•

One morning in January 2013, I was back on Huang Minpeng's sagging wicker sofa. The day was chilly and overcast. This time, Huang handed me a stack of papers for a new case he was working on. It concerned the death in 1997 of a young peasant, Liang Yuping, who had come to the city with his motorbike to try to earn some extra money. He was brutally beaten by a police officer in Tianhe District, not far from Xian Village, and later died in custody. His father, Liang Yuanxin, had spent the past fifteen years petitioning over the case. 'They were from a really poor village in the countryside,' said Huang. 'The economy was bad there. They just wanted to get to Tianhe District and scrape a bit of money together. He has spent so much time and energy, all for a bit of justice for his son. He's gone about it the wrong way, but no one has ever helped him.' Huang's 'letter of complaint' was addressed to the city's police chief, Xie Xiaodan, the very man he had tried to sue a few months earlier:

Respected Chief Xie,

To this day, police officer Chen Yumin . . . has escaped justice in the brutal death of citizen Liang
Yuping . . . His seventy-one-year-old father, trusting in the wisdom of the Chinese Communist
Party, trusting that the Constitution might clear his
son . . . has petitioned for the past fifteen years to
correct this injustice.[211]

I asked Huang Minpeng whether he had taken part in the protests at Guangzhou's *Southern Weekly* newspaper offices earlier that
month, against the draconian controls imposed on the newspaper's
staff. He fished out a stack of photographs. He hadn't been there,
but many of his friends had. On top was a time-stamped photograph in which a protester in a wheelchair held a hand-written banner: 'Support *Southern Weekly*, resist interference in the media.' In
the next photograph, an activist addressed the crowd with a megaphone as he stood next to a large blue 'Free China!' banner. 'He's
a friend of mine,' Huang said. He flipped through the stack until
he arrived at an old photograph from November 2011. It showed
him sitting in a park with the same activist. 'I did join that time,'
he said. He turned to the next photograph. It showed seven men
standing on the street with a banner that read: 'Freedom, democracy and human rights.' Huang was on the far right, his satchel
slung across his chest.

There was a chilly smattering of rain that afternoon as Huang
drove me back to the Jianggao Bus Station. We whirred past the old
ancestral temple: 'Serve the people.' A rooster beat its wings with
alarm, then strutted flamboyantly to the roadside. We pulled out
onto the main road. The viaduct of the high-speed railway line tow-
ered overhead. We gathered speed. The chilly air whipped over my
hands. On the right, between the road and some cabbage fields, a
river squirmed along like an oily black snake. The languid current

stuck in places, and there were glints of eerie green and swirls of sickly white foam. 'Look at that,' Huang Minpeng shouted over his shoulder, his voice gnarled with scorn. 'It's completely dead. Not a single fish can survive in there any more.'

•

The following month, I was huddled over my desk in Hong Kong when a message popped up on my Sina Weibo account. It was from Li Qizhong, writing in his nail-house holdout. 'Mr. Ban, Ah Peng has been arrested for taking part in a street banner protest.' Ah Peng was the name given to Huang Minpeng by his friends.

I posted back: 'What were they protesting? Where?'

'They were protesting the North Korean nuclear test. It was over near the Gongyuanqian Subway Station. They were eating lunch to-gether when they were attacked all at once.' Gongyuanqian was the stop at the entrance to the People's Park, where Huang and other rights defenders met regularly.

Police in fact detained at least sixteen protesters that day. They included Liu Yuandong, a local businessman and activist who with several others had started the Southern Street Movement in 2011. Liu's idea was that to have a real impact, activism had to be moved offline and into the public square. He was one of the activists who had delivered a public speech to the protesters outside the *Southern Weekly* offices the previous month. This time, he and others had or-ganised a protest to condemn a North Korean nuclear test. They were concerned about possible fallout from the test along China's border, and some believed China's government should join the inter-national push to impose heavier sanctions on North Korea. Huang Minpeng's interests had expanded from home-grown rights defence to broader issues of foreign policy.

For more than a week, the only news I could get of Huang was that he had been transferred to the authorities in Baiyun District, where he was serving administrative detention. I dialled his number repeatedly, but the tinny recording on the other end told me his phone was off. Finally, early in March, another message arrived from Li Qizhong: 'I'm hearing that brother Ah Peng has now been released.'

'Great news. I'll try giving him a call.'

Huang Minpeng eventually picked up later that night. 'Mr. Ban!' he boomed. I could tell he was in high spirits.

'How are you?' I asked. 'I was worried about you.'

'It was nothing,' he laughed. 'I've already got used to being locked up.'

'You were protesting the North Korean nuclear test?'

'That's right. We had just finished when the police picked us up.'

'Maybe you should stay at home and take it easy for a while.'

'I've already been into the city today,' he said. 'I just got back. I'm not afraid of them.'

●

The following July, I was back in Guangzhou. I planned to attend Huang Minpeng's court case at the Baiyun District Court to contest his administrative detention over the nuclear test protest. His assertion, as with his previous case, was that he had not 'disrupted public order' but had acted peaceably and within his rights.

Huang's court summons said the case would begin at 9:00 a.m. When I arrived at 8:30 a.m., Zhou Wentian, another rights defender, was just outside the guard station, getting ready to go through security. I slipped into line behind him. He smiled, then stepped forward at the female officer's command, fishing his belongings out of his pockets and placing them on the X-ray tray. For me, getting through the main gate was not a challenge, although the police were plainly dumbfounded by my presence. Their eyes tracked me uneasily as Zhou Wentian and I made our way up the stone steps, passing under the bright red disk of the national symbol, the Gate Tower of Tiananmen squatting beneath five golden stars wreathed with grain.

As the elevator doors opened onto the waiting area outside the courtroom, a cacophony swept over us. I could distinctly make out Huang Minpeng's voice booming down the narrow hall that led to the courtroom. Bai Pengjiang was standing in the waiting area with other rights defenders I knew: Guo Jianhe, a People's Park Thursday club regular, and Chen Zhiguang, a former soldier who had been jailed without trial after petitioning the Jiulong Township government in Guangzhou for back wages and pensions. 'What's going on?' I asked.

'They're not letting us into the courtroom,' said Guo Jianhe, shaking his fist at a pair of uniformed police standing guard at the mouth of the hallway. I could still hear Huang Minpeng's gravelly Cantonese tumbling out. 'What you're doing is illegal,' I thought I heard him say. 'They've filled the seats with plainclothes police and officials,' Guo Jianhe continued. 'They say the seats are full and there's no place for us. You know what they said? They said, "Why didn't you come early? These guys were here at 7:00 a.m."'

Twenty minutes later, Huang Minpeng emerged with a grin from the hall leading into the courtroom. He had told the court police that he refused to enter the courtroom until places were made for his friends. He wanted it put on record that the police had all arrived early for the hearing. 'I saw as soon as I looked into the courtroom that all the seats were taken up by these young police officers,' he said. Sitting in one of the plastic chairs against the wall in the entry hall, Bai Pengjiang wrote out a full account of what had happened. Everyone signed it, posed with it, photographed it. They presented it to the court officials. The standoff lasted for hours, until finally the court agreed to grant another hearing.

The court's ultimate decision was of no surprise. They upheld the decision of the police to sentence Huang Minpeng to administrative detention for 'disrupting the public order.' In a perverse sense, he was at least in good company. Four days later, rights lawyer Xu Zhiyong, the founder of the New Citizens Movement—who had peacefully called on the government to take real action against corruption and to respect the rule of law—was detained by police in Beijing for 'assembling a crowd to disrupt order in a public place.'[212]

Earlier that year, I had walked with Huang Minpeng past Xian Village's torn-down wall. As we waited at the red light on Huangpu Avenue West, I had asked for his thoughts on the Chinese Dream. What did he think it was? He fixed his eyes straight ahead. A satirical groan rumbled in his throat. 'That's exactly what it is: a dream,' he said, as the light changed. 'And then you awaken.'

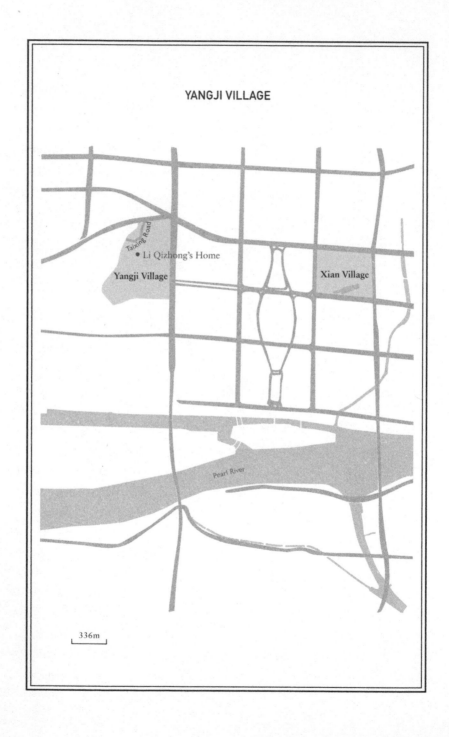

YANGJI VILLAGE

Taixing Road

• Li Qizhong's Home

Yangji Village

Xian Village

Pearl River

336m

13

A SILENT DEATH

Li Qizhong, Yangji Village, 2013

The message from Li Qizhong on March 19, 2013, carried a sense of urgency. 'Mr. Ban, they say they are going to forcibly demolish my place on March 25 at 9:00 a.m.'

'You've received a demolition notice?'

'Yes.'

'I'll arrive on the twenty-third.'

'Okay.'

On March 24, Huang Minpeng and I were in Li Qizhong's sitting room. Xu Zhihao, the villager from Pazhou, a little more than two miles southeast of Xian Village, who had unsuccessfully fought a forced demolition in court, was also there. We sat around an old card table with cartoon bunnies frolicking over the surface. As a precaution, we had left our mobile phones on top of the refrigerator in the next room; Li feared local police might be able to activate our microphones remotely and use the phones as covert listening devices. The table was piled with sunflower seeds and mandarin oranges. We built little hills of seed husks as we talked. Li was eager to discuss strategy. Negotiations had stalled, and tensions in Yangji Village were running higher than ever. He could feel the noose tightening. The time given on the demolition notice was just nineteen hours away. 'You could try filing a lawsuit against them.' The suggestion came from Xu Zhihao, whom the others called Ah Hao.

'Your laws!' The corners of Li's mouth curled into a grimace. 'I stopped believing in the law long ago. I'm happy to talk about principles. But if they don't respond to reason, the only thing is power.' He balled his hand into a fist and looked right into my eyes. 'You can only rely on *power*.' He said the word in English: *pow-wah*. 'What else is there to talk about? No more talking. Brother Ah Hao, I've heard everything there is to hear about this legal case of yours. My head is dizzy. I don't want to go to court. And going to court won't do anything.'

'You're right,' said Xu. 'There's no way they're going to rule in your favour.'

'Listen to me. My ideas have gone in another direction entirely,' Li said. He paused to crack a sunflower seed between his teeth. 'I know deep down that I don't have the slightest hope of winning a case. So what can you do? Even if I lived through the forced demolition of this place, I wouldn't take that route. I'd find my own way. I'd gather my own people together and then we could test our strength against theirs. If they had principles, they might listen, and this other way wouldn't be necessary. But what else is there?' No one spoke for a while. Everyone seemed to be casting about for an alternative. But there was only the cracking of seeds. 'If a thousand people surrounded my house, would they dare to demolish it?' Li continued. 'If ten thousand people were looking on, would they dare to demolish it? Everything depends on what we do. In a year, maybe two, at most three years, there will be tens of thousands of people like us. But we put all of our hope on legal cases.'

'I never had that much hope, actually,' said Xu.

'So you have to change your methods. You have to shift them back to reality. You have to show your strength and oppose them.'

Huang Minpeng chimed in. 'The important thing is to build a network,' he said.

'I get on Weibo and talk with people,' Li replied. 'That's the way I have to do it, because I can't go out. But you guys, you can get out there and meet others.'

Xu nodded. 'Lately,' he said, 'that's how I've spent all my time.'

The next morning, I arrived at the north gate of Yangji Village at around half-past eight. The gate was closed, but there seemed to be no activity. No police. No *chengguan*. Xu appeared at my side a few minutes later. 'I don't think it's happening today,' he said.

'Yes, it's very quiet.'

We stood there for a while before phoning Li Qizhong. He saw no signs of mobilisation either, he said. Xu and I walked to a restaurant up the street, where we kept vigil over tea and dumplings. Before long, it was clear the notice had been just another salvo in a protracted war of threats and counter-threats—probably meant to gnaw again at Li's ragged nerves.

Over the next couple of months I made several trips to Li Qizhong's nail house. It was an odd and unlikely meeting place, an outpost where rights defenders of all stripes could gather in relative safety under the slumbering cache of explosives. During the first week of April, He Jieling came too, trailing thirty minutes behind just in case she had coaxed along those persistent 'shadows' of hers, the state security police. Construction crews were busy at the northeast corner of the village, digging out the cube-shaped pit of a foundation. But whenever our talking stopped, there was an eerie silence in Li's sitting room—a disquieting sort of quiet, like that of a panther ready to pounce. For how long would local authorities allow the pilgrimages to the nail house to continue? How long before Li Qizhong was isolated entirely?

•

I was sitting on the front row of a packed university auditorium on April 10, listening to celebrity Chinese author Li Chengpeng as he talked about his new book, *Everybody in the World Knows*, when my phone buzzed to life in my pocket. The number was He Jieling's. I scuttled towards the back as Li berated his countrymen, drawing almost constant laughter, for what he saw as their chronic failure to stand against injustices like corruption. 'Mr. Ban!' He Jieling said breathlessly as I finally picked up. 'We came to see Ah Zhong here at Yangji Village. We left his house without incident, but the big iron gate was locked. Police from the Plum Flower Village Substation were waiting for us. They demanded to see our identification. They're still not letting us out.' Her voice brimmed with rage, but I could hear that she was on the verge of tears.

'Who are you with?' I asked.

'There are two other friends with me.' By 'friends,' she meant rights defenders. She added, shouting for the benefit of the police, 'We've taken photographs and videos of everything, including the vehicle and its plates. Ah Zhong has already made a post.' This was her best strategy. By calling on her network of online friends she hoped to preempt more assertive action by the police.

'Okay. I'll make a post on Sina Weibo immediately,' I said. 'Just be careful. I'll call you in fifteen minutes.' I slipped back into the auditorium and posted: 'Everyone please pay attention to "He Jieling, 138 Guangzhou Villages." As of tonight at 7:59 p.m., she was being kept inside the locked gates of Yangji Village by officers from the Plum Flower Village Substation.'

The storm had blown over by the time I called back. The police had returned the rights defenders' identification and let them through the gate. But He Jieling's anger had not subsided. 'I'm filing a complaint against the police,' she said in gasping breaths as they hurried off to the subway station. 'I'll take them to court.'

The episode at the gates was just the beginning of a spring of isolation and disquiet at Yangji Village. Five days later, discussions with the property developer collapsed again. Within hours, water and electricity to the village were shut off. Kuang Chunlian, one of the villagers who had set up the redwood sofa out in the rubble, had a spat with a group of thugs the villagers claimed were hired by the property company. You'll regret this, Kuang was told. The men roughed up his son the following day, so that his eye, as Li Qizhong told me, 'swelled up all blue.'

While Li found solidarity online, his isolation was in fact deepening. 'These past few days, the thugs haven't done anything,' he wrote to me on April 20. 'I think another storm is brewing.' On April 29, amid escalating tensions in the village, he wrote: 'My wife and kids moved out today. I have this deep feeling of sadness. Now that they've moved out, I know they'll never be able to come back.'

The departure of the children further encouraged the thugs. At 1:42 a.m. the following morning, Li sent me a lonely message that I didn't discover until daylight:

> Three thugs just busted out my windows . . .
> There's no sense in contacting the police. I'll
> wait until morning and see how bad the dam-
> age is. I don't feel angry. I'm ready for them . . .
> When the thugs came over I lit one of my firebombs,
> but the fuse just burned for a second before fizzing
> out. They went away after spending a couple of min-
> utes breaking out the windows.

Later that same day, the thugs attacked Li Biyun, the younger sister of Li Jianming, who had led the opposition to the village's eviction and demolition agreements outside their home. Li Biyun suffered serious head injuries and had to be hospitalised for two days.

On May 2, learning that Li Biyun had returned home from the hospital, He Jieling decided to pay a visit to her besieged friends. She was joined on her humanitarian mission by Ou Shaokun, or Uncle Ou, a sixty-year-old rights crusader who had become something of a folk hero (or, as he preferred, a 'grassroots celebrity') to many Chinese by campaigning against the abuse of public resources. He wandered the streets of Guangzhou snapping photographs of luxury sedans and SUVs with government registration plates as they were being used for unofficial business, then he posted the images to his Sina Weibo followers, of whom there were more than 60,000. I had met Uncle Ou back in December, when we had spent the afternoon in a quiet teahouse near the Canton Tower, across the Pearl River from Xian Village. His face had streamed with tears as he chronicled the intimidation he and his frail mother had suffered as a result of his activities. He was divorced, and estranged from his son. His family disapproved of his activism, which brought only trouble. 'But how do you know,' he asked, fixing me with moist eyes, 'that it won't be *you* who suffers next?' He was determined, he said, to fight corruption and to raise civic consciousness.

Guangdong Province had relaxed its restrictions on social organisations that past July, deeming that government sponsors were no longer necessary for the establishment of such organisations. Uncle Ou had tested the authorities' good faith by submitting an application to set up a nonprofit organisation called 'The Association for the Advancement of Justice and Transparency in Guangzhou.' The application was denied; he was told the name was too confrontational. He tried again, this time paying tribute to President Hu Jintao's political catchphrase, the 'harmonious society.' But 'The Association for the Advancement of Social Harmony' was equally rejected.

As He Jieling and Uncle Ou walked through the iron gates leading into Yangji Village, they were confronted by the same thugs who had beaten Li Biyun a few days earlier. The group's ringleader lunged at He, punching her across the right side of her face and breaking her nose, then struck her legs and arms as she tried to fend off the blows. 'If Uncle Ou wasn't here, I don't know what they would have done,' she said on the phone from the hospital, her voice crumbling. 'I think they might have killed me.' She and Uncle Ou had called the police. When they had arrived twenty minutes later, the officers had done nothing, even though He Jieling's attacker was standing close by. Later that night, Uncle Ou gave a full statement to police at the Plum Flower Village Substation. It was an empty formality. No action was ever taken. The thugs might strike blows with their own fists, but they did so with the blessing of more powerful interests.

•

I visited Li Qizhong's war room for the first time on June 10. He had moved his entire operation to the fourth floor after his wife and children moved out in April. The main room was stacked with supplies. There were even provisions suspended from ropes crossing the ceiling. Li slept—when sleep was possible—not more than ten paces from his homemade arsenal of explosives, kept in the small south-side bedroom. His surveillance monitors were housed in another room at the top of the stairs.

The afternoon was hot and listless. We had cracked open the east-facing windows, drawing in the rumble and whine of the earth-movers working in the foundation pit of a new tower, but the air was torpid. Mosquitoes droned around our sweating bodies. Li was shirtless, the hair tousled on the back of his balding head. I slumped on the sofa. With every stuffy breath, I drew in the sharp tang of black powder. We were waiting for Li Qizhong's brother, Li Qixun, to drop by with take-out for lunch. (It is ill-advised to cook at home when you live on top of a powder keg.) I noticed an odd green wire with no discernible purpose running across the wall to my right. 'What's this for, this green one here?' I asked, raising my index finger towards it.

'That's the tripwire,' Li Qizhong said. 'Cut that and this whole place explodes.'

Over the past couple of weeks, the stalemate in Yangji Village had erupted into open conflict as thugs and police made regular sorties on the nail houses, apparently trying to draw out their defences. On May 30, Li Qizhong had posted a detailed account on Sina Weibo of an assault on the nail house of Li Guojian, directly west of his property. A group of thugs had massed around the front door, a bulwark of reinforced steel, and tried to smash it down. Li Guojian had responded by hurling out a few firebombs. The men had scattered, but they regrouped for a second attempt the following week. This time, they had driven diggers right up to the edge of the house and started digging around the foundations. Li Guojian had thrown down two firebombs. 'I'll blow you all up!' he screamed. Another ten or fifteen men showed up. Then, from his roof, Li Qizhong had hurled a third, even larger firebomb across, a blazing show of solidarity. The crew had retreated, but there was no peace.

I hadn't yet heard the details of the second sortie, because the Nasdaq-listed Sina Corporation had by that time deleted Li Qizhong's Weibo account, expunging his entire user history. He had joined a growing number of social-media users targeted by China's censors in recent weeks. A concerted campaign was underway against the 'Big Vs,' users verified as using their real names rather than pseudonyms, who were often prominent personalities offline and had tens of thousands or even millions of followers (and therefore potentially immense influence over public opinion). Li Qizhong had just a few hundred followers, but his eyewitness reporting of local disharmony was nonetheless unwelcome.

At Yangji Village even the ruins were gone. And the final dominoes were falling one by one. The latest capitulation had come just days earlier. One of Li Qizhong's neighbours had arranged to meet with the property developer and came back with an agreement for 10,000 yuan, about $139, per square foot, foregoing a place in the resettlement block. The nail-house villagers had scoffed all along at the offer of resettlement housing. Building quality in commercial properties was often poor enough, as developers cut costs to chase enormous profits, but there was no commercial incentive to ensure quality for resettlement housing, and much of it was horribly substandard. However, the final settlement agreed by Li Qizhong's neighbour, which came out to 2 million yuan, was scarcely enough for a small apartment on the remote outskirts of the city. 'That morning, I kept telling him not to go,' said Li Qizhong. 'What he got can't possibly improve his life. He stood up to them for so long. And this land—our history is here. All of that is lost. It's like Li Jianming often says: "You're not taking what's theirs; you're fighting for what's yours." I have to fight on, no matter what. But this is a gamble with life.' Once all the others had fallen, the full force would turn on Li Qizhong. How long would he last? The more he was isolated, the bolder they became. What they feared most, in fact, was scrutiny. 'Actually, Mr. Ban,' Li said to me that afternoon, 'if you can come more often, they will be even less willing to make a move.' But as I left the nail house that day, the steel door shutting behind me with a bang like a thunderclap, I had a premonition it was my last visit.

●

Once Li Qizhong's account was eradicated from Sina Weibo, our interactions shifted to WeChat, a social-media platform that allows mobile voice and text messaging within private networks. The popularity of the service was surging in China as Sina Weibo came under attack from the leadership. Just before 11:00 a.m. on June 22, I received a frantic voice message from Li Qizhong. He had forgotten in his agitation that I couldn't speak Cantonese. I called him back. 'Ah Zhong, your message was in Cantonese just now. What's going on?'

'David! David! Right now, they're demolishing the house of Li Jianming's younger brother. They've almost knocked the whole thing down. Li Jianming has thrown out a few firebombs, but they've landed just to one side of the digger. They missed the digger.'

'Is anyone inside the house?'

'There's no one inside the house at the moment. I've filmed the entire thing.'

'Okay. Did they ever restore your electricity as they promised?'

'The water was reconnected the day before yesterday but not the electricity. I'm not sure if Li Jianming has electricity over there or not.'

'Take care of yourself. Let's keep talking.'

An hour later, Li Qizhong messaged an update: 'At present, the property company manager, Liu Jianhong, is on the scene with police. He's shouting at Li Jianming's little brother and his wife.' Finally, at 1:09 p.m.: 'Right now, Manager Liu is directing the crews to demolish the house of Li Jianming's younger sister too. This is banditry! They've not signed any agreement, and they're coming to demolish their properties like bandits!'

It was Li Qizhong's turn two days later. On the afternoon of June 24, a demolition crew swarmed around the house. The sound of an explosion rang across Yangji Village. Posted on Sina Weibo, an eyewitness photograph showed flames licking through the second floor of the tenement, which was encircled by black smoke. Li's wife, who had just left the house, told a *Southern Metropolis Daily* reporter that the crew surrounding the building had thrown something inside.[213] An anonymous spokesperson for the Plum Flower Village Subdistrict later said the crew had arrived to inspect the neighbouring property, which was Li Guojian's, and work out a plan for demolition, the owner having recently signed an agreement. Li Qizhong had been spooked when he saw the men and had tried to attack them with one of his firebombs, setting his own house on fire in the process.[214]

When Li messaged me on WeChat, three fire engines and an ambulance were already at the scene. 'I'm waiting on the roof for them to put out the fire. I think it's still smoking down there, but when I talked to my wife on the phone she said they've stopped spraying water. They say the fire is out. But smoke is still coming up. She needs to tell them to keep spraying.' Li soon became desperate. The smoke continued to rise. What if the flames, or some cinders, reached his arsenal on the fourth floor? He rushed downstairs. He could get safely to the fourth floor but no lower. He wrenched a window open and squeezed his body through, dropping to the earth and rubble below. The fall mangled his foot, twisted his back and damaged his knee. The skin was torn from his hands. He retreated to the only remaining stronghold: Li Jianming's nail house. It was from there that he sent me a voice message the next day: 'David, you know what happened yesterday. Now, my foot is hurt really bad. It's swollen and smells foul. I haven't eaten anything since it happened . . . I almost died yesterday.' He sent photographs of his hands, with ugly red gashes torn into his fingertips surrounded by chafed and blackened skin. I told him he needed to see a doctor. Two days later, he reported feeling better. His fever was down. He had eaten two bowls of rice congee. By that night, he felt well enough, in fact, to make his last audacious move. Hearing rumours that the police were going to make a final push to secure his house the next morning, he crept back over in the darkness and entered through one of the ground-floor windows. Early the next morning, a fire truck and a convoy of police vehicles pulled into the red-dirt road leading up to Li Qizhong's house. The vehicles stopped short of the property. Police poured out with riot shields and other equipment. There were more than a hundred special operations police, plainclothes police and firemen on the scene, news reports said. Li wrote to me:

> As soon as I saw them I was sure they were there to demolish my house. I was frantic. I shouted at them, 'If you want to demolish this house you'll have to trade deaths! A pot of fire for anyone who steps inside!' The police immediately drew back. They sent Officer Li and policeman Zhang Zhenqun over. They wanted me to come down so we could talk. They promised they hadn't come to demolish my house, only to inspect the scene of the fire. Later, Li Jianming came over and convinced me to come down. The police said they would ensure my safety. I went down eventually, listening to what Li Jianming said. The police escorted me to Li Jianming's house.

The police crews removed the explosives from Li Qizhong's nail house and stacked them out on the dirt road—petrol bombs, modified gas canisters and other deadly paraphernalia. They surrounded the house with a tall steel fence, bright blue, and posted 'No trespassing' notices. For the next ten days, the solitary nail house taunted Li Qizhong from Li Jianming's window. He sent me photographs of it. 'I've watched my house every day, unable to return there,' he wrote. 'I can't even explain how it makes me feel. What kind of world is this we live in? How do I respond to a society like this?'

The tense negotiations continued, the battle now centring on Li Jianming's house, a ragged tower in a red wasteland, the last occupied address in Yangji Village, the final chapter in its thousand-year history. As the anxious standoff entered its final days, relief was sometimes darkly comic: 'At 11:00 a.m. on July 3, a demolition negotiator came over shouting, "Fuck, fuck, fuck," over and over, his mouth full of trash. I couldn't help myself. I threw a knife down at him and it landed right under the balcony. His face turned green, the chicken shit, and he hightailed it out of there.'

On July 11, at 8:12 p.m., a surprise WeChat message arrived from Li Qizhong. 'This afternoon Li Jianming and I, both of our families, signed our demolition agreements.'

'Congratulations, Ah Zhong. I'll visit you tomorrow. I'll call you first thing in the morning.'

'Okay, David.'

The next morning, Li Qizhong was unreachable. His phone was off. His WeChat account was silent. I bought four chilly bottles of Pearl River Beer, sunflower seeds and fresh fruit on Taixing Street and walked through Yangji's north gate. The houses that had until recently stood around Li's nail house were gone, and it seemed lonelier than ever. Where Li Guojian's tenement had been, there was a towering hill of red earth with a single blue folding chair sitting enigmatically at its feet. Li Jianming's house looked abandoned, but from the rooftop garden a bright green sapling jutted skywards like a pennant, the last defiant stroke of

Yangji's ancient rural heritage. I dialled Li Qizhong's number again. Nothing.

I trudged through the red muck until I reached Li Jianming's house. I called up to the windows. No answer. No sign of movement.

The authorities wanted a silent death for Yangji Village. This much I understood when I finally heard from Li Qizhong, three days later. 'My heart feels so bleak . . . I hope next time you come to Guangzhou I will be free . . . Brother, it's all about what's unsaid.' What Li Qizhong meant, as I later learned, was that he would eventually be free to talk, for silence was a temporary condition of the payout he had been offered, a payout that at least afforded him and his family enough freedom to consider a decent apartment on the outskirts of the city. But there was no sense of victory, he told me over breakfast on August 1, an hour before the scheduled demolition of the two remaining nail houses. 'It's like instead of just stealing something that's yours, they force you to sell it at a 40 per cent discount,' he said. Another condition agreed informally in the final negotiations, in which the local government had become involved, had been that Li Qizhong and Li Jianming would be notified of the date and time of the demolition so they could look on with their families. Both planned to film what was for them a painful and important moment. I wanted to be there too, but I would have to find a vantage point of my own, apart from the families. I walked from the subway station to the north gate, but there was no activity at Yangji. A short time later, Li Qizhong phoned to say the demolition had been postponed. There was no indication of when it would happen; it might be quite some time, even. Officials at the Yuexiu District Renewal Office had said that onsite crews might use the houses during construction.

I returned to Hong Kong that evening after a spur-of-the-moment visit to Haipang Village, in Panyu District. There, hundreds of villagers had held a sit-in at the village office for five straight days, demanding officials reveal the truth about what they suspected was a dirty deal over the lucrative usage rights for a tract of village land next to the Asian Games sports complex. As I had walked up to the columned building, notebook in hand, a roar of wailing and applause had risen from the crowd of villagers, an utterly disquieting cry of lost hope. The government, the complaints office, the courts, the police: everything had failed them.

The next morning, a simple message pinged in from Li Qizhong: 'I just found out my ancestral home has been demolished. As I might have guessed, they did it secretly!' The demolition teams had gathered in the dark. Before sunrise, they had begun. By half-past eight, it had been over. The families had not been notified. Yangji Village had been extinguished with a broken promise.

Li Qizhong's dream had been so simple: to witness the end of something dear to him, something more than just bricks and mortar. 'What are they afraid of,' he wrote: 'that they are so deceitful?'

And I knew, because I had seen it in those despairing faces in Haipang Village the previous afternoon, hope was something that made them deeply fearful. Dreams are airy and intangible. But hope gives people the strength to build. Hope, unlike dreams, can be shared.

CLOSE-UP MAP OF XIAN VILLAGE

Huangpu Road West

Xian Village

Village pond • East Gate

Old Xian Village Sports Field

157m

14

TIGERS AND FLIES

Xian Village, 2013–2014

The storm of successive land confiscations, road expansions and demolitions in recent years has led me to a profound understanding: that so long as you have no regrets in your heart, so long as you act in the best interests of the majority of villagers, history will render a fair verdict.

—LU SUIGENG, *Xian Village Chronicle*[215]

On June 10, 2013, two days before the Dragon Boat Festival, the banquet cancelled back in April was finally held in Xian Village. As I approached the village that day, I got my first glimpse of the destroyed perimeter wall. The tenements along the north side of the village were now entirely exposed, the footpath lined with heaps of rubble mixed in with the sullied remnants of Lu Suigeng's pro-regeneration propaganda. I entered the village from the southwest corner and made my way along a narrow alley, almost pitch-black even hours before sundown. Faintly glowing bulbs dangled nakedly overhead, giving an obsidian sheen to the footpath. I mounted makeshift steps set into the side of a rubble heap at the east end of the village pond. Reaching the top, I could see a buzz of activity in the old sports field below. The villagers were setting up tables and plastic stools. Around the perimeter they had posted blank red flags. At the north end of the field I caught sight of Huang Minpeng, and He Jieling was there too. I also spotted the unmistakable figure of Uncle Ou in one of the brightly coloured Hawaiian shirts for which he had a penchant. The ancestral temple to the Lu clan sloped behind them, overshadowed by the tenements. By the time I had made my way over, Lu Zhaohui was standing with them. 'Is there no chance you'll parade the dragon boats this year?' I asked.

He shook his head. 'No,' he said, 'not until we've achieved a definite victory. We still don't know what's going to happen. We hear Lu Suigeng is being held somewhere outside the city, but we don't know for sure. And we have to keep fighting on the issue of the village's assets.'

In the mill of excitement, I came across an elderly villager I had met the year before, when a group of them were defending the village pond against crews they feared would fill it with rubble. 'So, no boat parades this year,' I said, shaking his hand.

'Not without a victory,' he said. 'Have you seen our couplet?' He pointed me over to the old temple. The heavy double doors in the stone entrance were chained shut. Pasted on either side was a red vertical banner. One read: 'In the churning waters of the dragon-boat race, the stain of the corrupt officials is washed away,' and the other: 'We invite our guests from the four corners on this Dragon Boat Festival day.'

Before long, the field was crowded with villagers. At least 800 people were there, old and young. When the food was ready, He Jieling led me over to a table for the cousins and sat me next to Uncle Ou. Villagers trotted over excitedly to pose for pictures with the scrappy old anti-corruption crusader. At one point, a proud grandmother brought her infant grandson across for him to cradle, a kind of sanctification. Our main course was a Cantonese specialty, a salmagundi of tender pork and chicken jumbled in with cabbage, lotus root, tofu, mushrooms and shrimp. The conversation stirred beneath the darkening tenements. Finally, bottles of clear rice wine were brought around to the tables. Beside me, Uncle Ou rose to his feet. 'A toast!' he called over the sea of heads, hoisting his clear plastic cup of wine. 'A toast!' There was a clamour as everyone pushed back their plastic stools and rose in their places, lifting their cups. I studied Uncle Ou. His glowing face. The straining muscles in his neck. The pulsing veins along his temple. 'Victory in the struggle!' he shouted, a husky cry ringing through the ruins.

And then the echo of the villagers. 'Victory *in the struggle*!' 'Victory in the struggle!' Uncle Ou roared again.

'Victory *in the struggle*!'

•

On August 19, I was back on the old sports field for another banquet, celebrating the fourth anniversary of the villagers' open protests against the village leadership. The mood of jubilation that night was unaffected by the occasional blast of a siren from one of the police vehicles processing around the outside of the village, as though the villagers rejoiced inside their own globe of self-assurance. The police presence on the periphery was a sinister reminder: here we are, said the declarative whoops, accented with whorls of claret light that played across the ruins of the primary school; we are biding our time. Bellies full, the villagers sat on plastic stools pulled up before a large projection screen just inside the entrance. The film was a gritty montage of past outrages captured on handheld video cameras and mobile phones. Whenever village cadres, cops or demolition personnel appeared on screen, they were greeted like film noir antagonists, with blithe jeers and boos.

The long-awaited denouement came the day after the celebration. 'Many cadres from Guangzhou urban villages under investigation for serious breaches of economic discipline,' read the headline of the official news report from China News Service. A single line in the article referenced Xian Village, paraphrasing an official government bulletin: 'According to the bulletin, the Guangzhou Commission for Discipline Inspection has opened an investigation into Xian Zhangming [Lu Suigeng's brother-in-law], the chairperson of Xian Village Industry Company Limited, and other relevant members of the leadership team for serious economic discipline violations.'[216] A report in Guangzhou's *Yangcheng Evening News* the next day said that members of the leadership of Xian Village were guilty of 'serious collective violations of discipline.' A spokesperson for the Guangzhou Commission for Discipline Inspection said that 'basically these violations involve the entire leadership group, with a serious negative influence.' According to the demands of provincial discipline investigators, the city had set up a special task force to look into the village's affairs.[217] *Nanfang Daily*, the official newspaper of Guangdong's Communist Party, said Xian Zhangming, formerly the deputy chairperson of Xian Village Industry, had taken up the post of chairperson following the removal of his brother-in-law, Lu Suigeng, in March.[218] So the news from Li Qizhong, hunkered down in his Yangji Village nail house, had been reliable after all. Lu Suigeng had indeed been forced out. But why, when he had dominated village affairs for more than three decades, was he not the focal point of this investigation?

A few days later, the *Yangcheng Evening News* added a smattering of details. A 'kinship group' topped by Lu Suigeng, and by his nephew Lu Youxing, the Party deputy chairperson, had controlled Xian Village. The junior managers of the village company were two more nephews, Chen Jianqiang and Lu Bingcan. The company accountant was Xian Zhangwei, Lu Suigeng's brother-in-law. Villagers had openly celebrated on the night the investigation was announced, said the newspaper. One villager had run through the tenements to spread the news. 'The corrupt official has been caught!' he shouted, no doubt assuming Lu Suigeng was among those detained. 'They did such a heap of horrible things,' another villager told the reporters. 'I could talk for three days and three nights and still not finish telling you!'[219] The sudden interest of provincial and city discipline inspectors was a bitter triumph for the villagers. For more than four years they had routinely petitioned leaders at the city, provincial and national levels only to be answered with inaction, intimidation and abuse.

•

Four months passed without fresh details about the investigation into Xian Village Industry, though a soft news piece in September reported that the Poly Real Estate Group was giving out moon cakes in Xian Village during the Mid-Autumn Festival. Villagers who visited the company's new Xian Village Regeneration Service Centre and presented identification could pick up their 'moon cakes of friendship.'[220] On October 1, China's National Day, *Guangzhou Daily*, the city's official Party newspaper, ballyhooed the city's stance in dealing with corruption, citing the case against Xian Zhangming. This case and a handful of other cases, the paper said, 'highlighted the resolve of Guangzhou's anti-corruption organs in striking "tigers" as well as "flies."'[221] The article was referring to a speech made by the nation's president, Xi Jinping, that January, when he had pledged to seize 'tigers as well as flies' in the fight against corruption[222]— meaning senior-ranking as well as junior officials. But where were the tigers? Xian Zhangming and Lu Suigeng, the latter still curiously absent from the news reports, were decidedly flies in the food chain of corruption.

The answer came on a cool night in late December, greeted with firecracker blasts that reverberated through Xian Village, and a chorus of excited shouts: 'Cao Jianliao has been arrested!' In a press conference earlier that day, corruption investigators had announced the removal of Cao Jianliao, the Guangzhou deputy mayor appointed in 2011 to a concurrent post as Party chairperson of the nearby satellite city of Zengcheng.[223] Cao, as I had learned in my investigation of Lu Suigeng, had held a number of important city posts over the past seventeen years and had presided over the transformation of many rural areas into urban centres, including Tianhe District. In Xian Village, Cao was known as Lu Suigeng's chief political ally, a man who had his fingers in village land-use rights and property deals. In nearby Liede Village, where anger over dirty land-use rights deals ran equally deep, the news of Cao's fall was also greeted with jubilation. Villagers there were reported to have made special offerings in their ancestral temple.[224] The official news was public the next morning, five days before Christmas, gift-wrapped in most of the city's major newspapers: 'Guangzhou deputy mayor Cao Jianliao under investigation.'[225] Here, at last, was the fall of a local tiger, the first senior-level government official in Guangdong to be placed under investigation in more than eleven years.

The spokesperson for the Commission for Discipline Inspection said investigators felt 'shock and regret' over the case, particularly considering the expanse of Cao's political career. He also insinuated a connection to Xian Village, saying that the probe had stemmed from 'information provided by the public' and was linked to other investigations. And he singled out Xian Village when explaining a new city measure to confiscate the passports of more than 2,000 village officials, preventing them from leaving the country. Corruption among village officials was epidemic, the spokesperson said, and if land-use rights and property issues were not handled properly at the 'rural grassroots,' these areas would become 'corruption disaster zones.' To give reporters an idea of how much wealth was involved in village corruption cases, the spokesperson said that, based on their preliminary findings, Xian Village's annual income from property rentals alone would be at least 100 million yuan, more than $16 million, if its contracts were properly renegotiated.[226] *Nanfang Daily* went further in drawing the connection between Cao Jianliao and Xian Village, confirming that the investigation had touched on the demolition and regeneration of Xian as well as other urban villages in the city centre.[227]

The official investigation into corruption in Xian Village eventually uncovered what discipline inspection authorities called an 'iron triangle of corruption' involving senior city officials, village officials and property developers. Once they had 'followed the trail of clues' during their investigation in August 2013, the authorities had 'discovered that serving Guangzhou deputy mayor Cao Jianliao had accepted massive bribes' from property developers to help secure favourable land deals with local villages.[228] The investigators estimated that Xian Village had five million square feet of property that collectively belonged to the villagers. Of this total, about three-quarters had been leased out for well below the market value, supporting the villagers' suspicions that the village leaders and more senior officials had taken under-the-table kickbacks from the developers. The highest rents negotiated by the village leadership, in fact, had been for just 25 yuan, or 37 cents, per square foot—meaning lessees were paying at most one-tenth the market rental rate as it was listed at the end of 2011.[229]

The findings of the investigation, shared in dribbles by China's official Xinhua News Agency, also named various companies of interest, two of which seemed like old friends: 'According to other accusations, from 2006 to 2013, Xian Zhangming provided lease and construction assistance to Guangzhou's Jiayu Group, Nanya Property Development Company Limited, Hejun Property Management Company Limited, Jiasheng Property Management Company Limited, the Chundu Hotel, Zhongju Property Management Company Limited and others in exchange for 233,200 renminbi and $130,000 (Hong Kong) in bribes, and 7,000-yuan-worth of gift cards.'[230] The Jiayu Group was the conglomerate behind the Home Garden complex and the parent company of the Guangzhou Jinyi Film & Television Group, which had talked up its favourable lease deal with Xian Village in its prospectus. Nanya Property Development was the mysterious company that villagers had claimed was linked to Cao Jianliao and that, according to business listings, 'holds many plots of land in the Pearl River New Town, but maintains a low profile.'[231]

Xinhua News Agency's reports suggested that the process of

urban development in Xian Village, and in other villages, had followed a pattern of corruption among local leaders, village chieftains and property developers. The agency reported that 'in the 1990s, the Pearl River New Town was developed largely by village collectives together with property developers, the one providing money, the other land.'[232] In cases where the rental price demanded by villages was high, the report said, 'property developers would engage in "public relations" with Cao Jianliao . . . Cao would help facilitate low-price cooperation. To express their "thanks," the property developers would either directly pay bribes to Cao Jianliao and village officials or agree to make future payments according to a percentage of the price difference.' In the high-stakes game of urban development, favourable terms came with a price tag. And the money and gifts amassed by Xian Zhangming, a character of relative unimportance, were just the tip of the iceberg:

> According to one corruption investigator, when holidays rolled around, developers were obliged to invite village chiefs to dinners at luxury hotels and proffer red envelopes of cash . . . Some developers, ahead of certain election times, would give several hundred thousand yuan to Lu Suigeng, the former Party chairperson of Xian Village Industry Company Limited, and Lu Suigeng would share this with other village cadres, having them 'spring into action' to buy votes. Later on, Lu Suigeng would offer property leases to the developers in return.[233]

General shareholder meetings and village assemblies, which should have allowed villagers to exercise and protect their rights and interests, had been bypassed in favour of 'family meetings,' said the investigators. Of the seven members of the Xian Village leadership team detained in July 2013, five were close family members of Lu Suigeng and two were former classmates.[234]

•

Nearly 200 villagers attended the trial of the seven-member lead-ership team of Xian Village Industry in July 2014.[235] In the court-room, the defendants sat cuffed before the judge in drab brown shirts with mustard-coloured stripes running down the sleeves. But the court proceedings that day, as reported in the media, dealt only with the crumbs of wrongdoing: the scheme by which the leadership team had awarded its own members spurious 'spiritual morality prizes' that came with generous cash awards drawn from the village's collective income. Xian Zhangming, the company's new chairperson and long-time legal representative, was accused of embezzling 770,000 yuan in public funds, or about $123,000, and accepting bribes of about half that amount. Lu Youxing, the village's second-in-command, was accused of embezzling the same amount and accepting bribes of over 1 million yuan. Lu Bingcan, Lu Suigeng's nephew who was one of the village company's junior managers (and director of Top Star Investments with Lu Suigeng's wife), was accused of embezzling 480,000 yuan in public funds, or about $77,000, and accepting bribes of 160,000 yuan. When the defendants tried to explain that Lu Suigeng had authorised their spiritual morality prizes with his signature and stamp, and that, in any case, the prizes had used village money, not public funds—chortles of scorn erupted from the gallery of the courtroom. 'I have my own opinion of these crimes,' said Xian Zhangming. 'I did take that much money, but I'm not guilty of corruption. Those were all bonus awards.' 'The chairman gave his approval,' said Lu Youxing, 'and so I took them.'[236]

Reports from the corruption investigators and records of the trial proceedings did not address the more serious issues of land-use rights requisition and related fees. There was no mention, for example, of the allotment or whereabouts of 600 million yuan in land-use rights requisition fees paid to the village in 1995, worth about $72 million at the time. This was the same year Lu

Suigeng's wife had formed Top Star Investments in Hong Kong with Lu Bingcan.[237] Nor was there any mention of the existence of documents reported by *Nanfang Daily*—copies of which I had managed to obtain—apparently showing a massive embezzlement of state funds in 1995 through the fraudulent reporting of the number of villagers eligible for resettlement compensation for the major farmland acquisition for the Pearl River New Town.[238] When the government had dispensed this resettlement compensation, the prescribed amount was 350 yuan per month for each eligible villager (of working age) for a period of thirty-six months. Documents showed that the village committee had reported there being 4,211 eligible villagers, a number verified in supporting documents signed and chopped by the governments of both Shahe Township and Tianhe District. The total compensation package was more than 53 million yuan, almost $9 million, paid out in full by Guangzhou's Land and Housing Office in July 1995. But a statistical report filed by the village committee in January 1996, and signed by Lu Suigeng himself, showed that in fact there were only 1,126 villagers of working age eligible to receive compensation. This meant that even if all the eligible villagers had been compensated appropriately—although most said they had never received a cent—an additional 38 million yuan, about $6 million, was unaccounted for. It was unlikely that such an error would simply have escaped township and district leaders, who asserted in handwritten notes that the numbers 'had been verified' and were 'accurate.'[239] At the time of the dispensation, Cao Jianliao was the Party chairperson of Tianhe District, its top leader, and rising quickly through the ranks of the city leadership.

Cao Jianliao reportedly took his fall with stoicism. An employee in the deputy mayor's office described to journalists how, nearly two weeks before the news was made public in December 2013, Cao stood for hours before the window of his office, tears pooling in his eyes as he gazed out over Zengcheng's picturesque Green Lake Park, an urban beautification project he had championed.[240]

As for how that other principal player in the drama, former Xian Village chief Lu Suigeng, had reacted to the news of the curtain's close, there is no record. Soon after the announcement of Cao Jianliao's ousting, the media reported that the investigation into the deputy mayor had been complicated somewhat by Lu Suigeng's escape from the country soon after his own removal back in March.[241] Thirty-four years after he came to power, the chief architect of Xian Village's misery had vanished into thin air. He was now hiding overseas, accompanied by his wife and two daughters. A few months later, official Communist Party media reported the saga's cruel punch line: Lu Suigeng was already an Australian citizen.[242]

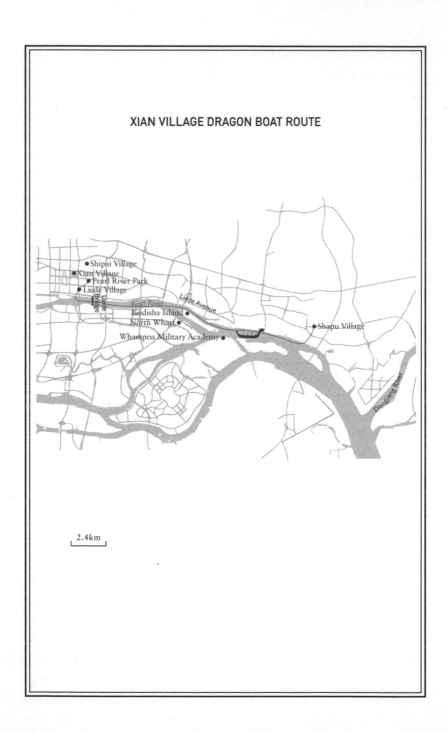

XIAN VILLAGE DRAGON BOAT ROUTE

Shipai Village
Xian Village
Pearl River Park
Liede Village
Liede Bridge
Pearl River
Liede Avenue
Beidisha Island
North Wharf
Shapu Village
Whampoa Military Academy
Dongjiang River

2.4km

15

THE WAKING OF THE DRAGONS

Xian Village, 2014

In 1981 . . . during the Dragon Boat Festival, Xian Village newly outfitted a pair of dragon boats, resuming a popular custom. Relatives in Hong Kong and Macau donated HK$40,750 and 452 renminbi for the cause. Beginning the same year, individuals throughout the village started raising pigs, and between January and December 8,902 pigs were raised, so that Xian Village became renowned as a 'pig-raising village' in Guangzhou's suburbs.

—*Xian Village Chronicle*[243]

Amid the clamour of gongs and the thunder of cow-hide drums, more than sixty Xian Village men removed their shoes beside a narrow river inlet in the cousin village of Shapu. It was mid-May 2014, two weeks before the Dragon Boat Festival. The time had come for the waking of the dragons, the ritual of *qilong*. When the village elders gave the word, the men trudged out into the water, groping along the mud bottom for the boats' outlines. As they heaved mud away from the flanks of the boats, the bright green water roiled with ink-like eddies. Meanwhile, men on the outside used banana plants and wooden stakes to build a clay bulwark holding back the river. When the boats were finally visible, their rims just above the water, they were bailed out, bucket by bucket, until they were exposed, ink-stone black, in their own muddy enclosure. Every now and again, as instructed by the elders, the men rocked the vessels back and forth, loosening the grip of the clay bottom. 'Way *way ow!*' they shouted to the clang of the gongs. They worked tirelessly, their legs and arms blackened with mud, bailing and rocking the boats by turns, until at last the time came to open gaps in the bulwark, allowing runlets of dark river water to flow in around the black frames—and the dragons rose.[244]

In Xian Village a week later, in a centuries-old rite known as Green Harvest, or *caiqing*, the boats were welcomed back from Shapu Village. The village priests gathered in teams of three or more in the ancestral temples, bringing out the dragon heads and tails that had been stored away. These they cleaned with oil, along with the drums, gongs and silken umbrella flags that would join the boats in their processions. The ritual artefacts were then marched out to the boats, along with bundles of green rice seedlings that in some villages were called 'dragon swords.' They traditionally bore the villagers' hopes for a bumper harvest and sometimes were placed around the mouths of the dragons in case they became hungry. Xian Village's Green Harvest ceremony had always been held at nighttime. This year's rites, the first in fourteen years, took place after midnight on May 25.[245]

The following week, as I hurried west along Jinsui Road, I saw that faded red flags still sagged from the rooftops of the Xian Village tenements. It was early morning on June 1, the eve of the Dragon Boat Festival, and the streets of the Pearl River New Town were almost tranquil as I passed Xingguo Road and the shuttered offices of Xian Village Industry. I quickened my step, my breath rasping through the pedestrian tunnel as I crossed under Liede Avenue. Up ahead, beyond a gated complex of luxury condominiums on former village land, I spotted a burst of flags hoisted on bamboo poles over the bridge that crossed the canal at Pearl River Park. A huge yellow flag, triangular with a saw-tooth hem, sailed over the top of the others. 'Xian Village,' it said in bright red characters.

I saw the boats as soon as I reached the bridge. They were drawn up to the opposite bank, already loaded with paddlers in white shirts and bright orange lifejackets. The walkway along the side of the canal stirred with activity. Villagers crowded up to the stone balustrade, beaming with excitement as they raised their cameras and mobile phones to capture video of the send-off. Behind this assemblage was a crew of village security guards in dark-blue uniforms, reclining against cardboard boxes of bottled water under the shade trees. Many of their faces were familiar—this was certainly not Lu Suigeng's ruthless old guard—and they smiled and barked 'Hello!' as I reached the top of the ladder leading down to the boats. 'Have you seen Zhaohui?' I asked a villager handing out paddles and lifejackets.

'Zhaohui?' he said, his eyes searching the boats below.

When Lu Zhaohui spotted us, he gave a broad wave from the long teak boat closest to the shore.

The dragon-boat ledger was opened for me to sign. As a ring of villagers gathered around me, I scribbled my name in Chinese, pressing a red fingerprint over the signature. I was handed a yellow baseball cap, 'Xian Village' embroidered across the brim, and cheerful shouts volleyed up as I pulled it on with a flourish.

I removed my shoes and placed them off to the side of the path, then stepped carefully down the ladder to the boats, wooden paddle in hand. Reaching my post at the tail of the boat was a treacherous balancing act. Boarding at the boat's midsection, I had to step past a dozen rows of seated paddlers, skirt the belly of the drum, swirl around the black flag of the Big Dipper and manoeuvre past the shiny aluminium box that stored the firecrackers.

The seven-star flag of the Big Dipper is an old symbol in the Pearl River Delta, as old as or older than Xian Village itself. The constellation is thought to drive out evil and corruption, restoring order and balance—an omen of peace and good fortune. My running of the gauntlet was made across a bobbing teak boat smeared with oleaginous river clay, and as one of the final stragglers, I had three full dragon-boat crews as a captive audience. They gave shouts of 'Woah!' several times as I nearly pitched into the canal before thankfully being steadied by surer hands and shoulders, some on the neighbouring boat. When at last I made it safely to the rear, I was seated behind Lu Zhaohui's teenage son and side by side with another young villager. Lu Zhaohui sat directly behind me, the last paddler before the tail, where two village priests in gold silk robes stood together on the narrow stern deck. Once I was settled in my seat, Lu Zhaohui passed a bottle of water over my shoulder, a gesture of welcome and encouragement. 'Do you know how to swim?' he asked.

A villager in the teak boat to my left grinned and gave me a thumbs-up as he pointed to my cap. He wore a broad-brimmed straw hat with 'Xian Village' in red characters on the dome. The same characters had been stamped onto our paddles. The villager warned me to keep my hands clear of the gap between our boats, which might pinch together in the current. Farther out in the canal, on the outside of his vessel, was the golden spruce boat I had visited in the warehouse at Shangjiao Village two years earlier. It was shorter and more lightweight than its teak brothers, designed for greater speed.

I searched the faces around me for Lu Qiang, and for the needled grey head of Lu Nianzu, the villager who had shared with me the story of his unlawful incarceration and had pledged that afternoon at the warehouse that this day would come. I could spot neither of them, but I reckoned there were at least 200 men on the boats. While villages sometimes field women's teams for dragon-boat racing events, the dragon-boat parades are still an all-male affair, steeped in superstitions about the unpropitious effects of female presence. 'Have you seen Lu Qiang and Lu Nianzu?' I asked, over my shoulder.

Lu Zhaohui sighed. 'A group of villagers has broken off from the rest of us,' he said. 'Xian Yaojun, Lu Qiang and some of the others, including Lu Nianzu. They don't agree with how the village business is being handled now, so they're not joining the dragon boats today. They think we haven't achieved a clear victory yet.

'It's tough to be united at the moment,' he continued, a bit sadly. 'We can say we've achieved a partial success. But there are still some shareholder representatives from the old leadership group. We haven't entirely thrown them out . . . And the issue of getting the property back will be very difficult.'

Xian Yaojun was the villager whose home had been broken into in 2011 by a gang of plainclothes men, who had cuffed him and his wife in front of their nine-year-old son. He had served twelve months of reeducation through labour.[246] In early 2014, cases like Xian Yaojun's had prompted calls by a top Guangzhou court official for the city to lead the country in dismantling its labour reeducation system.[247] 'Xian Yaojun doesn't know how to compromise,' said Lu Zhaohui. 'He's always right. His way of doing things is always the only way.'

•

New lines of division, it seemed, had been marked out in Xian Village since the formal collapse of Lu Suigeng's reign in the wake of the Cao Jianliao scandal. In December 2013, several weeks before discipline inspectors formally announced the investigation of the deputy mayor, Tianhe District officials had quietly installed a new Xian Village leadership team.[248] The chief executive of the village company was now Xian Qifa, a fifty-one-year-old villager who had been an influential supporter of the protest movement. Villagers described him as a self-made man with a gift for doing business. He had started out as a fruit seller in Liede, his wife's native village, and had later gone into clothing wholesale and had opened a successful local bar. Like everyone on the new leadership team—voted

in by eighty-eight shareholder representatives, many of them hang-
overs from the Lu Suigeng era—Xian Qifa was a Communist Party
member.[249]

The next item of business after the appointment of the new
leadership had been to decide measures for dealing with Xian Village's property holdings. In a letter posted to villagers in January,
the leaders had announced the decision to marginally raise rents for
existing contracts in order to increase village revenue. Next, 'when
conditions were mature,' they would explore the recovery of village
property through litigation. This plan had met with staunch resistance. Many villagers said they wanted swifter action to reclaim
village properties. More pointedly, having fought for years against
the secretive regime of Lu Suigeng, they resented the idea that this
opaque group of shareholder representatives was making decisions
on their behalf. This was not a democratically elected body and
therefore not at all representative. Responding to these concerns,
the village's new leadership had called a general meeting of village
shareholders to decide how to deal with the question of collective
properties. In March, more than 4,000 shareholders had crowded
into the brightly lit auditorium of the Tianhe District People's Government and had voted to recover their collective property and re-
negotiate for more favourable terms. Many villagers had rejoiced at
the opportunity to put their future to a vote, breaking with more
than three decades of black-box politics under the leadership of Lu
Suigeng.[250]

However, by June, just three months after that flash of self-
determination, renewed accusations were being made of deceit and
inaction. Some villagers objected to the pace at which the new leadership and its appointed Property Recovery Group were moving to
reclaim the village's assets. But property recovery was a difficult business. The village had hired Wang Cailiang, a well-known Beijing
lawyer, and the disputes had to be dealt with on a case-by-case basis,
through lawsuit after lawsuit.

•

The deafening clatter of the gongs and the visceral roar of the drums soon announced the start of the dragon-boat parade. The drums in the centre of the boats were beaten with heavy sticks by pairs of powerful drummers. Screeching whistle blows, from silk-clad priests standing on the stern and bow decks, accented the unstressed beats. Closest to the shore, we were the last to pull away. I followed the lead of the other paddlers, digging my paddle to the rhythm of the drums, soaked almost immediately by the water's surge over the side; the gunwale was at most a hand's length above the surface. Our boats slid north towards the bridge, across which the villagers had unfurled a long red banner: 'We warmly invite the various villages to Xian Village for the Dragon Boat Festival.' The act of 'visiting relatives' is an ancient tradition of friendly exchange among the villages of the Pearl River Delta; it both highlights and reinforces village connections through intermarriage. The point is not competition over speed, but friendly rivalries of pep and excitement in which the dragons are meant to come alive.[251] As we laboured with our paddles, our mettle measured by our unity of rhythm, the drummers and priests turned the dragon boats into a floating carnival of colour and noise.

Soon after we started, when the boats were far enough apart, a villager standing a few rows from me, his steep black hat blazoning a yin-yang symbol, started lighting the firecrackers. This involved stuffing bandolier-like strings of red firecrackers into a metal basket fastened to the end of a bamboo pole. Once the fuse was lit, the cage was held out over the water, where the firecrackers exploded in white-orange stars before sending up mushroom clouds of white smoke. In the ritual of the village dragon-boat visits, the elders onboard the visiting boats direct their crews in setting off the firecrackers, a way of saying (how else could anyone hear?), 'Cousins, we have arrived.' The first barrage came as something of a shock to me and many of the younger paddlers, those of us who had not had the foresight—as the older men had—to stuff our ears with toilet tissue. The red paper cinders from each blast drifted down over my straining body, singeing the hairs on my forearms and stinging my eyes. All the while the drums beat furiously, taunted by the crazed whistles. The drummer closest to me, a powerfully built villager with sun-darkened skin, had a belly as round as the drum itself. He wore a bandanna fastened around his forehead, and a pair of Oakley sunglasses. His face streamed with perspiration. Behind me, the pair of priests in gold robes danced up and down on the stern deck, wagging the dragon's tail.

Before the dragon's whiskered head had reached the bridge, the drummers executed a succession of quick strikes. The paddlers rose from their seats. 'Whenever you hear that, it means we have to turn around,' Lu Zhaohui explained, and I twisted my body to face the other direction. We found our rhythm again, this time pulling south. The non-rowing villagers crowded up on the walkway, smiling and waving their straw hats. The firecrackers seemed to explode on all sides, enveloping us in sulphurous smoke. We had travelled a short way towards the next bridge when the drum signal urged us to change direction once more. Lu Zhaohui explained, over my shoulder again, that according to tradition the boats had to parade back and forth in this way before arriving at or departing from a village.

After a sufficient round of back-and-forth paddling, we continued south towards the Pearl River, travelling past the transposed ancestral temple of Liede Village, the first urban village in Guangzhou to actually undergo regeneration, under a plan announced by the city government in 2010. Over much of the past two years, Guangzhou leaders had touted Liede as a model for other villages in the city.[252] But Liede's public 'success' cloaked its own scandal involving misappropriated land and purloined millions. The fiction had collapsed in November 2012 when the village's top leader escaped to Canada.[253] Festivities in Liede were a burst of yellow, the village's traditional colour. The crowds waved and set off firecrackers as we surged past, our drums throbbing with a fury that burned through my arms and across my back. The sun was scorching already. When I reached up to adjust my glasses, which had slipped to the end of my nose, my hand came away with a charcoal smear of cinder dust.

Soon we passed out of the canal into the massive brown expanse of the Pearl River. Just ahead and to the right was Haixinsha Island. Over our heads loomed the arch supports of the Liede Bridge. Before us sat a barge that was waiting to convey us and our boats farther downstream. The river is wide, and sizeable waves are whipped up by passing barges and cruise boats—not ideal conditions for dragon boats weighed down by sixty men each, the gunwales just inches above the water's surface. Once we had all clambered aboard and the boats had been hitched up, the barge took us downstream, past Beidisha Island, the North Wharf and the old Whampoa Military Academy, the Soviet-funded training ground that had produced many of China's most famous commanders at the beginning of the twentieth century. As we lounged aboard the barge, an open tub with high sides whose belly we accessed by skirting down wooden planks, I chatted with Lu Zhaohui over the chug of the engine.

Before we reached the mouth of the Dongjiang River, where it empties into the Pearl, our barge stopped at a small port. We boarded the dragon boats once again, paddling into a narrow canal hung densely with trees and vines. Wen Village lay somewhere ahead, and we announced our approach with a cacophony of drums, gongs and firecracker barrages. The red paper cinders left behind by our strident passage bobbed like flotillas of cherry blossom on the surface of the water. In the local villages connected to the river by networks of canals and inlets, crowds of villagers pressed up to the muddy banks or stone piers, straining to see the boats. As we made our approach, our changes in direction became more frequent, demanding agility and strength. The priests danced at bow and stern, banners waved, drums and gongs thundered, and firecracker blasts crackled incessantly. At least three passes of the dragon boats are generally required before crews can pull up and go ashore.[254] The passes are an expression of gratitude, as the host villages then receive the paddlers with bottles of water, savoury and sweet dragon-boat cakes, cigarettes and sometimes cups of tea. It is also tradition to present visiting village elders with brush-written welcome cards to take back to their ancestral temples.

The culmination that day was our parade before the cousin village of Shapu, where Xian Village's pair of teak dragon boats—including the one in which I was paddling so furiously—had hidden for nearly five years, waiting for their opportunity. We seemed to parade endlessly before the village's stone promenade, executing turn after turn. The beaming crowds under the shade trees urged us on through milky curtains of smoke, as the firecrackers burst all around us, the hot cinders swirling like snowflakes.

Later that afternoon, we returned to the broad expanse of the Pearl River, where the barge waited to take us back to the mouth of the canal outside Xian Village. Under the shadow of the wheelhouse, many of the paddlers nodded off, their hats tugged down over their faces. As the boat pulled west towards the heart of the city, I asked Lu Zhaohui about some of the dragon-boat customs. He explained that the bundled branches fastened to the tops of flags on the dragon boats came from the wampee tree. A medicinal herb, the leaves could offer protection to the paddlers. He was less certain about the significance of the umbrellas hoisted at the centre of the boats. These ceremonial silk canopies, shaped like giant jellyfish, were used for royal processions in dynastic times, and they are still a part of local pageants in southern China that celebrate folk deities like Guandi, the god of war. 'There are a lot of traditions and taboos around the Dragon Boat Festival,' Lu said. 'Most villagers don't know why we do them, but the village priests pass them along from generation to generation.'

When the barge reached the mouth of the canal, we stepped back down into the boats and paddled to Xian Village for our final parade of the day. We were again enveloped in a white haze, as the firecracker salvos rent the air all around us. The gold-clad priests on the bow and stern decks leaped up and down, animating the dragons. By the time we pulled up to the muddy bank, the husks of the firecrackers had formed a red skin over the surface of the canal. I could barely hear Lu Zhaohui through the white noise in my ears as we struggled up the bank with our paddles and life-jackets. 'Next year there won't be so many firecrackers,' he said. 'A lot of people have complained that it's too loud.'

As soon as we reached the stone walkway, I saw Lu Qiang walking over with a wide grin from the direction of Jinsui Road, his eleven-year-old son at his side. Lu Zhaohui acknowledged them with a nod—a bit constrained but not unfriendly. 'We were watching you from the bridge,' Lu Qiang said. 'How was it?'

'I'm exhausted, but it was great,' I said. 'We missed you out there,' I added, clapping his son on the shoulder.

'I *wanted* to go,' he said, choking out the words.

Lu Qiang's smile soured with unease. 'Are you joining the boats tomorrow?' he asked. The Dragon Boat Festival was a multiday affair, with parades scheduled at various villages on appointed days.

'No,' I said, 'but I'll come and watch them.'

'We can watch them together. I have something I want to give you.'

Lu Zhaohui walked ahead of us in the direction of the village. 'Okay. We really should talk,' I said.

'Yes, we should,' he said, casting a glance at Lu Zhaohui's retreating figure.

•

The canal buzzed with activity the next day, the official calendar day of the Dragon Boat Festival. People from all over the city crowded into Pearl River Park to cheer on the dragon boats. From time to time, crews from visiting villages climbed up the ladder to the stone

walkway and straggled over to the Xian Village pavilion for water
and cakes. Lu Qiang and I met under the shade trees. 'Here,' he
said, handing me a red plastic bag. It was identical to the one he
had given me two years earlier, which had contained my copy of
the village's demolition agreement. Through the filmy material of
the bag I could feel a heavy slab of neatly folded fabric. 'You don't
need to open it here,' he said, stilling my hand. 'Just keep it safe.
It's my flag of the Big Dipper. During the darkest days, around the
time we met, this flag flew over the roof of my home. I hope it helps
you remember.'

I slipped the package into my satchel. 'Of course, I'll never forget,' I said.

Later that afternoon, I stood with Lu Qiang on the bridge at
Jinsui Road and watched as the Xian Village boats returned after
a day out on the river visiting Yangji and other cousin villages. The
dragons paraded through billowing clouds of white smoke, their
teeth bared over their bright red tongues, their whiskers jouncing
with bravado. Lu Qiang watched silently. 'However things stand,
you must be moved by the sight of this,' I said.

'Actually, I really wanted to be out there with the boats yesterday. But it's too early to say we have achieved victory,' he said. 'I
don't mean Xian Qifa is a bad man. He's okay. But the city leadership has tied his hands already.' Lu Qiang explained how even the
paddles for the dragon boats had been changed before the festival
to formalise the new leadership and its links to the Communist
Party bureaucracy. The paddles had originally read 'Xian Village'
on one side and 'Villagers' on the other, asserting the popular and
spontaneous nature of their struggle for justice. But now they said
only 'Xian Village,' stressing the administrative unit over the convictions of the villagers themselves. This symbolic obliteration of
the villager—for that was exactly how Lu and the other dissenting
villagers viewed it—had come with a notice posted outside the village's ancestral temples. Ahead of this year's Dragon Boat Festival,
the notice had said, each of the villagers would be compensated in

full for the money they had donated in 2009 for the construction of the dragon boats. For some, like Lu, it seemed as though the original act of unity and defiance had been undone. 'I'll stick to my position over the village affairs,' he said, not taking his eyes off the boats. 'But this is a great way to come together. It's a really great way to come together.'

As the boats pulled up to the bank at last, we walked over to welcome the crews. 'Are you finished for today?' I asked one paddler as he heaved himself onto the stone walkway and dropped his paddle and lifejacket atop the others.

'Almost,' he said. 'We just need to parade up at Shipai Village.'

Lu Qiang and I sat quietly on red stools under the shade trees, eating sweet dragon-boat cakes. Against the backdrop of celebration he looked sullen and contemplative. Finally, he turned to me and said, 'I've decided we're joining the boats for the parade at Shipai. I'll bring my son back over in a bit.' The tide had pushed the water level in the canal to within inches of the underside of the bridge. Only when it receded, in an hour or so, would there be enough clearance to guide the boats through to the Shipai Village launch on the northern side. Lu Qiang suggested we walk back to the village and wait there.

We lounged under a canopy of shade cloth on a leafy patio on the southeast side of the village pond. It was the same spot where I had spent the afternoon two years earlier with the troupe of elderly villagers defending the pond from demolition crews, but it was almost unrecognisable. Over the past few months the area had been transformed. Where hills of rubble had once tumbled right up to the footpath, villagers had built a terraced wall of salvaged stones and glass bottles. They had set out lacquered chairs and a tea table. As a breeze shifted over the ancient pond, we reminisced about the past—how we had met on almost exactly this spot two years earlier. But the question of what lay ahead for Xian Village lingered over our reminiscences. Soon there would be a new agreement for the redevelopment of the village. What sort of future would it mediate for this centuries-old community? Could village brothers overcome their divisions and find concord once again? For how many more generations would the dragons parade in 'Diamond Village,' the hallowed place of their treasured heritage?

A call buzzed in to Lu Qiang's mobile. 'It's my son,' he said. 'He's really anxious. He's afraid we're going to miss the boats. We'd better go.' The boy joined us on the footpath at Liede Avenue. As we hurried through the tunnel at Jinsui Road, he scampered ahead of us, wheeling around impatiently. His eyes pleaded, *Hurry, hurry!* As soon as we emerged on the north side of the street we could hear the rumpus of the drums. Lu Qiang's son turned to face his father with a look of the profoundest heartbreak. Our fears were confirmed as we reached the bridge: the Xian Village boats were in the water already, parading before the crush of onlookers. As we reached the waterfront the boy's head was turned down, his eyes pooling with tears. 'He's a bit upset with me,' Lu Qiang said, his face reddening. We stood and watched the boats as they made their jubilant passes, the excitement crackling through the air. But I could sense that Lu was brooding over his son's disappointment.

When the boats pulled back to the bank and the crews climbed up for their dragon-boat cakes, we walked over and spoke to one of the villagers. 'Are the parades finished now?' Lu Qiang asked.

'No, there's just one more,' he said.

'Do you have space for us?'

'No problem.'

As the crews straggled back down the bank, Lu Qiang and his son hustled on their lifejackets. 'Okay, let's get our shoes off,' he said. 'Quickly. Set them there.' They climbed down the ladder to the muddy bank and found seats at the back of one of the teak boats. As they waited for the send-off, Lu Qiang demonstrated how to use the paddle. *That's right,* his motions urged, *a strong grip there at the neck. Long, even strokes, like this.* The drums and gongs thundered to life. The boy was hesitant at first, swiping his paddle over the surface of the water. Lu Qiang encouraged him. *Dig in deeper, like this—in time with the drumbeats.* The boy's strokes were laggard and irregular. But as the boat edged north under a firecracker barrage, his timing improved. *That's right, that's right,* Lu Qiang nodded, his back straining against the heft of the water. As the drumbeats thundered in quick succession and the crews turned, Lu Qiang tapped his son on the shoulder. The boy twisted awkwardly in his seat and brought his paddle over to the other side. As they started up again his strokes were more even, just a heartbeat behind those of his father. The drums roared as the boats sped back towards us. The boy's paddle strokes deepened and strengthened until finally he was in harmony with his father and the rest of the village crew. And just as the dragon nudged past the launch, powering south with its heaving arms, a smile turned up to where I stood on the walkway and lingered there amid the clamorous music.

EPILOGUE

The custodial sentences handed down to the rights-defence petitioners recorded in this book, while ostensibly justified in the name of public order, reflect a chronic instability. China's economic boom has created greater prosperity, but disaffection and social unrest have surged in its wake. Under the strain of social demands arising from unequal development, China's intransigent, Leninist political institutions are incapable of responding with anything but repression. Commanded by a closed and unrestrained political system, economic dynamism is twinned with the manufacture of discontent. Land use, as we have seen, offers a prime example. The social impact of land seizures alone has been immense. By 2005, China was, according to conservative estimates, generating at least three million landless peasants every year,[255] and by 2013 the total number of landless peasants was estimated at fifty million[256]—equivalent to the population of South Korea and approaching two-thirds of the national membership of the Chinese Communist Party.[257] There are more than 100,000 mass incidents in China every year (some estimates are double that number), of which at least half are related to land use. But land financing, the primary source of income for most cities and a chief enabler of the expanding property bubble, continues to fuel land grabs. China's cities are addicted to land, a problem so prevalent that a senior Party

251

official warned in 2013 that overdependence on the land-financing model is creating a disaffected underclass.[258]

Rural Chinese are losing out most often, whether they are landless peasants, the besieged denizens of the urban villages or part of the forever-uprooted mass of migrant labour. One of China's leading thinkers on rural policy, Zhang Musheng, summed up the situation somewhat provocatively in 2011. He matter-of-factly described China's economic rise—what some have dubbed the 'China model'—as the plunder of rural land and people. Peasants, he said, had contributed usage rights for more than 77,200 square miles of land at rock-bottom prices over three decades. They had also provided the cheap labour that drove Chinese manufacturing. Booming cities might be the engine of China's ascendance, but rural land and people were the blazing fire in the furnace. Months before the Party's general secretary, Xi Jinping, publicly asserted his 'Chinese dream' of national revival and strength, Zhang Musheng stated in a media interview, speaking of his own country, that 'to dream of being a powerful nation is to be a nation dreaming of plunder.'[259]

A flexible response to growing demands for fairness would necessitate political reform, including the protection of basic civil liberties and sounder rule of law. But that, many officials fear, could undermine the rule of the Communist Party. And it would certainly erode the lucrative monopolies Party elites currently have on resources, including land. So China's leaders have responded to the rising tide of social unrest by building a bulwark against it. Beginning in the early 1990s, the government mobilised an extensive system of 'stability maintenance' against its own society. By 2011, spending on public security in China—including paramilitary police, secret police and surveillance—surpassed military spending. The gap widened further the next year.[260]

As stability maintenance is the overriding priority for the Party leadership—'Stability before all else,' the slogan goes—the petitioning system has become an enormous dragnet. It is no longer capable of, or even concerned with, resolving appeals. In fact, according to one of China's preeminent experts on the petitioning system, only about 2 in every 1,000 petitions is ever properly resolved.[261] The petitioning system is braided together with stability maintenance. Every petition points to a potential threat. The wronged are criminalised, and therefore revictimised, as possible menaces to public order. In 2005, President Hu Jintao introduced his signature concept of the 'harmonious society,' a vision of a stable nation that gave a rhetorical nod to deepening social inequality. The 'harmonious society' must incorporate democracy, rule of law and justice, said Hu, so that all Chinese could share in the wealth of society.[262] But Hu's real legacy was an overbearing system of stability maintenance.

●

Hu Jintao's successor, Xi Jinping, has made the fight against corruption within the Party's ranks a defining feature of his legacy, an attempt to rebuild the Party's standing among the people. In the months before Xi came to power, anti-corruption had already become a life-and-death matter for the Chinese Communist Party. There was a growing sense among the masses that corruption—now aired in cathartic waves of scandal on a new generation of social media—was at the very heart of Party politics. 'It's impossible not to be corrupt,' goes a common refrain in private conversations. 'A clean official would be a pariah!'

On the occasion of the Party's ninetieth anniversary in July 2011, President Hu Jintao warned that the Party risked 'alienation from the people' if it failed to deal with corruption.[263] In September 2012, appearing on China Central Television, the Party's anti-corruption tsar and China's discipline inspection chief, He Guoqiang, said the Party needed to 'strengthen the campaign against corruption, creating a favourable public opinion climate for the success of the Chinese Communist Party's eighteenth National Congress.'[264] And in his political report to the National Party Congress in November 2012, Hu

Jintao, soon to be succeeded, warned of the dangers of corruption and said the Party must 'resolutely investigate major and important cases, doing its utmost to resolve the problems of corruption happening right beside the masses.'[265]

As he took control of the Chinese Communist Party at the November congress, Xi Jinping warned his comrades that corruption could 'doom the party and the state.'[266] He followed quickly with a moratorium on official banquets, the lavish dinners at public expense that had come to epitomise government waste and greed.[267] Initially, at least, there were encouraging signs that Xi Jinping might also seek to grapple with the 'problems of corruption happening right beside the masses' by empowering citizens to defend their interests against entrenched Party elites. Marking the thirtieth anniversary of China's Constitution on December 4, 2012, Xi said, 'We must firmly establish the authority of the Constitution and the law throughout society, enabling the masses to fully trust in the law.'[268] Perhaps, thought some, the new leadership would make good on long-dormant constitutional pledges like human rights, freedom of expression and an independent judiciary.[269]

On December 13, 2012, a group of Chinese lawyers, activists, writers and scholars issued an open letter calling on China's top 205 officials to make full disclosure of their assets. The initiator of the call was Beijing lawyer and rights advocate Xu Zhi-yong, who had launched a nationwide initiative seven months earlier called the 'New Citizens Movement,' dedicated to the peaceful promotion of freedom, democracy, rule of law and constitutionalism.[270] For the movement's emblem Xu Zhiyong had chosen the Chinese characters for 'citizen,' written in the hand of the twentieth-century revolutionary leader Sun Yat-sen.[271]

But in the months that followed Xi Jinping's speech on constitutionalism, hopes that the Chinese Communist Party might relax controls on political engagement by China's citizens progressively unravelled. In the first week of January, staff at Guangzhou's *Southern Weekly*, a newspaper known for its more freewheeling coverage, began a strike action to protest draconian controls that threatened their legacy as one of China's most progressive newspapers. *Southern Weekly*'s New Year's edition had been eviscerated by propaganda officials and internal monitors, the culmination of many months of worsening censorship.[272] The original draft of the paper's popular New Year's editorial had been called 'The Chinese dream: the dream of constitutionalism.' Inspired by Xi Jinping's now pervasive concept of the 'Chinese dream,' the editorial had been a bold call for greater rights and freedoms. But the editorial was gutted in favour of a bootlicking paean to China's feats of development, even quoting from a passage published in the Party's official *People's Daily*.[273] On January 7, in the first large-scale public demonstration calling for freedom and democracy in China since mass student protests in Tiananmen Square in 1989, several hundred protesters gathered outside the *Southern Weekly* offices.[274]

The new administration seemed at first to hesitate. This was a serious test of Xi Jinping's sincerity and resolve. He had spoken gravely about the need to fight corruption. How would he deal with public concerns over the crippling of what had once been the country's staunchest muckraking newspaper? For three days, police waited in force behind the offices of *Southern Weekly*, in a back lot butting up against the red wasteland that had once been Yangji Village, where just twelve or thirteen nail houses now stood defiantly as construction work commenced around them. Finally, on January 10, police began dragging protesters away[275]—the message for those who had taken Xi Jinping's overtures of openness at face value: enough is enough.

On a Friday in February 2013, several weeks after the *Southern Weekly* incident, there was a light knock on my office door at the University of Hong Kong. It was an unexpected visit from Xiao Shu, a social critic and former *Southern Weekly* columnist who was involved in the New Citizens Movement. He stood in my doorway, grinning from ear to ear. 'Brother,' he said, 'I have something that might interest you.' The document on Xiao Shu's laptop was the first draft of a letter calling on China's leaders to ratify the International Covenant on Civil and Political Rights, the United Nations' treaty committing parties to measured progress on core values like freedom of speech, freedom of assembly and due process. Framed as 'a citizen proposition,' the letter argued that ratification of the covenant would promote real progress to 'protect the life and authority' of China's Constitution, which enshrined these rights, though only in name. The letter had been signed already by more than a hundred Chinese from varied backgrounds—lawyers, writers, economists, doctors and business people—including some of the country's most recognisable public intellectuals. It was addressed to the National People's Congress, the rubber-stamp legislature that in three weeks' time would formally elect Xi Jinping as China's new head of state. In part, it read:

> The establishment of a nation of human rights, a China in which the Constitution has real force, is the only true and fundamental measure—for citizens, for the government and for our country—of the excellence of our achievements and our dreams. We must foster the creation of a civil society rooted in fairness, peace, rationality and openness. We must build a decent system of politics, based on love and justice.[276]

'Where do you plan to publish this?' I asked.

'The idea is to run it in *Southern Weekly* next week. A test. But of course we're not sure that can happen.' A test indeed. Despite the conviction among some liberal intellectuals, Xiao included, that Xi Jinping was a determined reformer who would outline bolder steps after the National People's Congress, the inclinations of the top leadership remained a mystery. As for *Southern Weekly*, the protests of January had so far had little impact. The editor-in-chief had survived staff calls for his removal. The provincial propaganda officials behind the affair were similarly unscathed. Unfortunately, the authorities learned of the letter sometime over the weekend and leaned on some of the signatories, inviting them to tea. Xiao's only choice was to post it online four days earlier than it had been due to be published, hoping it would capture attention.[277]

By April 2013, hopes that President Xi Jinping was a determined reformer had evaporated. A high-level Chinese Communist Party document came to light in which cadres were warned about ideological threats to the Party's leadership, including civil society and constitutional democracy. 'We must not permit the dissemination of opinions that oppose the Party's theory or political line . . . [or] defame the image of the Party or the nation,' said the document.[278] It alleged that dissidents had 'stirred up trouble about disclosing officials' assets, using the internet to fight corruption, media control and other sensitive topics, to provoke discontent with the Party and government.'[279] On April 12, the founder of the New Citizens Movement, Xu Zhiyong, was placed under house arrest. The following July, he was charged with 'gathering crowds to disrupt public order' and eventually was sentenced to four years in jail.[280]

On May 9, writer Murong Xuecun, one of the country's most outspoken critics of state censorship, posted on Sina Weibo: 'This is my Chinese dream: to have no illusions about evil, to understand that its rot will only spread; and yet, not to lose heart, not to despair—to begin from zero, from less than zero, and to build in the midst of the ruins.' His account was deleted two days later.[281]

•

Few would question the robustness of Xi Jinping's anti-corruption drive. In 2014 alone, the campaign brought investigations against sixty-eight high-level officials, or 'tigers,' and some 70,000 lower level officials, or 'flies.'[282] In July 2014, anti-corruption officials announced the launch of a global 'fox hunt' to track down corrupt officials who had fled overseas;[283] according to the Chinese Academy of Social Sciences, an estimated 18,000 escaped between 1990 and 2011, whisking away some $126 billion.[284] In September 2014, reports surfaced that the Chinese government had approached police in New Zealand about interviewing the wife, daughter and alleged mistress of Cao Jianliao, the former Guangzhou deputy mayor involved in the Xian Village case.[285]

Xi Jinping's campaign against corruption has been matched, however, with an equally resolute campaign against dissent. The examples are too numerous to recount, but one of the most egregious cases has been the persecution of rights lawyer Pu Zhiqiang, a self-described political moderate who has worked within the Chinese system to represent clients—including the artist Ai Weiwei—on a range of cases dealing with such questions as press freedom and political dissent.[286] Pu, who has always scrupulously followed the letter of the law, was detained in July 2014 for unspecified crimes. For months, investigators probed for any sign of corruption or treason, a hook on which to hang their case against him.[287] Unable to uncover anything incriminating, they settled in January 2015 on a group of twenty-eight posts that Pu had made on Sina Weibo.[288]

What sustainable progress can be made by a top-down purge of corruption within the Party's ranks when the process of supposed justice can unfold only as a political prerogative of the Chinese Communist Party, and when citizens like Pu Zhiqiang and Xu Zhiyong are persecuted for having the same agenda? The proceedings against Pu Zhiqiang recall those cases fabricated against Xian villagers Lu Nianzu and Xian Yaojun, both of whom, like Pu, dared to speak out against real injustices. They recall the tribulations of He Jieling, the Ha Street campaigner, whose respect for the law pitted her against those whose duty it was to enforce the law. Such is the madness of China's 'stability preservation' regime—that adherence to the letter of the law becomes a radical act of civil disobedience. At present, much of the resilience and dynamism of Chinese society is lost in the single-minded pursuit of what scholar Yu Jianrong has called 'rigid stability,' a fragile stability achieved through coercion and 'founded upon the exclusive and closed nature of political power.'[289]

The stories in this book iterate a point over which no doubt should be entertained to begin with: that Chinese citizens are ready and able to play a more active role in their own destinies. As Pu Zhiqiang said to me and others during a visit to Hong Kong in October 2013, 'I believe the Chinese Dream is about the freedom to dream, and it should be the dream of each and every individual.' For this to happen, institutions in China will have to find a way to accommodate the voices of Chinese citizens. The voice of conscience will have to be normalised, at which point it ceases to become a source of (perceived) instability and becomes instead a force for the betterment of society.

ACKNOWLEDGEMENTS

A few years back, Jo Lusby at Penguin spoke six insistent words, dusting off a project on China's urban villages that I had nearly set aside: 'David,' she said, 'you have to write this.' So thank you, Jo. And thanks to the whole Penguin team—to Imogen Liu, Mike Tsang and my eagle-eyed editor Penny Mansley—for making it happen.

For the earliest inception of this book, I have two people in particular to thank. In 2005, Professor Lu Xinyu of Fudan University loaned me a stack of gritty documentaries from China's nascent independent film movement. Among these was *Sanyuanli*, a black-and-white film about the Guangzhou village of the same name by artist and activist Ou Ning. I was captivated by Ou's sympathetic view of urban villages. One trip into the dim alleys of Sanyuanli and there was no turning back.

Many other people helped me along the way. Thanks in particular to Emma Dong, Karen Zhang and Dorothy Dong for key advice; to Gene Mustain, who offered early encouragement; to Patrick Boehler and Alf Romann, for the rudiments of adventuring through Hong Kong's Company Registry and other document troves; to Virginia White, Jessica Hefes, Laura Lau (and Alf once again), for moral support and the occasional daycare so essential to solitude; and to Dr. Alex Chow, who got me back on my feet in time for the waking of the dragons in Xian Village. I owe a special debt to filmmaker and friend Zhao Dayong, whose home was often my Guangzhou base camp. Above all, my heartfelt thanks goes to Qian Gang and Yuen-ying Chan of the University of Hong Kong's China Media Project, which for the past twelve years has nurtured and inspired my work.

I thank my entire family for their unfailing support and patience through the long process. All of you are now freed (for a time anyway) from that de rigueur greeting: 'So, how's the book going?' Thanks, Mom, for encouraging an indulgent love of language before words were even on my tongue.

Finally, to my wife Sara, whom I was so lucky to meet all those years ago at a Mid-Autumn Festival in Nanjing—my deepest love and thanks. Patiently, Sara offered direction and encouragement through the twists and turns, as the project stretched from months into years. Sometimes I needed a kick, other times a kind word. But she was always in my corner.

Notes

PROLOGUE

1. Lu Suigeng, ed., «冼村村志» [*Xian Village Chronicle*], Xian Village Industry Company Limited, Guangzhou, December 2008, p. 7.
2. Huang Liao, «龙的传人» ['Descendants of the Dragon'], 番禺日报 [Panyu *Daily*], June 23, 2012, pyrb.dayoo.com/html/2012-06/23 /content_1744174.htm.

INTRODUCTION

3. «三元里人民抗英斗争纪念馆» ['Sanyuanli People's Resistance to the English Commemorative Museum'], 广州市人民政府 [People's Government of Guangzhou Municipality], March 21, 2013, www.guangzhou.gov.cn/node_2790/node_2792/2013/03/21/13638 53753406089.shtml.
4. Zhang Ming, «耳熟能详的"叁元里抗英"不过是一场小闹剧» ['The "Resistance to the British at Sanyuanli" We Are So Familiar with Was Just a Small Drama'], 人民网 [*People's Daily Online*], March 19, 2013, history.people.com.cn/BIG5/198467/17429020 .html.
5. «百个爱国主义教育基地(058):三元里人民抗英斗争纪念馆» ['One Hundred Patriotic Education Sites (058): Sanyuanli People's Memorial to the Struggle of Resistance Against the En-

glish'], Wenming.cn, September 22, 2008, archive.wenming.cn
/hsly/2008-09/22/content_14456956.htm.

6.   'China Pledges Steady, Human-Centered Urbanization,' *Xinhua
     News* 273 NOTES *Agency*, December 14, 2013, news.xinhuanet
     .com/english/china/2013-12/14/c_132968136.htm.

7.   Karin C Seto, 'Urban Growth in China: Challenges and Pros-
     pects,' presentation slides, Center for Integrated Facility Engineer-
     ing Seminar, Stanford University, January 31, 2007, web.stanford
     .edu/class/cee320/CEE320B/Seto.pdf.

8.   'Urban Population (% of Total),' World Bank, n.d., data.world-
     bank.org/indicator/SP.URB.TOTL.IN.ZS.

9.   Seto, 'Urban Growth in China.'

10. 《深圳城中村村民成"房爷":房租普遍月入十万》['Shenzhen Urban-
     Village Villagers Become "Property Bosses," with Monthly Rents
     of 100,000'], 上海证 券报 [Shanghai *Securities News*] (via *Xin-
     hua News Agency*), February 19, 2013, news.xinhuanet.com/for-
     tune/2013-02/19/c_124361393.htm.

11. Zhang Yue and Huang He, 《深圳新土改:城中村"更新"博弈》
     ['Shenzhen's New Land Reforms: The Game for Urban-Village
     "Renewal"'], 南方周末 [*Southern Weekly*] (via *iNFZM*), August
     15, 2014, www.infzm.com/content/103213.

12. Fan Gang, 《"城中村"两面观》['The Two Sides of "Urban Vil-
     lages"'], 新华社 [Xinhua News Agency] (via *Cityup*), February
     17, 2009, www.cityup.org/topic/chzhcgz/chzhcgz/20090217/65102
     .shtml.

13. Luo Aihua, 《广州100亿元改善城中村》['Guangzhou Earmarks
     10 Billion to Improve Urban Villages'], 人民日报 [*People's Daily*],
     May 8, 2014, paper.people.com.cn/rmrb/html/2014-05/08/nw
     .D110000renmrb_20140508_3-04.htm.

14. 《2013年广州市人口规模及分布情况》['Scale and Distribution
     Data for Guangzhou City Population, 2013'], 广州统计局 [Guang-
     zhou Office of Statistics], March 19, 2014, www.gzstats.gov.cn
     /tjgb/qtgb/201403/t20140319_35845.htm.

15. Li Ruihe, 《我区打响"城中村"改造攻坚战》['My District's Deter-
     mined War for Regeneration of "Urban Villages"'], 包河区政府
     [Baohe District Government], May 26, 2008, www.baohe.gov.cn
     /Tmp/News_wenzhang.shtml?d_ID=2025.

16. Glossary of Statistical Terms: Urbanization, Organisation for Eco-
     nomic Co-operation and Development, September 25, 2001, stats
     .oecd.org/glossary/detail.asp?ID=2819.

17. Han Yi, «年轻妈妈骑摩托车回家看儿子» ['Young Mother Rides Motorbike to Go Home and See Her Son'], 重庆晚报 [*Chongqing Evening News*], January 19, 2011, p. 22.

18. Qin Hui, «从南非看中国» ['Viewing China Through the Lens of South Africa'], 财新网 [*Caixin Media*], March 25, 2010, qinhui .blog.caixin.com/archives/5363.

19. «太原"城中村"改造难在哪里?» ['Where Is the Difficulty in Regenerating Taiyuan "Urban Villages"?'], 太原日报 [*Taiyuan Daily*] (via *Xinhua News Agency*), November 4, 2014, www.sx.xinhuanet .com/newscenter/2014-11/04/c_1113102686.htm.

20. «"土地财政依赖症"出路何在?» ['Where Is the Road Out of "Land-Financing Addiction"?'], 光明日报 [*Guangming Daily*] (via *Guangming Online*), July 27, 2014, news.gmw.cn/2014-07/27/content_12190231.htm.

21. Bai Xuemei, Jing Chen and Shi Peijun, 'Landscape Urbanization and Economic Growth in China: Positive Feedbacks and Sustainability Dilemmas,' *Environmental Science and Technology*, 2012, Vol. 46, No. 1, pp. 132–39. pubs.acs.org/doi/pdf/10.1021/es202329f

22. Bill Gates, 'A Stunning Statistic About China and Concrete,' *GatesNotes: The Blog of Bill Gates*, June 25, 2014, www.gatesnotes .com/About-Bill-Gates/Concrete-in-China.

23. Ibid., p. 25.

24. «潘石屹:要降低地方政府对土地财政依赖性» [Pan Shiyi: 'We Must Lower Local Governments' Reliance on Land Financing'], 财经 [*Caijing*], April 16, 2011, www.caijing.com.cn/2011-04-16/110694010.html.

25. Land Administration Law of the People's Republic of China (People's Republic of China), National People's Congress Standing Committee, August 28, 2004 (originally adopted June 25, 1986), art. 2, www. npc.gov.cn/englishnpc/Law/2007-12/12/content_1383939.htm.

26. Li Zexu, «解读股份改革中的"绝对权力"» ['Explaining "Absolute Power" in Stockholding Reform'], 新民周刊 [*Xinmin Weekly*] (via Yuhuan.com), June 15, 2005, www.yuhuan.com/news/show .asp?url=NewsNews/c/2005-06-15/16006951141.shtml.

27. Clarissa Sebag-Montefiore, 'Shanty China,' *New York Times*, May 14, 2013, latitude.blogs.nytimes.com/2013/05/14/even-slum-dwellers-in-china-are-upbeat-about-progress/.

28. Liu Chen, «解决城中村须"破旧立新"» ['Resolving Urban Villages Requires "Destroying the Old and Raising the New"'],

广东建设报 [*Guangdong Construction News*], June 20, 2003, Wise-News.

29. Organic Law of the Villagers Committees of the People's Republic of China (People's Republic of China), National People's Congress Standing Committee, Order No. 9, November 4, 1998, arts 2, 16, 19, www.npc.gov.cn/englishnpc/Law/2007-12/11/content_1383542.htm.

30. Angela Meng and Minnie Chan, 'Anti-Graft Drive Will Go On as China Can't Afford to Lose Corruption Battle: PLA Daily,' *South China Morning Post*, December 17, 2014, www.scmp.com/news/china/article/1663532/anti-graft-drive-will-go-china-cant-afford-lose-battle-against-corruption (subscription required).

31. Jamil Anderlini, 'Arrest of "Tiger" Zhou Yongkang Sheds Light on China Graft Purge,' *Financial Times*, December 8, 2014, www.ft.com/intl/cms/s/0/57042e30-7ebe-11e4-b83e-00144feabdc0.html#axzz3Qky5GyMD (subscription required).

32. China Development Research Foundation, *China's New Urbanization Strategy*, Routledge, New York, 2013, p. 72.

33. Yi Peng, «媒体析"新四化"新意:从以物为主转向以人为本» ['Media Explicate the New Meaning of the "Four New Modernisations"'], 人民日报 [*People's Daily*], January 17, 2013, politics.people.com.cn/n/2013/0117/c30178-20235053.html.

34. You Shanshan, 'The New Urbanites,' *China Pictorial*, April 28, 2013, www.chinapictorial.com.cn/en/features/txt/2013-04-28/content_538365.htm.

CHAPTER 1: LU SUIGENG'S SECRET EMPIRE

35. Lu Suigeng, ed., p. 5.

36. «村民上访揭发村官涉嫌违法犯罪遭打击报复» ['Those Facing Demolition in One Guangzhou Village Demand That Village Officials Step Down First'], 了望东方周刊 [*Oriental Outlook*] (*Xinhua News Agency*, via Sina.com), August 2010, news.sina.com.cn/c/sd/2010-08-24/112020963814_2.shtml.

37. Wang Zechu, «城中村改造须尊重村民大会决定权» ['Urban-Village Regeneration Must Respect the Decision-Making Power of General Village Meetings'], 南方日报 [*Nanfang Daily*] (via *Xinhua News Agency*), August 22, 2013, p. GC02, news.xinhuanet.com/2013-08/22/c_125225654. htm.

38. «冼村往事» ['Past Events in Xian Village'], 时代在线 [*Time-*

Weekly], March 20, 2014, www.time-weekly.com/index.php?m=content&c=ind ex&a=show&catid=10&id=24231.

39. Lu Suigeng, ed., p. 3.

40. 'Heirs of Mao's Comrades Rise as New Capitalist Nobility,' *Bloomberg Business*, December 27, 2012, www.bloomberg.com/news /articles/2012-12-26/immortals-beget-china-capitalism-from-citicto-godfather-of-golf.

41. Lu Suigeng, ed., pp. 3, 35.

42. Ibid., p. 54.

43. «冼村:亚运会前完成清拆» ['Xian Village Demolition to Be Completed Before Asian Games'], 羊城晚报 [*Yangcheng Evening News*], July 31, 2009, p. A7.

44. 'Guangzhou Asian Games, Asian Para Games to Cost Over $18 Billion,' *Xinhua News Agency* (via *People's Daily*), english.people .com.cn/90001/90779/90867/7165523.html.

45. 'Guangzhou South Axis,' Heller Manus Architects, n.d., accessed June 15, 2012, www.hellermanus.com/Guangzhou_South_Axis .html; 'About the Firm,' Heller Manus Architects, n.d., accessed June 15, 2012, www.hellermanus.com/firm.html.

46. Jeffrey Heller, 'Repositioning Guangzhou,' *Building Journal*, January 18, 2010, pp. 54–9 (p. 56), www.building.hk/forum/2010 _0118repositioning.pdf.

47. 'Heller Manus Architects Selected to Lead the Design and Construction of Downtown Guangzhou, China,' San Francisco Office of Economic and Workforce Development, 2009 (web page no longer available), copy in author's possession.

48. «搬家公司进村等生意» ['Moving Companies Enter a Village Waiting for Business'], 信息时报 [*Information Times*], August 18, 2009, p. A7 City.

49. «请大家听听冼村"城中村"拆迁居民哭诉无门的求救声!» ['Please, Everyone, Listen to the Helpless Voices of Those Facing Demolition in the "Urban Village" of Xian Village!'], 房天下 [*SouFun*], August 22, 2009, xiangjinghyuan.soufun.com/bbs/2811 007506~-1/42961916_42961916.htm.

50. «林永健:从捡家具到非著名演员» ['Lin Yongjian: From Furniture Mover to Non-Famous Actor'], 信息时报 [*Information Times*], August 20, 2009, p. A33 Entertainment.

51. «卢穗耕,冼村村民喊你回家吃饭了!» ['Lu Suigeng: The Villagers of Xian Village Call You Back to Eat!'], 开心网 [*Kaixin Net*], September 2009, www.kaixin001.com/repaste/10321967_521038041.html.

52. 《广州市天河区冼村村民集体讨伐贪官》['Villagers in Xian Village in Guangzhou's Tianhe District Unite in a Crusade Against Corrupt Officials'], 新闻论坛 [*News Forum*] (via QQ.com), August 20, 2009, bbs.news. qq.com/t-156590-1.htm.

53. Mu Hong (lyrics), 《团结就是力量(歌曲)》['Unity Is Strength'], song, available at 百度百科 [*Baidu Baike*], baike.baidu.com/subview/252130/15416875.htm.

54. 《广州市天河区冼村村民集体讨伐贪官》['Villagers in Xian Village in Guangzhou's Tianhe District Unite in a Crusade Against Corrupt Officials'].

55. Deng Boxiong, 《杨箕村的"城中村拆迁"受关注》['The "Urban-Village Demolition" at Yangji Gets Attention'], 凤凰博报 [*Phoenix Online Blog*], September 19, 2009, blog.ifeng.com/article/3179225 .html.

56. 《杨箕贪官》['Yangji's Corrupt Officials'], chat thread, 大洋社区 [*Club Dayoo*], October 18, 2009, club.dayoo.com/view-1154572-1-1.html.

57. 《天河区城改办解答冼村改造九大疑问》['Tianhe District Urban Redevelopment Office Answers Nine Questions on the Xian Village Regeneration'], 南方日报 [*Nanfang Daily*], April 21, 2010, p. AII03.

CHAPTER 2: PICKING QUARRELS AND PROVOKING TROUBLE

58. Lu Suigeng, ed., p. 14.

59. Tan Xiying and He Ping, 《冼村市场要拆:四祠堂将易位》['Xian Village Market Faces Demolition: Four Ancestral Temples to Be Relocated'], 南方都市报 [*Southern Metropolis Daily*], November 26, 2009, p. AII14.

60. 《冼村前晚拆违未發生衝突》['No Conflict Occurred During the Demolition of Illegal Property in Xian Village the Night Before Last'], 新快报 [*New Express*], August 21, 2010, p. A05.

61. 《9大"城中村"亚运前拆完》['Nine Major Urban Villages to Be Demolished Before the Asian Games'], 信息时报 [*Information Times*], February 25, 2010, p. A11.

62. 《村破"困"街坊开签改造协议》['Xian Village Breaks Through "Troubles" to Get to Agreement Signing'], 新快报 [*New Express Daily*], April 2, 2010, p. A21.

63. All quotations in this section relating to the demolition agreement are reproduced from 《冼村整体改造拆迁补偿安置协议》

['Demolition, Compensation and Resettlement Agreement for the Integral Transformation of Xian Village'], Xian Village Industry Company Limited, Guangzhou, April 2010, copy in author's possession.

64. Contract Law of the People's Republic of China (People's Republic of China), National People's Congress, Order No. 15, March 15, 1999, art. 3, www.npc.gov.cn/englishnpc/Law/2007-12/11/content _1383564.htm.

65. «广州市长自曝还没买房住130平米宿舍月租600元» ['Guangzhou Mayor Reveals He Has Not Bought a Home, Lives in 130-Square-Metre Apartment for 600 Yuan a Month'], 南方日报 [*Nanfang Daily*], January 7, 2011, news.sohu.com/20110107/n278739874 .shtml.

66. «冼村70%村民已签约» ['Seventy Per Cent of Villagers in Xian Village Sign Their Agreements'], 广州日报 [*Guangzhou Daily*], April 28, 2010, p. A21 City Districts.

67. «冼村拆迁:按时签订协议即刻兑奖1万» ['The Xian Village Demolition: Those Who Sign on Time Can Get an Award of 10,000 Yuan'], 南方都市报 [*Southern Metropolis Daily*], April 28, 2010, p. AII06.

68. «冼村改造六成村民已签约» ['Sixty Per Cent Sign Agreement for Xian Village Regeneration'], 南方日报 [*Nanfang Daily*], April 28, 2010, p. AII03.

69. «冼章海等寻衅滋事案» ['Picking Quarrels and Causing Trouble Case Against Xian Zhanghai and Others'] 广东省广州市天河区人民法院:(2010)天法刑初 字第119号 [Criminal verdict, People's Court of Tianhe District, Guangzhou, Guangdong Province, case no. 119 (2010)], January 30, 2011.

CHAPTER 3: A SUDDEN-BREAKING INCIDENT

70. «广东技术师范学院征地拆迁补偿协议签约仪式在江高镇举行» ['Jianggao Township Holds Agreement-Signing Ceremony with Guangdong Polytechnic Normal University for Land Requisition Compensation'], 广州市白云区 政府 [Baiyun District Government], August 24, 2009, www.by.gov.cn/publicfiles/business /htmlfiles/jgz/zxdt/200908/259883.html.

71. «广东技术师范学院征地拆迁补偿协议签约仪式在江高镇举行» ['Jianggao Township Holds Agreement-Signing Ceremony with Guangdong Polytechnic Normal University for Land Requi-

sition Compensation], 广州市国土资源和房屋管理局白云区分局 [Guangzhou Baiyun District Land and Housing Office (Sub-Bureau of Land Resources and Housing Management)], November 9, 2009, baiyun.laho.gov.cn/zwgk_1367/gzdt/200911/t20091109 _296981.htm.

72. Wang Yong, 'The Chengguan's Parent-Child Relationship,' *Caixin Online*, November 16, 2012, english.caixin.com/2012-11-16/100461535.html?po.

73. 《网友曝光城管"打人不见血"教材》 ['Web Users Expose Urban Management "Hit Without Drawing Blood" Manual'], 南方都市报 [*Southern Metropolis Daily*], April 22, 2009, p. A32, news.oeeee .com/a/20090422/720376.html.

74. 《江高镇依法开展广东技术师范学院江高新校区建设项目收 地工作》 ['Jianggao Township Carries Out Land Requisition for Guangdong Polytechnic Normal University New Campus Development Project in Accord with the Law'], 广州市白云区政 府 [Baiyun District Government], May 13, 2010, www.by.gov.cn /publicfiles/business/htmlfiles/byqzf/qqdt/201005/290306.html.

75. 《2010年第二季度各街道办事处,镇人民政府,区应急委各成员 单位突发事 件信息报告情况》 ['County People's Government, District Emergency Management Committee Member Units' Information Report on Sudden-Breaking Incidents: April 1, 2010, to June 30, 2010'], 广州市白云区政府 [Baiyun District Government], Guangzhou, July 2010, items 73, 104.

CHAPTER 4: URBAN DREAMS IN RURAL GUANGZHOU

76. 《哈街举行开业典礼》 ['Ha Street Holds Opening Ceremony'], 番禺日报 [*Panyu Daily*], May 2, 2011, p. A1.

77. 《番禺哈街7月1日迎客》 ['Panyu's Ha Street to Welcome Guests on July 1'], 新快报 [*New Express*] (via XKB.com), March 26, 2011, p. D02, epaper.xkb.com.cn/view/491593.

78. 《违法商业街》 ['The Illegal Commercial Street'], 社会纵横 [*Society Focus*], television program (archived), 广东电视台 [Guangdong *Television*], September 2011, available at *Youku*, v.youku.com/v_ show/id_XMzExODk4NjUy.html.

79. 《我会常务副主席程良洲在中山传递亚运圣火》 ['Our Foundation's Deputy Chairman Cheng Liangzhou Carries the Asian Games Torch in Zhongshan'], 广东宋庆龄基 金会 [Guangdong Soong Ching Ling Foundation], October

20, 2010, www.gdsclf.org/news/ShowArticle.asp?ArticleID =290.

80. «"都市笑口组"助阵番禺哈街开业上演爆笑小品» ['"Metro Comedy Troupe" Stages Comedy Sketch for Opening of Panyu's Ha Street'], 新浪广东 [*Sina Guangdong*], May 1, 2011, ent.gd.sina.com .cn/news/2011/05/01/665994.html.

81. «番禺哈街7月1日迎客» ['Panyu's Ha Street to Welcome Guests on July 1'].

82. «祈福水城:威尼斯式园林小区» ['Clifford Waterfront: A Venetian-Style Garden Neighbourhood'], property listing, 58.com, September 1, 2013, gz.58.com/ershoufang/15040549689481x.shtml.

83. 'Hotel About,' Agile Hotel Guangzhou, n.d., agilehotelguangzhou .com.

84. «番禺南区大型商业街哈街二期招商» ['Ha Street, Large-Scale Commercial District in South Panyu, Seeks Merchants in Second Round'], 南方都市报 [*Southern Metropolis Daily*], June 1, 2010, p. D02.

85. «信访回复[2011]116号» [Letters and calls response (2011) no. 116], 广州市城市管理综合执法局番禺分局 [Guangzhou Urban Administrative and Law Enforcement Bureau, Panyu Branch], December 1, 2011, copy in author's possession; shown in «违法商业街» ['The illegal commercial street].

86. Xiao Han, «太石村事件评论之一至三» ['Xiao Han: Taishi Village Commentaries 1–3'], 博迅 [Boxun.com], October 6, 2005, www .boxun.com/news/gb/china/2005/10/200510060648.shtml.

87. He Jieling, «何洁凌面向全国转发的遗书» ['He Jieling's Death Note to the Entire Nation'], PY168.com, July 31, 2011, bbs.py168 .com/thread-1316304-1-1.html.

CHAPTER 5: TROUBLEMAKING VILLAGERS

88. Lu Suigeng, ed., p. 12.

89. «冼村肉菜市场部分旧档主欲转战石牌村» ['Some Old Stall Holders in the Xian Village Wet Market Fight Their Way to Shipai Village'], 信息时报 [*Information Times*], July 15, 2010, p. C4.

90. Video footage described in this section was filmed by Xian Villagers and shown to the author in the course of the research for this book. Footage is also available at «8月13日廣州冼村村民被警察武力震壓 . . . 被逼退守 家園1.MOD» ['August 13 Villagers of Guangzhou's Xian Village Are Forcibly Suppressed by

Police, Forced to Retreat from Their Homes'], YouTube.com, posted August 16, 2010, www.youtube.com/watch?v=6dtVgbhF8PQ.

91. «深痛8.13背后的序幕» ['Prologue to the Deep Pain of August 13'], open letter from Xian Villagers, Guangzhou, 2010, copy in author's possession.

92. Yao Yiqu and Hong Yiyi, «阻挠清拆影响施工14名滋事村民被带走审查» ['Fourteen Troublemaking Villagers Taken Away for Investigation After Impeding Demolition Work'], 南方日报 [Nanfang Daily], August 14, 2010, p. 4 Current Affairs.

93. Tan Xiying, Zhang Zhitao and Tian He, «冼村拆违出动警力不属实» ['Word That Police Were Mobilised for Demolition of Illegal Construction in Xian Village Is Not True'], 南方都市报 [Southern Metropolis Daily], August 21, 2010, p. A09.

94. «公安部下发"意见"严禁民警参与征地拆迁» ['Ministry of Public Security Releases "Notice" Banning Police Participation in Demolitions'], 报刊文摘 [Press Digest], March 9, 2011, p. 1.

95. «天河通报冼村两次拆违具体情况» ['Tianhe Makes Official Release on Specifics of the Two Xian Village Demolitions'], 羊城晚报 [Yangcheng Evening News], August 21, 2010, p. A06.

96. «广州冼村拆迁引发数千人冲突村民质疑违章建筑定性» ['Demolitions in Guangzhou's Xian Village Spark Conflict Involving Thousands: Villagers Take Issue with Designation as Illegal Construction'], 财新网 [Caixin Media] (via Ifeng), August 23, 2010, finance.ifeng.com/a/20100823/2540629_0.shtml.

97. «冼村爆发» ['Xian Village Explodes'], 财新网 [Caixin Media], August 23, 2010, magazine.caixin.com/2010-08-21/100172650.html.

98. «冼章海等寻衅滋事案»['Picking Quarrels and Causing Trouble Case Against Xian Zhanghai and Others'] 广东省广州市天河区人民法院: (2010)天法刑初 字第119号 [Criminal verdict, People's Court of Tianhe District, Guangzhou, Guangdong Province, case no. 119 (2010)], January 30, 2011.

99. Ibid.

100. Tan Xiying, «冼村全拆整村拆迁改造方案待审批,有消息称这一地块被保利 相中» ['Xian Village Regeneration Plan Still Awaiting Approval, Sources Say Land Settled for Poly'], 南方都市报 [Southern Metropolis Daily], August 12, 2009, p. AII17.

101. Guo Hetang, «冼村高门槛"招婿"欲结7年拆迁拉锯战» ['A Seven-Year Seesaw Battle over Demolition as Xian Village "Seeks a Partner" with High Expectations'], 信息时报 [Information Times] (via

Sina.com), December 2, 2011, gd.news.sina.com.cn/news/20111202 /1207965.html.

102. Tan Xiying, «冼村改造招合作企业要求身家不低于500亿» ['Xian Village Regeneration Seeks Partner Enterprise, Demands Assets of No Less Than 50 Billion'], 南方都市报 [*Southern Metropolis Daily*], December 2, 2011, p. AII10.

103. Hai Pengfei, «冼耀均被收容教育的釘子戶» ['Xian Yaojun: A Nail Houser Sentenced to Labour Re-Education'], 南方人物周刊 [*Southern People Weekly*] (via Hexun.com), January 26, 2013, news .hexun.com.tw/2013-01-28/150675824.html.

CHAPTER 6: DANCING WITH SHACKLES ON

104. Luo Yanghui, «理发店被查封店员工资无着落» ['Hair Salon Shut Down, Employees Can't Get Wages'], 信息时报 [*Information Times*], August 6, 2011, p. A10.

105. «违法商业街» ['The Illegal Commercial Street'], 社会纵横 [*Society Focus*], television program (archived), 广东电视台 [Guangdong Television], September 2011, available at Youku, v.youku.com /v_show/id_XMzExODk4NjUy.html

106. «电影院停业引发的哈街违建争端» ['Closure of a Cinema Causes Illegal Construction Controversy at Ha Street'], 南方都市报 [*Southern Metropolis Daily*] (via *ND Daily*), November 25, 2011, p. GA01, gcontent.oeeee.com/3/2e/32e05616c8ed6594/Blog/4bd/0d16f8 .html.

107. «预留征地款无明细村民申请重审计» ['With No Details on Land Acquisition, Villagers Apply for Re-Audit'], 南方都市报 [*Southern Metropolis Daily*], August 8, 2011, p. AII08.

108. Law of the People's Republic of China on Assemblies, Processions and Demonstrations (People's Republic of China), National People's Congress Standing Committee, Order No. 20, October 31, 1989, art. 1, www.npc.gov.cn/englishnpc/Law/2007-12/12/content _1383911.htm.

109. «广东省实施"中华人民共和国集会游行示威法"办法» ['Guangdong Province Implements Measures for "Law of the People's Republic of China on Assemblies, Processions and Demonstrations"'], 深圳市公安局 [Shenzhen Public Security Bureau], February 24, 2009, www.szga.gov.cn/ZWGK/ZCFG/JD_ZAGL/201305/t2013 0529_36869.htm.

110. He Jieling, «在中国:公民依法申请示威游行会被批准吗?» ['In

China: If a Citizen Legally Applies for a Demonstration, Will It Be Approved?'], January 8, 2012, copy in author's possession.

111. «番禺区沙湾镇原副镇长等 涉向非国家工作人员行贿» ['Former Township Chief of Panyu District's Shawan Township and Others Involved in Bribery of Non-Government Official'], 新快报 [*New Express*], August 15, 2012, p. A15.

112. Li Bin, «习近平在参观"复兴之路"展览时强调:承前启后继往开来继续朝着 中华民族伟大复兴目标奋勇前进» ['Xi Jinping Emphasises During Visit of "Road to Revival" Exhibition: Following the Past and Heralding the Future, Continuing to Move Forwards in the Great Struggle of Revival for the Chinese People'], 新华网 [*Xinhua Online*], November 29, 2012, news.xinhuanet.com/politics /2012-11/29/c_113852724.htm.

113. 'The Rocky Road to Revival,' *Economist*, December 15, 2012, www .economist.com/news/china/21568392-region-ponders-policy-chinas-new-leaders-over-disputed-waters-and-shudders-rocky.

114. Li Bin.

115. He Jieling, p. 6.

116. Ibid., pp. 14, 17.

CHAPTER 7: DISRUPTING PUBLIC ORDER

117. «孙中山许多重大决策就在广州这些故地诞生» ['Many Major Decisions by Sun Yat-sen Happened in Guangzhou's Older Areas'], 中国共产党新闻网 [Chinese *Communist Party News Online*], June 17, 2011, www.lib.zhjnc.edu.cn/tuyan/study/show.asp?id=658.

118. Sun Yat-sen, 'The Principle of Democracy,' 1924, available at Asia for Educators, Columbia University, afe.easia.columbia.edu/ps/cup /sun_yatsen_democracy.pdf.

119. «举报信» ['Petition Letter'], Maogang, Yuzhu Subdistrict, Huangpu District, Guangzhou, 2012, copy in author's possession.

120. Liu Guannan and Ma Weifeng, «违章建筑变合法村官骗领700万征地补偿 款» ['An Illegal Building Is Made Legal, and a Village Official Pockets 7 Million Yuan in Land Requisition Payments'], 南方日报 [*Nanfang Daily*], July 31, 2013, epaper.southcn.com /nfdaily/html/2013-07/31/content_7212229.htm.

121. Quotations referring to Huang Minpeng that are not attributed in a note have been reproduced from documents collected, signed and presented to the author by Huang Minpeng on December 14, 2012.

122. Huang Wei, «穗首宗土地征用强制执行案办结» ['Guangdong's First Case Dealing with the Forced Implementation of Land Acquisition Is Resolved'], 南方日报 [*Nanfang Daily*], November 9, 2012, p. GC05.

123. «广州市白云区江高镇叶边村强制性征地» ['Forced Land Confiscation in Yebian Village, Jianggao Township, Baiyun District, Guangzhou'], 百度贴 吧 [*Baidu Tieba*], December 16, 2010, accessed October 7, 2014, tieba.baidu.com/p/960757822.

124. Steven Lee Myers and Mark Landler, 'Frenzied Hours for U.S. on Fate of a China Insider,' *New York Times*, April 17, 2012, www.nytimes.com/2012/04/18/world/asia/details-emerge-on-us-decisions-in-china-scandal.html?pagewanted=all&_r=0.

125. Law of the People's Republic of China on Penalties for Administration of Public Security (People's Republic of China), National People's Congress Standing Committee, Order No. 38, August 28, 2005, art. 82, www.npc.gov.cn/englishnpc/Law/2007-12/13/content_1384114. htm.

126. Constitution of the People's Republic of China, art. 35, available at National People's Congress of the People's Republic of China, www.npc.gov.cn/englishnpc/Law/2007-12/05/content_1381903 .htm.

CHAPTER 8: A LIMITED-LIABILITY POLICE FORCE

127. Mimi Lau, 'Villagers Flock to Rare Trial of Top Policeman,' *South China Morning Post*, July 6, 2012, www.scmp.com/article/1005984 /villagers-flock-rare-trial-top-policeman.

128. «冼村实业有限公司» ['Xian Village (Xian Village Industry Company Limited)'], in «天河年鉴» [*Tianhe Annual Survey* (2011)], ed. Lin Daoliang, Tianhe District Government, 2012, xiancun.thnet .gov.cn/v2011/jgdh/gzgs/201202/t20120210_480705.html.

129. Lu Suigeng, ed., p. 238.

130. Ibid., pp. 229–30, 258.

131. «举报信» ['Petition Letter'], from Xian Villagers to Central Commission for Discipline Inspection, 2009, p. 6, copy in author's possession.

132. «冼村往事» ['Past Events in Xian Village'], 时代在线 [*Time-Weekly*], March 20, 2014, www.time-weekly.com/index.php?m=-content&c=index&a=show&catid=10&id=24231.

133. Lu Suigeng, ed., pp. 3, 43.

134.   «保利房地产(集团)股份有限公司首次公开发行股票招股意向书摘要» ['Poly Real Estate (Group) IPO Prospectus Summary'], 上海证券报 [*Shanghai Securities News*], July 5, 2006.

135.   «寺右联社,广州丰伟合作开发房地产合同纠纷» ['Siyou Stock-holding Co. Operative of Guangzhou, Tianhe District, Liede Subdistrict v Guangzhou Feng Wei Real Estate Development Company Limited'] 广东省高级人民 法院民事判决书:(2008)粤高法民一终字第161号 [Civil verdict, Guangdong Supreme People's Court, case no. 161 (2008)], March 16, 2009, p. 2, available at Yifake.com, www.yifake.com/judge/14463.html.

136.   Mark Stokes and Russell Hsiao, *The People's Liberation Army General Political Department: Political Warfare with Chinese Characteristics*, Project 2049 Institute, October 14, 2013, p. 60, www.project2049.net/documents/PLA_General_Political_Department_Liaison_Stokes_Hsiao.pdf.

137.   Cheng Xue, «远华案背后的黑幕» ['Unveiling the Yuan Hua Case'], Mirror Books, Hong Kong, 2009, chap. 3, available at Boxun.com, blog.boxun.com/hero/200904/lianhuaxiaofo/17_1.shtml.

138.   «寺右联社,广州丰伟合作开发房地产合同纠纷» ['Siyou Stock-holding Cooperative of Guangzhou, Tianhe District, Liede Subdistrict v Guangzhou Feng Wei Real Estate Development Company Limited'].

139.   Li Lin, «保利地产入住丰兴广场» ['Poly Real Estate Enters Fengxing Plaza'], 羊城晚报 [*Yangcheng Evening News*], November 14, 2005, www.ycwb.com/GB/content/2005-11/14/content_1019211.htm.

140.   «粤数千市民消费者权益日泄愤» ['Thousands of City Residents in Guangdong Vent Their Anger on World Consumers Day'], 澳门日报 [*Macau Daily*], March 16, 2002, p. B03.

141.   Li Lin.

142.   Ni Ming, «19家房地产开发企业上黑榜» ['Nineteen Property Development Enterprises Blacklisted'], 广州日报 [*Guangzhou Daily*] (via Sina.com), May 24, 2006, news.sina.com.cn/o/2006-05-24/06209007799s.shtml.

143.   «品牌发展不忘慈善» ['In Brand Development Do Not Forget Charity'], 南方都市报 [*Southern Metropolis Daily*], March 30, 2007, p. 10.

144.   Xiang Zi, «花木地块:价高者与最佳者的抉择» ['The Land of Flowers and 285 NOTES Trees: Deciding Between the Highest and the Best'], 第一财经日报 [*First Financial Daily*], September 22, 2006, p. C08.

145. Maggie Farley, 'Chinese Investment Firm GITIC Collapses,' *Los Angeles Times*, January 12, 1999, articles.latimes.com/1999/jan/12 /business/fi-62726.

146. Ngai-Ling Sum, '(Post-) Asian "Crisis" and "Greater China": On the Bursting of the "Bubbles" and He-Tech (Re-)Imaginations,' in Jurgen Haacke and Peter Preston, eds., *Contemporary China: The Dynamics of Change at the Start of the New Millennium*, Routledge, London and New York, 2013, pp. 190–220 (pp. 196–97).

147. Ngai-Ling Sum, '(Post-) Asian "Crisis" and "Greater China": On the Bursting of the "Bubbles" and He-Tech (Re-)Imaginations,' in Jurgen Haacke and Peter Preston, eds., *Contemporary China: The Dynamics of Change at the Start of the New Millennium*, Routledge, London and New York, 2013, pp. 190–220 (pp. 196–97).

148. Zhao Fulin, «混沌初开:中国房地产市场与大亨纪实» ['A Chaotic Beginning: A Record of Big Shots in China's Real-Estate Market'], 中外房地产导报 [*Chinese and Foreign Real Estate Times*], November 1994, pp. 55–56.

149. Wang Jun and Zou Aoshan, «历数"城中村"弊端种种天河区委书记进行村镇 改造总动员» ['Many Hurdles in the "Urban Villages": Tianhe District Secretary Carries Out General Mobilisation for Village and Township Regeneration'], 南方都市报 [*Southern Metropolis Daily*], May 11, 2000, p. 3.

150. Lu Suigeng, ed., p. 21.

151. «广州两大地产老板涉曹鉴燎案滞留境外» ['Two Major Guangzhou Real-Estate Bosses Linked to Cao Jianliao Case Now Overseas'], 财新网 [*Caixin Media*], August 23, 2014, china.caixin.com /2014-08-23/100720503.html.

152. «举报信» ['Petition Letter'], p. 7.

153. «四航局签订广州中交南雅投资有限公司出资协议» ['CCCC Fourth Harbor Engineering Signs Investment Agreement with Nanya Investment Company in Guangzhou'], press release, 中交第四航务工程局有限公司 [CCCC Fourth Harbor Engineering Company Limited], April 30, 2010 (web page no longer available), copy in author's possession.

154. «城启天鹅湾PK博雅首府» ['Cheng Qi Tian'e Wan v Boya Shoufu'], *Soufun.com* (via *Fang.com*), accessed September 5, 2014, newhouse.gz.fang.com/zt/200806/8PK.html.

155. You Xingyu, «曹鉴燎(广州市副市长)抓食品安全雷厉风行» ['Cao Jianliao (Guangzhou Deputy Mayor) Gets a Tight Grip on Food Safety'], 南方都市报 [*Southern Metropolis Daily*] (via *Wen.*

oeeee.com), August 14, 2012, wen.oeeee.com/a/20120814/1049094 .html.

156. «增城市委书记曹鉴燎:坚决把腐败分子清除出干部队伍» ['Old Articles: Zengcheng Party Secretary Cao Jianliao; Resolutely Rooting the Corrupt Out of Our Party Ranks'], 财经网 [*Caijing Online*], December 19, 2013, politics.caijing.com.cn/2013-12-19/113713772.html.

157. «举报信» ['Petition Letter'], pp. 2, 10.

CHAPTER 9: DUBIOUS RICHES

158. Lu Suigeng, ed., p. 275.

159. «首次公开发行股票招股说明书» ['IPO Prospectus'], 广州金逸影视传媒股份 有限公司 [Jinyi Film & Television Group], April 2014, p. 181, available at Chinese Securities Regulatory Commission, www.csrc.gov.cn/pub/zjhpublic/G00306202/201404/P020140422590778756843.pdf; «首次公开发行股票招股说明书» ['IPO Prospectus'], 广州金逸影视传媒股份有限公司 [Jinyi Film & Television Group], June 19, 2012, pp. 20, 37, available at Chinese Securities Regulatory Commission, www.csrc.gov.cn/pub/zjhpublic /G00306202/201206/P020120627552897961348.pdf.

160. «首次公开发行股票招股说明书» ['IPO Prospectus'], June 19, 2012, pp. 20, 37.

161. «走进嘉裕» ['Entering Jiayu'], 走进集团 [Jiayu Group], n.d., accessed July 2014, www.jiayuchina.com.cn/topic.php?channelID=39&topicID=226.

162. Zhao Xiarong, «嘉裕地产:1000万起家4年投资超百亿» ['Jiayu Property, the Pearl River New Town's Biggest Landholder: Started with 10 Million, Investments Exceed 10 Billion'], 时代周报 [*Time Weekly*] (via *Sohu.com*), May 24, 2012, business.sohu.com/20120524/n343952418.shtml.

163. Ibid.

164. Ibid.

165. Dong Liang, «金逸影视80后董事长被指"拼爹"公司存关联交易隐忧» ['Jinyi Film & Television's Post-80s Chief Executive Accused of "Relying on Family Background": Concerns of Related Party Transactions at the Company'], 价值线 [*Value Line*], May 12, 2014, available at JRJ.com, stock.jrj.com.cn/ipo/2014/05/12113417191285.shtml.

166. Li Cheng, «新年新气象广州3大卖场要变身» ['New Year, New

Climate: Three Big Merchandisers in Guangzhou Change Faces'],
羊城晚报 [*Yangcheng Evening News*], February 16, 2007, Furniture
Weekly.

167. Land Administration Law of the People's Republic of China (People's Republic of China), National People's Congress Standing
Committee, August 28, 2004 (originally adopted June 25, 1986),
arts 43–44, www.npc.gov.cn/englishnpc/Law/2007-12/12/content
_1383939.htm.

168. «2006年9月"国有土地使用证"登记结果» ['"State Land Use Permit" Registration Results'], 广州市国土资源和房屋管理局天
河分局 [Tianhe District Land and Housing Office], September
2006, tianhe.laho.gov.cn/zwxxjb/tddjjg_2691/200711/W0199902
060000000000425.xls.

169. «2012年半年年度报摘要» ['Interim Report 2012'], 青海坚成矿
业股份有限 公司 [Qinghai Xiancheng Mining Company Limited], August 31, 2012, available at CNINFO, www.cninfo.com
.cn/finalpage/2012-08-31/61512613.PDF.

170. Yuan Mingfu, «资本玩家黄贤优的腾挪玄机» ['The Mystery of
Capital Speculator Huang Xianyou'], 南方周末 [*Southern Weekly*]
(via *iNFZM*), July 31, 2012, www.infzm.com/content/78970.

171. «广东省广州市越秀区人民法院公告» ['Notice from the Yuexiu
District Court, Guangdong Province, Guangzhou City'], 人民
日报 [*People's Daily*] (via *PeopleGonggao.com*), November 1, 2013,
www.peoplegonggao.com/e/action/ShowInfo.php?classid=2&id=
122222.

172. 'Circular: Major Transaction; Disposal of Subsidiary,' Kaisa Group
Holdings Limited, Cayman Islands, August 26, 2010, copy in author's possession; 'About Kaisa: Group Profile,' Kaisa Group Holdings Limited, n.d., accessed August 2014, www.kaisagroup.com
/english/aboutUs/Default.aspx.

173. 'Evergrande to Buy Guangzhou Kaisa Plaza for 1.9B Renminbi,'
Asset, August 27, 2010, preview at www.theasset.com/PRINT
/A20100827PJ7Hi/18315.html (subscription required for full
article).

174. «走进嘉裕» ['Entering Jiayu'].

175. «维家思广场» ['Home Garden'], 嘉裕集团 [Jiayu Group], n.d.,
www.jiayuchina.com.cn/topic.php?channelID=48&topicID=254.

176. «首次公开发行股票招股说明书» ['IPO Prospectus'], June 19,
2012, p. 224.

177. «举报信» ['Petition Letter'], from Xian Villagers to Central Com-

mission for Discipline Inspection, 2009, p. 3, copy in author's possession.

178. Ibid.

179. 《广州翠亨村酒店管理有限公司等诉李钟泉租赁合同纠纷案》 ['Guangzhou Tsui Hang Village Restaurant Company Limited and Others in Contract Dispute v Li Zhongquan'], 民事判决书 [Civil verdict], 广州市中级人民法院 [Intermediate People's Court of Guangzhou], (2012) 穗中法民五终字 第3888号 [Case no. 3888 (2012)], shlx.chinalawinfo.com/Case/displaycontent.asp? Gid=119689296&Keyword=.

180. Annual return, Grand Fortune Food & Beverage Company (Company no. 61307), 1994 (made up to June 20, 1994), p. 3, Integrated Companies Registry Information System.

181. Yang Wei Jennifer and Mannix Holdings Limited v HSBC Private Trustee (Hong Kong) Limited, as personal representative of the estate of . . . Albert B C Young, High Court of the Hong Kong Special Administrative Region, Court of First Instance, HCA 5073/2001 and HCAP 11/2002, Action no. 5073 (2001), www .lawyee.org/Case/Case_Other_HK_Display.asp?lang=2&ChannelID=2030200&RID=35499.

182. 'Young, Albert Bing Ching,' Webb-site.com, n.d., accessed March 12, 2015, webb-site.com/dbpub/positions.asp?p=3695.

183. Lu Suigeng, ed., pp. 3, 35.

CHAPTER 10: KICKING THE PIG

184. Feng Haiyong, 《杨箕村生死录》 ['A Record of Life and Death in Yangji Village'], 天涯社区 [Tianya], April 2013, bbs.tianya.cn /postno004-2291673-1.shtml.

185. Descriptions of events and quotations unattributed in a note in this section were sourced from 《广州强拆第一跳续:李洁娥绝望一跃连续慢 镜》 ['Video: Guangzhou's First Case of Suicide Jump over Forced Demolition; Continuous Slow-Lens of Li Jie-e's Leap of Despair'], video, 南都网 [Southern Metropolis Daily Online], May 10, 2012, available at Youku, v.youku.com/v_show/id_XMzkoMjE3NjYw.html; and 《广州强拆逼 死女户主李洁娥:邻居怒鸣不平》 ['Video: Forced Demolition in Guangzhou Forces the Suicide of Li Jie'e; A Neighbour Is Furious'], Youku.com, May 2012, v.youku.com/v_show/id_XMzk2MzI5MTA0.html.

186. Feng Haiyong.

187. «4万人两月搬空杨箕已成空村小偷横行» ['40,000 People Moved Out in Two Months: Yangji Village Becomes an Empty Village and Thieves Run Amok'], 新快报 [*New Express*] (via *XKB.com.cn*), June 28, 2010, news.xkb.com.cn/guangzhou/2010/0628/73306.html; «杨箕村拆迁补偿为猎德村1.5倍» ['Yangji Village Demolition and Removal Compensation 1.5 Times That of Liede'], 南方都市报 [*Southern Metropolis Daily*] (via *House.163.com*), August 15, 2009, gz.house.163.com/09/0815/07/5GO9SQ1N00873C6D.html.

188. Hai Pengfei, «被判3日内腾空搬走杨箕6钉子户终审败诉» ['With Ruling Ordering Clearance Within Three Days, Six Yangji Nail Housers Lose Their Case'], 南方都市报 [*Southern Metropolis Daily*], December 17, 2011, p. A09.

189. «广州杨箕村城中村改造拆迁补偿安置协议» [Demolition, compensation and resettlement agreement for the urban-village regeneration of Yangji], 广州市天河区杨箕股份合作经济联社 [Guangzhou Tianhe District Yangji Stockholding Cooperative], May 3, 2010, copy in author's possession.

190. Wang Cailiang and Zhu Ming, «城中村改造不能违法进行:李建明,曾桂婵, 李竹林,刘福祥刘福朝四户与广州市天河区河南街杨箕股份合作经济联社 宅基地纠纷案二审» ['Urban-Village Regeneration Cannot Proceed Illegally: Argument for Li Jianming, Zeng Gui in Appeal Ccase over Housing Plot Dispute with Guangzhou, Tianhe District, Henan Subdistrict, Yangji Stockholding Cooperative'], July 28, 2012, copy in author's possession.

191. Organic Law of the Villagers Committees of the People's Republic of China (People's Republic of China), National People's Congress Standing Committee, Order No. 9, November 4, 1998, art. 19, www.npc.gov.cn/englishnpc/Law/2007-12/11/content_1383542.htm.

192. Wang Cailiang and Zhu Ming.

193. Lian Qingqing, «杨箕村改造纠纷判村民限时交屋» ['Yangji Village Regeneration Dispute Ruling Gives Villagers Time Limit to Relinquish Properties'], 南方日报 [*Nanfang Daily*], December 3, 2011, gzdaily.dayoo.com/html/2011-12/03/content_1549237.htm.

194. Zhang Ningdan, Deng Xinjian and Yue Yan, «广州杨箕村"城中村"改造纠纷 二审宣判» ['Guangzhou Yangji Village "Urban-Village" Regeneration Dispute Heard on Appeal'], 法制日报 [*Legal Daily*], January 17, 2013, epaper.legaldaily.com.cn/fzrb/content/20130117/Article08003GN.htm.

CHAPTER 11: TEAR DOWN THIS WALL

195. Lu Suigeng, ed., p. 9.

196. 'Hotel Information.' *Leeden Hotel*, 2009, www.gzleedenhotel.com
/eng/home.asp.

197. Liu Litu, 《冼村拆迁局中局保利陷广州旧城改造泥潭》 ['Move
After Move in the Xian Village Demolition: Poly Gets Stuck in the
Mud of Urban Regeneration in Guangzhou'], 华夏时报 [*Huaxia
Times*] (via *Sina.com*), July 14, 2012, finance.sina.com.cn/chanjing
/gsnews/20120714/082312567673.shtml.

198. 《广州冼村改造签约率超九成》 ['More Than 90 Per Cent Sign Regeneration Agreement in Guangzhou's Xian Village'], 广州日报
[*Guangzhou Daily*] (via *Xinhua News Agency*), July 8, 2012, www
.gd.xinhuanet.com/newscenter/2012-07/08/c_112385627.htm.

199. 'Family Bonds, Civil Strife,' *China Media Project*, October 29,
2012, cmp.hku.hk/2012/10/29/28228.

200. 《广州拆迁户废墟上摆千人宴》 ['Villagers Facing Demolition in
Guangzhou Hold 1,000-Person Banquet'], 南方都市报 [*Southern Metropolis Daily*] (via *News.163.com*), February 20, 2013,
news.163.com/photoview/00AP0001/32014.html?from=tj_xgtj
#p=8O556O2D00AP0001.

201. 《钉子户废墟摆千人宴》 ['Nail Housers Hold 1,000-Person Banquet in the Ruins'], 明报 [*Ming Pao Daily News*], February 21,
2013, p. A22.

202. 《村民不满镇政府偷偷征地堵路维权掀翻警车》 ['Unhappy with
Secret Land Seizure by the Township Government, Villagers Block
Roads and Overturn Police Cars'], 南方农村报 [*Southern Rural
News*] (via *Ta Kung Pao*), February 1, 2013. news.takungpao.com
.hk/society/topnews/2013-02/1420041.html.

203. 《警民大战!重伤数人江门市新会睦洲南安村》 ['War Between the
Police and the People! Many Injured in Jiangnan City's Nan'an
Village, Xinhui County'], 天涯社区 [*Tianya*], January 15, 2013,
bbs.tianya.cn/post-funinfo-3895941-1.shtml.

204. 《湛江警助强征地,拆屋搞观光》 ['Police in Zhanjiang Aid Violent
Demolition, Houses Demolished for Tourism'], 东方日报 [*Oriental Daily News*], April 16, 2013, p. A34.

205. 《端午将至,潜龙出水四月初八起龙舟》 ['The Dragon Boat Festival Draws Near: The Dragons Underwater Will Rise on the Eighth
Day of the Fourth Lunar Month'], 南方都市报 [*Southern Metropolis Daily*], May 20, 2013, p. AII10.

206. «广州冼村村民对开发商不满引数百村民聚众推倒围墙» ['Vil-lagers from Guangzhou's Xian Village Unhappy with Developer, Hundreds of Villagers Gather and Push over Surrounding Wall'], 人民网 [*People's Daily Online*], May 24, 2013, vip.people.com.cn /do/userbuy.jsp?picId=2630042&aId=336238.

207. Sina Weibo, website search for «冼村» ['Xian Village'], accessed May 23, 2013, partial results in author's possession.

CHAPTER 12: THE CHINESE DREAM

208. Kuang Da, «农民工博物馆» ['Museum to the Migrant Worker'], 阳光时务周刊 [iSun *Affairs*] (Hong Kong), no. 37, January 3, 2013, available at Google+, bit.ly/17ZmbOM.

209. Zhong Ruijun and Yu Siyi, «慢一点,中国» ['Slow Down, China'], 南方都市报 [*Southern Metropolis Daily*] (via *ND Daily*), January 21, 2012, p. RB01, gcontent.oeeee.com/f/3e/f3e52c300b822a81/Blog /41f/0a4502.html.

210. «广东村民选举形同虚设,黑帮团伙被当选» ['Guangzhou Villag-ers' Election Is Rigged, Gang Is Elected'], 大记元 [*Epoch Times*], April 8, 2011, www.epochtimes.com/gb/11/4/8/n3222627.htm.

211. Quotations referring to Huang Minpeng that are not attributed in a note have been reproduced from documents collected, signed and presented to the author by Huang Minpeng on December 14, 2012.

212. Chris Buckley, 'Case Against Activist Xu Zhiyong to Focus on Pub-lic Protests,' *Sinosphere* (blog), *New York Times*, December 16, 2013, sinosphere.blogs.nytimes.com/2013/12/16/case-against-activist-xu-zhiyong-to-focus-on-public-protests/?_r=0.

CHAPTER 13: A SILENT DEATH

213. Li Nengzhong and Huang Qiuxia, «6月24日杨箕村留守户火灾称系开放商点 火» ['Yangji Village Holdout Experiences Fire on June 24, Claims Developer Set It'], 南方都市报 [*Southern Me-tropolis Daily*] (via *Bendidao.com*), June 25, 2013, gz.bendibao.com /news/2013625/content127753.shtml.

214. «广州"钉子户"惊心动魄维权路,险遭击毙» ['Guangzhou "Nail Houser"s' Chilling Rights-Defence Road Takes Him Close to Death'], 博迅 [Boxun.com], July 5, 2013, www.boxun.com/news /gb/china/2013/07/201307051606.shtml#.VQEPcRypoZE.

CHAPTER 14: TIGERS AND FLIES

215. Lu Suigeng, ed., p. 5.

216. Wang Hua and Zhang Li, «广州多名城中村干部因涉严重经济
违纪问题被 查» ['Many Cadres from Guangzhou Urban Villages
Under Investigation for Serious Breaches of Economic Discipline'],
中国新闻社 [*China News Service*], August 20, 2013, www.china
news.com/fz/2013/08-20/5185612.shtml.

217. Sun Chaofang, «萝岗村干确系戴罪"留任"冼村窝案目前正在调
查» ['Xian Village Collusion Case Under Investigation'], 羊城晚报
[*Yangcheng Evening News*], August 21, 2013, p. AO7G.

218. Cheng Xi and Liang Jingying, «广州市纪委举行新闻发布会通
报» ['Guangzhou Commission for Discipline Inspection Holds
Press Conference'], 南方日报 [*Nanfang Daily*], August 21, 2013,
p. A02.

219. Li Wenjie, Tang Mingming and Wang Yancan, «冼村人争说村官
那些事» ['Xian Village Villagers Talk About the Affairs of Those
Village Officials'], 羊城晚报 [*Yangcheng Evening News*], August
26, 2013, p. A13G.

220. Li Guangjun, «保利中秋冼村送月饼联谊» ['Poly Gives Out
Moon Cakes of Friendship in Xian Village for Mid-Autumn Festival'], 南方日报 [*Nanfang Daily*], September 13, 2013, p. B08.

221. «广州纪委每月"晒家底"晒足一年» ['Every Month This Year
Guangzhou's Commission for Discipline Inspection Has "Shone
Light Under the House"'], 广州日报 [*Guangzhou Daily*], October
1, 2013, p. LD03.

222. Ben Blanchard and Sui-Lee Wee, 'China's Xi Urges Swatting
of Lowly "Flies" in Fight on Everyday Graft,' *Reuters*, January 22,
2013, uk.reuters.com/article/2013/01/22/uk-china-corruption-xi-
idUKBRE90L0A920130122.

223. «曹鉴燎落马引村民点鞭炮庆祝:被曝控制土地渔利» ['Cao Jian-
liao's Fall Celebrated with Firecrackers: Revealed That He Controlled Land Profits'], 第一财经日报 [*China Business News*] (via
MSN), July 12, 2014, money.msn.com.cn/internal/20140712/0813
1705885.shtml.

224. Ibid.

225. Lin Chunting and Zhang Liang, «广州市原副市长曹鉴燎被立案
调查» ['Guangzhou Deputy Mayor Cao Jianliao Under Investigation'], 第一财经日 报 [*China Business News*], December 20, 2013,
p. A04.

226. Huang Qiong, «2014名村官要上交护照统一保管» ['2014 Village Officials Submit Their Passports for Safe-Keeping'], 新快报 [*New Express*], December 21, 2013, p. A02.

227. Cheng Xi, «广州出台"关于加强和规范村'两委'班子主要成员出国 (境)管理　意见"2014名"村官"护照统一上缴保管» ['Guangzhou Puts Out "Management Opinion for the Regulation of Overseas Travel by Village 'Two Heads'": 2014 Passports Confiscated from Village Leaders'], 南方日报 [*Nanfang Daily*], December 21, 2013, p. A03.

228. «黄金路段的土地白菜价成交市长村官开发商成了"腐败铁三 角"» ['Mayor, Village Officials and Developers Became an "Iron Triangle of Corruption"'], 新华社 [*Xinhua News Agency*] (via *Hangzhou Daily Press Group*), August 18, 2014, hzdaily.hangzhou .com.cn/dskb/html/2014-08/18/content_1784078.htm.

229. Kelvin Wong, 'China Trade Hub Guangzhou Booms as New Area Rises from Dirt,' *Bloomberg Business*, March 15, 2012, www .bloomberg.com/news/2012-03-14/china-trade-hub-guangzhou- booms-as-new-district-rises-from-dirt.html.

230. «这一家子搭冼村"班子"把公家的钱当自家的使» ['This Xian Village Family "Clique" Used Public Money as Its Own'], 新华社 [*Xinhua News Agency*], July 22, 2014, news.xinhuanet.com/photo /2014-07/22/c_126780308. htm.

231. «城启天鹅湾PK博雅首府» ['Cheng Qi Tian'e Wan v Boya Shoufu'], *Soufun.com* (via *Fang.com*), accessed September 5, 2014, newhouse. gz.fang.com/zt/200806/8PK.html.

232. «黄金路段的土地白菜价成交市长村官开发商成了"腐败铁三 角"» ['Mayor, Village Officials and Developers Became an "Iron Triangle of Corruption"'].

233. Ibid.

234. Ibid.

235. «广东冼村实业原董事长及亲友贪污700余万受审»　['Former Chairman of Guangdong's Xian Village Industry Company Limited and Relatives and Friends Are Tried in 7-Million-Yuan Corruption Case'], 新快报 [*New Express*] (via *Sina.com*), July 22, 2014, gd.sina.com.cn/news/b/2014-07-22/0504114398.html.

236. Ibid.

237. Wang Zechu, «城中村改造须尊重村民大会决定权» ['Urban- Village Regeneration Must Respect the Decision-Making Power of General Village Meetings'], 南方日报 [*Nanfang Daily*] (via *Xin- hua News Agency*), August 22, 2013, p. GC02, news.xinhuanet.com /2013-08/22/c_125225654.htm.

238. Ibid.

239. «关于请求对广州市土地开发中心征用冼村村农地过程中违法犯罪违纪 问题进行查处:举报信» ['Petition Letter: Concerning the Request for an Investigation into Illegalities and Violations of Discipline Occurring in the Process of the Requisition of Xian Village Farmland by the Guangzhou Land Development Centre'], from Xian Villagers to Guangdong Commission for Discipline Inspection, July 25, 2010, obtained with supporting documents, in author's possession.

240. Li Wen, Liu Jun, Wang Daobin, Xiong Wei, Xu Yan, Liu Xue, Tan Xiying and Liu Qijing, «涉嫌严重违纪被立案调查曹鉴燎曾主政天河海珠增城» ['Under Investigation for Serious Discipline Violations, Cao Jianliao Was Leader in Tianhe, Haizhu and Zengcheng'], 南方都市报 [*Southern Metropolis Daily*], December 20, 2013, p. AII04.

241. «广州城中村窝案牵出副市长曹鉴燎» ['Guangzhou Urban-Village Corruption Case Implicates Deputy Mayor Cao Jianliao'], 财新网 [*Caixin Media*], December 23, 2013, china.caixin .com/2013-12-23/100620495.html.

242. «"蚁官"巨贪» ['An "Ant Official" Commits Massive Corruption'], 南方日报 [*Nanfang Daily*], July 14, 2014, www.nfyk.com/nfgz /ShowArticle.asp?ArticleID=5864.

CHAPTER 15: THE WAKING OF THE DRAGONS

243. Lu Suigeng, ed., p. 19.

244. Zheng Yunan, Xia Jiawen, Ye Ziwen, Yang Ning, Ye Siming and Wen Jing «端午将至涌中龙船透底挖» ['As the Dragon Boat Festival Approaches Dragon Boats Are Dug Up from the Bottom'], 南方都市报 [*Southern Metropolis Daily*] (via *Nandu.com*), May 15, 2014, gd.nandu.com/nis/201405/15/216349.html.

245. «龙船采青搅热大小河涌» ['Dragon Boat Green Harvest Ceremonies All the Rage in Canals Large and Small'], 南方都市报 [*Southern Metropolis Daily*] (via Sina.com), 22 May 2014, p. AII11, news.sina.com.cn/c/2014-05-22/064030194200.shtml.

246. Hai Pengfei, «冼耀均被收容教育的钉子户» ['Xian Yaojun: A Nail Houser Sentenced to Labour Re-Education'], 南方人物周刊 [*Southern People Weekly*] (via *Hexun.com*), January 26, 2013, news .hexun.com.tw/2013-01-28/150675824.html.

247. Wu Sunlin and Mai Yicong, «建议广州率先停用收容教育制

度» ['Guangzhou CPPCC Deputy Chairperson, Guangzhou Intermediate Court Vice-President Yu Mingyong Proposes Guangzhou Be First to Stop Use of the Labour Re-Education System'], 南方都市报   [*Southern Metropolis Daily*], February 19, 2014, p. AA07.

248. «冼村街党工委关于冼村股份合作经济联社(冼村实业有限公司)党政领导　班子成员分工的批复» ['Xian Village Subdistrict Work Committee Official Reply Concerning Work Tasks of the Party-Government Leadership Group of the Xian Village Stockholding Economic Association (Xian Village Industry Company Limited)'], 天河区政府 [Tianhe District Government], January 13, 2014, xiancun.thnet.gov.cn/v2011/zwgk/bzfg/201401/t20140113_759601.html.

249. He Xuehua, «任务分解到21名市管干部» ['Tasks Given to Twenty-One City Cadres'], 广州日报 [*Guangzhou Daily*], February 16, 2014, p. LD02.

250. «冼村举行全体股东大会,打破30多年来股东代表决定集体重大事项惯例逾4000村民投票收回集体物业» ['Xian Village Holds General Meeting, Breaking with More Than Thirty Years of Decision-Making on Collective Affairs by Shareholder Representatives'], 南方都市报 [*Southern Metropolis Daily*], March 4, 2014, p. GC04.

251. «端午节龙舟«探亲»拉开序幕　冼村12年重启庆典» ['The Visiting of Relatives by Dragon Boat Begins During the Dragon Boat Festival: Xian Village Renews Celebrations After Twelve Years'], 网易网 [*Netease Property*], May 30, 2014, gz.house.163.com/14/0530/16/9TGNECII00873L40.html.

252. Liao Jingwen, «"城中村"改造应采取猎德模式实现"零强拆"» ['"Urban-Village" Regeneration Should Employ the Liede Model of "Zero Forced Demolition"'], 广州日报 [*Guangzhou Daily*] (via *Dayoo*), January 23, 2013, news.dayoo.com/guangzhou/201301/23/73437_28597362.htm.

253. «大城里的小村如何治理腐败?» ['How Can Corruption Be Controlled in Small Villages in the Big City?'], 新闻1+1 [*News 1+1*], 中国中央电视台 [China Central Television], September 22, 2014, news.cntv.cn/2014/09/22/VIDE1411398157249996.shtml.

254. Zhu Yuanbin and Guo Ketang, «百余龙舟猎德趁景» ['One Hundred Boats Visit Liede'], 信息时报 [*Information Times*], June 27, 2014, informationtimes.dayoo.com/html/2014-06/27/content_2672582.htm.

EPILOGUE

255. 《如何解决失地農民問題?》 ['How Can the Problem of Landless Farmers Be Solved?'], 人民日报 [*People's Daily*], December 9, 2005, theory.people.com.cn/BIG5/40553/3929253.html.

256. Liu Qi, 《中国失地农民面临四大难题》 ['China's Landless Farmers Face Four Major Problems'], 中国发展观察 [*China Development Observation*] (via *People's Daily Online*), August 5, 2013, theory.people.com.cn/n/2013/0805/c83865-22447864.html.

257. Dexter Roberts, 'China's 85 Million-Strong Communist Party Wants to Slim Down,' *Bloomberg Business*, June 12, 2014, www.bloomberg.com/bw/articles/2014-06-12/chinas-85-million-strong-communist-party-wants-to-slim-down.

258. 《陈锡文: 城镇化切忌过分依赖土地财政》 ['Chen Xiwen: Urbanisation Must Avoid Over-Reliance on Land Financing'], 人民网 [*People's Daily Online*] (via *Sina.com*), March 7, 2013, finance.sina.com.cn/nongye/nygd/20130307/103114752004.shtml.

259. David Bandurski, 'Turning Back to "New Democracy"?,' *China Media Project*, May 19, 2011, cmp.hku.hk/2011/05/19/12486.

260. Chris Buckley, 'China Internal Security Spending Jumps Past Army Budget,' *Reuters*, March 5, 2011, www.reuters.com/article/2011/03/05/us-china-unrest-idUSTRE7222RA20110305; Chris Buckley, 'China Domestic Security Spending Rises to $111 Billion,' *Reuters*, March 5, 2012, www.reuters.com/article/2012/03/05/us-china-parliament-security-idUSTRE82403J20120305.

261. Yu Jianrong and Minxin Pei, 'Seeking Justice: Is China's Administrative Petition System Broken?,' *Carnegie Endowment for International Peace*, April 5, 2006, carnegieendowment.org/2006/04/05/seeking-justice-is-china-s-administrative-petition-system-broken/zv4.

262. Building Harmonious Society Crucial for China's Progress: Hu,' *People's Daily Online*, June 27, 2005, en.people.cn/200506/27/eng20050627_192495.html.

263. 'Full Text of Hu Jintao's Speech at CPC Anniversary Gathering,' *Xinhua News Agency*, July 1, 2011, news.xinhuanet.com/english2010/china/2011-07/01/c_13960505_5.htm.

264. 《粉碎与习近平遇车祸传言贺国强重新露面》 ['He Guoqiang, Rumoured to Have Been in an Accident with Xi Jinping, Re-Emerges'], 南洋商报 [*Nanyang Commercial Daily*], September 14, 2012, p. A28.

265. Hu Jintao, «胡锦涛在中国共产党第十八次全国代表大会上的报告» ['Hu Jintao's Report to the Eighteenth National Congress of the Communist Party of China'], 新华社 [*Xinhua News Agency*], November 17, 2012, news.xinhuanet.com/18cpcnc/2012-11/17/c_113711665.htm.

266. Edward Wong, 'New Communist Party Chief in China Denounces Corruption in Speech,' *New York Times*, November 19, 2012, www.nytimes.com/2012/11/20/world/asia/new-communist-party-chief-in-china-denounces-corruption.html.

267. Brian Spegele, 'Xi Eats Plainly amid Focus on Official Waistlines,' *China Real Time* (blog), *Wall Street Journal*, December 31, 2012, blogs.wsj.com/chinarealtime/2012/12/31/xi-eats-plainly-amid-focus-on-official-waistlines.

268. Zhao Yinan, 'Uphold Constitution, Xi Says,' *China Daily USA*, December 5, 2012, usa.chinadaily.com.cn/china/2012-12/05/content_15985894.htm.

269. Constitution of the People's Republic of China, arts 33, 35, 126, available at National People's Congress of the People's Republic of China, www.npc.gov.cn/englishnpc/Law/2007-12/05/content_1381903.htm.

270. 'For Freedom, Justice, and Love: Xu Zhiyong's Closing Statement to the Court,' *ChinaFile*, January 26, 2014, www.chinafile.com/freedom-justice-and-love.

271. Nozomu Hayashi, 'Civil Rights Movement Gains Momentum in China, Alarms Government,' *Asahi Shinbun*, October 29, 2013, ajw.asahi.com/article/asia/china/AJ201310290052.

272. David Bandurski, 'Inside the Southern Weekly Incident,' *China Media Project*, January 7, 2013, cmp.hku.hk/2013/01/07/30402.

273. David Bandurski, 'A New Year's Greeting Gets the Axe in China,' *China Media Project*, January 3, 2013, cmp.hku.hk/2013/01/03/30247.

274. 'Chinese Stage Rare Protest over Newspaper Censorship,' *Guardian*, January 7, 2013, www.theguardian.com/world/2013/jan/07/chinese-rare-protest-newspaper-censorship.

275. 'China Censor Row Paper Southern Weekly Back on Stands,' *BBC News*, January 2013, www.bbc.com/news/world-asia-china-20968170.

276. 'Open Letter to the National People's Congress on Human Rights,' trans. David Bandurski, *China Media Project*, February 26, 2013, cmp.hku.hk/2013/02/26/31531.

277. Olivia Rosenman, 'Chinese Activists Seek Approval of Rights Treaty,' *Asia Sentinel*, March 21, 2013, www.asiasentinel.com /society/chinese-activists-seek-approval-of-rights-treaty.

278. 'Document 9: A ChinaFile Translation,' *ChinaFile*, November 8, 2013, www.chinafile.com/document-9-chinafile-translation.

279. Chris Buckley, 'China Takes Aim at Western Ideas,' *New York Times*, August 19, 2013, www.nytimes.com/2013/08/20/world/asia /chinas-new-leadership-takes-hard-line-in-secret-memo.html.

280. 'China Detains Activist Xu Zhiyong,' *BBC News*, July 17, 2013, www.bbc.com/news/world-asia-china-23339401; Jonathan Kaiman, 'China Upholds Four-Year Sentence of Activist Xu Zhiyong,' *Guardian*, April 11, 2014, www.theguardian.com/world/2014/apr /11/china-upholds-sentence-activist-xu-zhiyong.

281. Murong Xuecun, 'Chinese Internet: "A New Censorship Campaign Has Commenced,"' *Guardian*, May 15, 2013, www.theguardian .com/world/2013/may/15/chinese-internet-censorship-campaign.

282. Adam Connors, 'A Growing List of "Tigers" Snared by Chinese President Xi Jinping's Anti-Corruption Campaign,' *ABC News* (Australia), January 16, 2015, www.abc.net.au/news/2015-01-14 /chinas-tigers-downfall-timeline/6016714.

283. Tom Phillips, 'China Launches Global "Fox Hunt" for Corrupt Officials,' *Telegraph*, July 25, 2014, www.telegraph.co.uk/news /worldnews/asia/china/10991255/China-launches-global-fox-hunt-for-corrupt-officials.html.

284. Connors.

285. Jamil Anderlini, 'Bribe Case Highlights West's Dilemma over China's Overseas Probes,' *Financial Times*, September 16, 2014, www .ft.com/intl/cms/s/0/a90c00e8-3d70-11c4-8797-00144feabdc0 .html.

286. William Dobson, 'The World's Toughest Job,' *Slate*, June 6, 2012, www.slate.com/articles/news_and_politics/foreigners/2012/06 /dictator_s_learning_curve_pu_zhiqiang_is_one_of_china_s_ leading_free_speech_attorneys_.html.

287. Perry Link, 'China: Inventing a Crime,' *New York Review of Books*, February 9, 2015, www.nybooks.com/blogs/nyrblog/2015/feb/09 /china-pu-zhiqiang-inventing-crime.

288. Chris Buckley, 'Comments Used in Case against Pu Zhiqiang Spread Online,' *Sinosphere* (blog), *New York Times*, January 29, 2015, sinosphere.blogs.nytimes.com/2015/01/29/comments-used-in-case-against-pu-zhiqiang-spread-online/?_r=0.

289. Yu Jianrong, 'Reassessing Chinese Society's "Rigid Stability": Stability 297 NOTES Preservation through Pressure, Its Predicament and the Way Out,' *China Story*, January 27, 2013, www.thechinastory.org/2013/01/chinas-rigid-stability-an-analysis-of-a-predicament-by-yu-jianrong.

Index

ABOUT THE AUTHOR

DAVID BANDURSKI is an award-winning journalist whose work has appeared in *The New York Times* and *The Wall Street Journal*. He received a Human Rights Press Award in 2008. He produces Chinese independent films and documentaries through his production company, Lantern Films.